FUNDRAISING

for

Social Change

FUNDRAISING

for

Social Change

Kim Klein

Third Edition, Revised and Expanded

CHARDON PRESS
Berkeley, California

Chardon Press
P.O. Box 11607
Berkeley, CA 94712
510 704-8714
chardon@aol.com

Printed in the United States of America.
Library of Congress Catalog Card Number: 94-72320
ISBN 0-9620222-3-3

Editing: Nancy Adess
Design: Robert Cooney
Layout: Julia Gennert, Deborah Anker

Printed on recycled paper with soy ink.

To Rosie and Myles,
without whom this book would have
been completed much faster

Table of Contents

Preface to the Third Edition

I have worked full time in fundraising — as staff, consultant, trainer, writer — for seventeen years. During that time, fundraising for and running grassroots nonprofits has changed considerably. The entire budget of the first grassroots organization I worked for was $36,000. That supported three staff people, an office, a newsletter and an organizing program. We created a program to encourage people to give $50 and $100 to the group and called it a "major donor program." Fifty dollars went a long way in a $36,000 budget, and it represented a large gift from the person who gave it. Fundraising has gotten a lot harder because $50 is still a large gift for most people, but today it doesn't go very far at all in most grassroots organizations.

The first edition of this book was published in 1985 and I learned to use a computer to write it. Most small nonprofits didn't have computers then; I was ahead of my time. But time has raced ahead and now almost everyone has computers, printers, fax machines and modems. These innovations have made many aspects of fundraising easier at the same time as they have made all of fundraising more expensive.

There are two basic premises of fundraising that haven't changed and they never will. Luckily, these premises are also the most important ones:

1. If you want money, you have to ask for it
2. If you ask enough people, you will get your money.

Almost all of the fundraising I do is with groups and people working for social justice. Like most people in this field, I started out to be something else — in my case, a minister. I studied at Pacific School of Religion in Berkeley and volunteered in a shelter for battered women in San Francisco. Later, I helped to start a shelter in Oakland. I soon realized that good groups often foundered for lack of money and yet most people would do anything for their group except raise money. My work has always been to change those two realities. I want my obituary to say, "She taught a lot of people how to ask for money."

People sometimes ask me how I can talk to people about money so much of the time. Don't I get tired? Don't I get cynical? What grassroots fundraisers understand is that we don't talk to people about money very much at all. We talk to people about ideas, about vision, about what the world could be like if certain changes were made. Then we talk about how much those changes will cost and ask if the person wants to help. The world I talk about with people and the world I work for — characterized in all its parts by justice and equality — cannot be bought. But neither will it ever exist without massive resources invested in organizations that know how to create the changes that the world needs. Being in fundraising has kept me in touch with some of the most creative and compassionate people on the planet, and I hope that all the people who use this book have the same experience.

Kim Klein
Berkeley, CA
April, 1994

Acknowledgments

First and foremost, I want to thank my best friend, colleague and editor, Nancy Adess. Nancy gets credit for editing this book, but the word "edit" doesn't come close to describing the level of work she has performed to get this book (and the previous two editions) into print. She is so thorough and extraordinary an editor that some chapters should be labelled, "as told to Nancy Adess." She also understands the field of fundraising, having done it for many years professionally and as a volunteer. Much of what I learned early on about fundraising was learned with her as we tried out every strategy and idea we could think of to raise money for various women's health issues. In addition to editing this book, she also managed its production, and she and I together distribute it through Chardon Press. She is also the editor of the magazine that I publish, *Grassroots Fundraising Journal*.

My early fundraising teachers, Hank Rosso, Joan Flanagan, Si Kahn, Mary Harrington and Kat Thomas have to be thanked for providing the theoretical basis for my fundraising knowledge, and for continuing to enrich the whole field with their contributions.

Of course I have learned the most from the thousands of organizations and individuals I have worked with over the years — in training, consulting, as a staff member or board member. At the risk of hurting some people's feelings by leaving them out, I have to thank some of the people and groups from whom I learned more than I ever taught: Marya Grambs and Tracy Gary who supported me in my first volunteer fundraising efforts with La Casa de las Madres, and continue their fundraising work to this day; Mary Foran, Pat Cody, Ellie Friedman and the dozens of women I worked with at the Coalition for the Medical Rights of Women to make it one of the first grassroots organizations in the United States to have a major donor program; Vicki Quatmann and all the folks at SOCM (Save Our Cumberland Mountains) who actually took most of my advice over many years so I could see what worked and what didn't in a rural setting; Peggy Mathews and the founders of the Appalachian Community Fund and Community Shares; the many staff and board members I worked with in the Funding Exchange network;

9

Gary Delgado and the people at the Center for Third World Organizing; Lisa Honig, who co-founded and ran the *Grassroots Fundraising Journal* with me for its first 10 years; and all the people who have written and called me for the past decade with questions, comments and their own stories — many of which are incorporated in this book.

Finally, I want to thank my life partner, Stephanie Roth, who keeps me grounded in more ways than she knows. Stephanie is a fine fundraiser, organizer and activist in her own right. She helped formulate and clarify many of the ideas in this book, and is the co-publisher of the *Grassroots Fundraising Journal*. She keeps me laughing, she laughs at and with me, and understands me so well that she was not offended when I told her I was dedicating this book to our cats.

Introduction

The purpose of this book is to provide low-budget organizations — those with budgets under $500,000 — with the information they need to establish, maintain, and expand successful community-based fundraising programs. Successful grassroots fundraising will allow them to move away from reliance on foundations, corporations, and government assistance.

Low-budget groups need to keep in mind that their fundraising efforts take place in a context different from those of more traditional community service organizations, such as large hospitals, voluntary health agencies, or major arts groups.

First, many people will not agree with or even understand what your group is trying to do. Your organization probably has little immediate public recognition and, if you are seeking to change the status quo, people may feel threatened by your program. Even those in sympathy with what you are trying to accomplish may think that you are hopelessly naive or idealistic, and you may often be told to "face reality."

Second, you probably have little or no front money and not enough staff; therefore, you cannot afford to invest in large-scale fundraising strategies, such as large direct-mail campaigns. Without a cushion of money, you are either just holding your own financially or falling behind.

Third, your board, volunteers and staff are likely to be unfamiliar with fundraising strategies and may not be comfortable with even the idea of fundraising.

Traditional fundraising strategies need to be re-thought with these three premises and their attendant implications in mind and translated into workable terms for grassroots groups. This book does that. All of the strategies recommended here have been successful for small groups. Not every strategy will work for every group, but the discussion of each strategy will allow you to decide which strategies will work for your group and how to expand the strategies you are already using.

Fundraising without planning, without a strong, committed group of volunteers, without a workable organizational structure, or without understanding the basic components of all fundraising plans is practically impossible. The appropriate staff of every organization should read the first two sections of the book to learn the context for successful fundraising.

The next sections present detailed descriptions of how to carry out strategies to acquire, retain and upgrade donors to your organization. These proceed from the most impersonal — direct mail appeals and special events — to the most personal — solicitation by telephone and in person. Special attention is given to the difficulties most people have asking for money, offering concrete ways to overcome them. Finally, the book covers the rudiments of setting up a fundraising office, record keeping, and hiring fundraising staff or consultants. Special circumstances are also covered, such as raising money in rural communities, for coalitions, in times of financial crisis, and so forth.

I will take this opportunity to deliberately state the obvious: All of the reading of fundraising literature, planning, strategizing, writing case statements, and attending fundraising trainings cannot and will not raise money. Only implementing your plan — taking action — will raise money. So make this your motto: **"Today someone has to ask someone for money."**

SECTION 1
Fundraising Framework

1.

Philanthropy in America

The word *philanthropy* comes from two Greek words meaning "love of people." In modern times, this love is usually expressed in donations of property, money, or volunteer work to worthy causes. Similarly, the word "charity" comes from a Latin word meaning "love" in the sense of unconditional lovingkindness, compassion and seeking to do good. The roots of these words remind us of the fundamental reasons for the work of most nonprofit organizations.

The United States of America has the largest system of private philanthropy in the world. In this country, non-governmental organizations have been created — and funded through private sources — to provide services that in countries with greater government commitment to social welfare are provided through taxation. If charity were a single industry, it would rank as the nation's largest income producer and one of its biggest employers, accounting for more than 5 percent of the workforce. As of 1993, more than 500,000 organizations had been recognized by the Internal Revenue Service as tax exempt and qualified to receive tax-deductible donations. These organizations are commonly called by their IRS designation: 501(c)(3). There are 400,000 more organizations that are tax exempt, but donations to these groups — service clubs, trade associations, political action committees and the like — are not tax deductible. Thousands more small grassroots organizations that are doing important charitable work are not registered with the government and have no formal tax status. These groups include organizations just getting started, organizations that come together for a one-time purpose, such as cleaning up a vacant lot or protesting something, or those that don't wish to have a structural relationship with the state or federal government.

Because of the size and increasing sophistication of the nonprofit sector, there is a corresponding interest in the sector by government officials, researchers, academics and many members of the general public. Some agencies and organizations are seeking ways to regulate how nonprofits function, while others believe that increased public awareness and voluntary compliance with accepted ethical standards of accounting, personnel and fundraising will provide sufficient self-regulation. As the American Association of Fund Raising Counsel puts it in their 1992 annual report, *Giving USA*, "We are at a point in our understanding of these organizations where we are increasingly cognizant of the line between the right of citizens to have access to information about those organizations which receive preferred tax treatment in exchange for a commitment to operate in the public interest and the liberties of their organizations to function without undue restraint."

Nonprofit status is a public trust and tax exemption is, in effect, a public expense. Even if an organization has no formal tax status, if it seeks to raise money from the public it has the same moral duty as registered nonprofits to operate ethically, be truthful with donors, and provide the highest quality services to clients.

Sources of Charitable Giving: Myths and Facts

Ask almost anyone, "Who donates the most money to nonprofit causes?" and seven out of 10 times the reply will be, "Corporations and foundations." This myth is a tribute to the power of these entities to get the most public relations mileage from their charitable giving, but it has no relationship to the truth. Nonetheless, the myth that most nonprofit funding comes from corporations and foundations has burdened people's understanding of where to look for money for their nonprofits.

Despite successful self-promotion by corporations and foundations, the truth is far different: most charitable dollars come from government programs, collectively known as "the public sector." This fact holds true despite the extensive cutbacks in government funding that characterized the 1980s and early 1990s. These funds rarely support grassroots organizations.

Following government dollars, individuals give more money to nonprofit organizations than any other source, including corporations and foundations combined. This book focusses almost entirely on how to raise money from that enormous market.

Giving USA studies and identifies economic and social trends in American philanthropy. Every year since 1935, the authors have also calculated just how much money was given away to nonprofits and by whom. They have identified four sources of gifts from the private (non-governmental) sector: living individuals, bequests (a cash or other donation an individual arranges to be given to a charity on their death), foundations and corporations.

Their research shows that the proportion of giving from each of these sources remains constant, varying from year to year by only two or three percentage points, with gifts from individuals (living or deceased) exceeding the rest by nine to one. Perhaps more shocking are their findings that 85 percent of the money given away by individuals is given by families with incomes of less than $50,000 and that poor and working-class people tend to give away more money as a percentage of income than upper-middle-class or wealthy people.

In 1995, the latest year for which figures are available, giving from these sources totaled $143.85 billion.

Sources of Contributions

Contributions from	(in billions)	As a percent of total
Individuals	$116.23	80.8%
Foundations	10.44	7.3%
Bequests	9.77	6.8%
Corporations	7.40	5.1%

Given these facts, an organization should have no trouble knowing where to go for money: individuals provide the vast bulk of support to nonprofits. Foundations and corporations, which have the false reputation of keeping charity alive, are overrated as a source of funds and the help they can provide is often misunderstood. While foundation and corporate giving will always play a vital role in the nonprofit sector, the limitations of that role must be clearly understood.

Foundations

Foundations have relatively little money and that money is in very great demand. Some of the larger foundations report receiving 100 proposals for every two they are able to fund. And the demand has increased as foundations have released more information about their giving. Guidebooks to foundations by state or by subject proliferate as do data bases to help potential grantees identify more and more sources. Computers have made it easier to write proposals and to adjust them to fit the guidelines or format of each foundation.

While many nonprofits, especially new or small organizations, think foundation funding would be the answer to their money problems, in fact foundation funding is designed to be used only for short-term projects. These include the start up of a new organization and its first few years of operation, special capital improvements, endowments (rarely), one-time projects such as conferences, or help through a particularly rough period in the life of an organization for which it has a good excuse and a workable recovery plan.

If an organization has become reliant on foundation funding, decreasing that reliance should be an important part of its financial planning. If an organization has never become reliant on foundation funding, it should plan not to, and not make the mistake that many small organizations make of seeking more and more foundation funding as the years pass rather than less and less.

Corporations

Corporations are different from foundations in a key way: unlike foundations, whose job it is to give money away, corporations exist to make money. Giving money away is primarily an activity that a corporation hopes will directly or indirectly help it to make more money. In fact, only 11 percent of corporations give away any money at all, and the average amount these companies give away is 2 percent of their pre-tax profits, although they are allowed to give up to 10 percent of those profits. Corporations generally give money to the following types of organizations or activities:

- ◆ to organizations that improve the life of the community where the corporation's employees live (symphonies, parks, museums, libraries)

- ◆ to organizations that provide volunteer opportunities for employees, or to which employees make donations (sometimes the corporate giving is in the form of matching employee donations)

- ◆ to groups that help their employees be more productive by addressing problems employees have (such as alcohol and drug abuse or domestic violence)

- ◆ to research efforts that will help the company invent products or market existing products (various departments in universities get much of their funding for such research from corporations)

◆ to education programs for young people to ensure an adequate workforce for the company in the future (literacy programs, innovative schools, scholarships).

Corporations also make valuable donations besides money, such as expertise (loaning a worker to help a nonprofit with accounting, marketing, personnel), space (free use of conference or meeting rooms), office equipment (computers, fax machines, copy machines), printing, furniture, building materials, and the like.

Recently, many corporations have joined with charities in "cause-related marketing" efforts, in which a corporation donates a certain percentage of its profits or a certain amount of each sale to a particular group. The group and the corporation advertise the arrangement and encourage people in choosing among similar products to choose the one that also benefits the charity.

Many organizations using this book will not be able to get corporate funding because their work is too controversial; many others will not seek corporate funding because they wish to avoid appearing to endorse a corporate product or a particular corporation's way of doing business.

The Power of Individual Giving

A broad base of individual donors provides the only reliable source of funding year in and year out, and the growth of individual donations to an organization is critical to its growth and self-sufficiency. Further, relying on a broad base of individuals for support increases an organization's ability to be self-determining, making it unnecessary to determine program priorities based on programs that foundations, corporations or government agencies will fund.

Recipients of Charitable Giving

To understand private-sector giving, it is important to look at not only who gives this money, but who receives it. Again, with only a few percentage points of variation from year to year, a consistent pattern of giving has been demonstrated through *Giving USA*'s reporting. Over half of all money given away in America goes to religious organizations, with education a distant second, followed by health, human services, the arts and four other categories that receive small percentages of giving.

1995 Uses of Contributions

Contributions to	(in billions)	As a percent of total
Religion	$56.71	45.6%
Education	17.94	2.5%
Health	12.48	8.8%
Human Services	11.70	8.1%
Arts	9.96	6.9%
Gifts to Foundations	7.43	5.2%
Public/Society Benefit	7.10	4.9%
Environment/Wildlife	3.98	2.8%
International affairs	2.06	1.4%
Unallocated	7.64	5.3%

(Source: *Giving USA, 1996*)

The rest of this chapter examines why religious organizations are such successful fundraisers.

Religious Organizations: A Model

Religion as a category receives almost half of every charitable dollar, yet only a small percentage of giving to religion is from foundations, and virtually none of it comes from corporations. Because of the constitutional separation of church and state, religion receives no government funding either. The conclusion is obvious: the most successful nonprofits in America rely almost entirely on individuals for the funding they need.

Why do religious organizations receive so many of the private-sector dollars? The answer is simple and it is one of the most important things to understand for successful fundraising: Religious institutions offer ideas and commitments that are of great value, but the real reason they get so much money is that *they ask for it.*

Let's look at the elements of a typical church fundraising program. (Churches are used here because they are the dominant religious form in the United States and because of my familiarity with them. People from other religious traditions will see that fundraising techniques are similar in their tradition.)

♦ Churches ask regularly. In most churches a basket is passed around during the collection each Sunday. Any gift is acceptable, from small change to large checks. Everyone, whether out-of-town visitor, occasional church-goer, or loyal and generous congregant, has an opportunity to give, and almost everyone does. The ushers or ministers are not concerned about offending someone by asking too often. They would never say, "Don't pass the basket to Mrs. Faithful, she just bought the new carpet."

♦ Churches make it easy to give. In the great majority of churches, if you are a regular congregant someone will come to your house to discuss your giving plan. He or she may ask you to tithe, or to pledge a certain amount per week or month, or to give a one-time gift to the ongoing work of the church. The option of monthly or quarterly payments allows people to give a great deal more over the course of a year than they could in a single lump sum.

♦ Churches provide a variety of programs to which you can give as you desire. If you are particularly interested in the youth program, you can give to that; you can buy flowers for the altar in someone's honor; you can support the music program or the overseas mission programs. Most churches have any number of scholarship funds, homeland missions, soup kitchens and other social programs for which your donation is needed and gratefully accepted. If you are a "bricks-and-mortar" person — that is, you prefer to buy things with your gifts — you can buy a new window, new Bibles, a new carpet, or a whole new sanctuary.

♦ Any size of donation is appropriate. You can belong to a church by making a gift of any amount. While some churches suggest guidelines for giving and the Bible suggests 10 percent of income as the appropriate tithe, the church always leaves the amount of giving up to the donor.

All groups should try to institute this type of diversity in giving. In the chapters that follow I will show you how.

2.

Principles of Fundraising

If one were to ask, "What is the purpose of fundraising?" many people would think, "What a stupid question," and would answer, "To raise money." In fact, the purpose of fundraising is to build a base of donors; if you do that you will raise money.

Focussing on building a donor base rather than on simply raising money means that sometimes you will undertake a fundraising strategy that does not raise money in the first year, such as direct mail, or for several years, such as planned giving. It means that you will relate to your donors as individual human beings rather than as money faucets that you turn on when you want money and off when you don't. It means you will plan for both the short term and the long term and think through the consequences of any fundraising effort for both the next month and the next few years.

Three principles of fundraising underpin any successful fundraising program. Understanding these principles will give you a basis on which to plan your own fundraising. They are:

1) Fundraising programs must build on a diversity of sources

2) People give for a variety of reasons that relate to their self-interest

3) Anyone can participate in fundraising.

Diversifying Sources

Focussing on building a donor base means deliberately and systematically diversifying sources of funding, and getting a large number of people helping you to raise money. The need for diversity is not a new lesson. Factory towns face high unemployment when their single industry closes or cuts back. People with only one skill have a more difficult time finding employment than those with a variety of skills. And, in the last decade, thousands of nonprofits were forced to curtail their services severely or close their doors because they were so heavily reliant on government funding that ceased to be available.

Yet many organizations continue to look for the ideal special event that will provide for their entire budget, or they search for the one person, foundation, or corporation to provide most of the money they need, or they try to hire the perfect fundraiser who will raise all their money without anyone's help. These groups reason that if they could use one fundraising strategy that was absolutely certain, tried and true, their money worries would be over. Unfortunately, no fundraising device or person fits that description. In fact, only if they maintain a diversity of sources will an organization survive for the long term.

Organizations should not receive more than 30 percent of their funding from any one source. An organization could lose 30 percent of its funding and probably survive, though it would be difficult, but the loss of more than 30 percent of funding would put any organization in dire straights. This rule means that while you could have more than 30 percent of income coming from membership (and many groups do), you cannot have one member providing 30 percent of all an organization's money. The IRS recognizes this principle with their "one-third rule." This rule of thumb that says if more than one-third of an organization's total income comes from one person, foundation or corporation, that organization does not meet the test of a public charity (that is, a 501(c)(3) organization) and if this condition persists for five years or more, an organization risks losing its public charity status. Public charities are to be supported by the public — a broad spectrum of the public — and are not to serve as hobbies or forums for any one person or corporate entity.

There is no set number of sources that constitutes healthy diversity. Much will depend on the size of your budget, your location and your work. However, the more people that give you money, the better.

Why People Give:
Appealing to Self-Interest

Approximately seven out of ten people regularly make donations to nonprofits. Of those who do give, most support between five and eleven organizations, giving away a little over 2 percent of their personal income. All fundraising efforts should go toward trying to become one of the groups that the givers give to, rather than trying to become the first charitable donation of a previous non-giver. People who give your organization money are not taking it from what they would have spent on food or shoes for their children; these people are dedicated givers, and your group's job is to make them dedicated to the work of your organization. To do that you must carefully examine what makes a person a giver.

At the level of pure exchange, people give to organizations because they like the newsletter or because they receive a free tote bag, bumper sticker or some other tangible item. Sometimes they give to a certain group because everyone in their social circle gives to that group or because it is a family tradition. Giving may be the only way to get something the organization offers (classes, theater seats, entry to the swimming pool).

At the altruistic level of motivation, people give because they care about the issue, they believe in the group, they think the group's analysis of a problem and vision of a solution is correct. Often people give either because they or someone they know were once in the position of the people the group serves (alcoholics, abused women or children, unemployed or homeless people), or because they are thankful that neither they nor anyone they know is in that position.

People give because they feel guilty about how much they have or how little service they have done in their own life, and a gift relieves that guilt. In the case of some religious giving, people give in order to feel more assured of salvation and eternal life.

People give because the group expresses their own ideals and enables them to reinforce their image of themselves as principled people — for example, as feminists, environmentalists, pacifists, equal rights advocates, good parents, concerned citizens, or whatever image is important to them. Through their giving, they can say in truth, "I am a caring person," "I have deep feelings for others," "I am helping others."

People give because they are asked, and being asked reminds them what they care about. When they are asked personally by a friend or someone they admire, in addition to feeling good about giving to the organization, they get to show themselves as principled and generous people to someone whose opinion they value. Although these motivations for giving are what impels most people to give, most nonprofit organizations appeal to two other motives that are not very persuasive. These are, "We need the money," and "Your gift is tax deductible." Neither of these reasons distinguishes your organization from all the others. All nonprofit organizations claim to need money, and most of them do. The fact that the gift is tax deductible is a nice touch, but gifts to several hundred thousand other nonprofits are tax deductible too. Neither need nor tax advantage makes your organization special.

The 70 percent of Americans that give away money pay nonprofits to do work that can only be accomplished by group effort. There is very little one person can do about racism or gay bashing or sexual assault. Only as part of an organization can an individual make a difference in these or any other pressing social problems. Certainly, one person cannot be a theater or a museum or an alternative school. Donors need the organization as much as the organization needs them, and the money is given in exchange for work performed. In a very important way, donations are really fees for service.

Involving Everyone in Fundraising

Finally, and most important for small organizations, it is critical to understand that fundraising is easy to learn. In the last ten years, there has been an increasing emphasis on fundraising as a "discipline." Colleges and universities now offer courses on various aspects of fundraising, sometimes as part of degree programs in nonprofit management, and professional organizations offer certification programs in fundraising. There are more and more professional fundraisers.

All of these things are important and contribute to the health and well-being of the nonprofit sector. But college courses or professional standing are not required in order to be good at fundraising and they will never take the place of the only three things you really need to be a fundraiser: simple common sense, a commitment to a cause, and a basic affection for people.

Fundraising is an acquired taste. Probably no one says at the age of 12, "When I grow up, I want to be a fundraiser." Most people are drawn to the profession by a cause, an idea, an issue, or an organization in need of money. They decide to help with fundraising even though it is not their first choice and even though they may have at first found the idea slightly distasteful or a little frightening. With time and experience, many of these people find that fundraising is not as difficult as they had imagined and they begin to like it. They realize that people feel good about themselves when they make a donation to an organization they believe in, and that to ask someone for money actually means to give that person an opportunity to express traditions or beliefs that are important to them.

People asked to raise money often confuse the process of giving money with the process of asking for it. In fact, there is a significant difference between the two. People feel good about giving money, but rarely do people feel good asking for money until they get used to doing it. People asking for money for their cause tend to project their feelings of discomfort in asking onto the potential donor and then describe the donor in words such as these: "I really embarrassed that person when I asked him," or, "I could tell she wanted to leave the room when I asked her," or, "They were so upset that they just looked at each other and finally said yes but I know they wanted to say no." These descriptions of how the donor supposedly felt (embarrassed, humiliated, upset) are more likely to be descriptions of how the asker was feeling. The potential donor was more than likely flattered, pleased to be included, thinking about what amount he or she could give, or wondering if the asker was feeling all right.

Feelings of discomfort in asking for money are normal and in Chapter 12, Personal Solicitation, I will talk about them and how to deal with them. For now, simply understand that asking and giving are two very different experiences, even when they happen in the same conversation. When people are recruited to ask for money, they must reflect on what they like about giving, not on what they hate about asking.

When an organization has a diversity of ways to raise money, it can use the talents and abilities of all the people in the group to help with fundraising. As volunteers and board members learn more about fundraising and experience success, they will be willing to learn new strategies and they will begin to like asking for money. Further, an organization that has only one or two people raising its money is not much better off than an organization that has only one or two sources of money. In the chapters that follow, I discuss identifying appropriate fundraising strategies and building a team of volunteer fundraisers.

3.

Fundraising Needs and Strategies

Organizations have three types of funding needs: the money they need to operate every year, called the Annual Fund; money they need to improve their building or upgrade their capacity to do their work, called a Capital Fund; and money they need to ensure financial stability and assist long term planning, called an Endowment Fund. In addition, each organization has a series of strategies — from acquisition through retention and upgrading — to move each donor's giving to the organization toward being more and more thoughtful. Usually, the largest gifts a group will receive are capital and endowment gifts, and these gifts will come from the most thoughtful donors. The types of funding needed, the process of a donor moving from being an impulse to a thoughtful donor, and the strategies needed to acquire, retain and upgrade donors are all described in this chapter.

Types of Funding Needs

The Annual Fund

Because the overall purpose of fundraising is to build a base of donors who give you money every year to support your operations, it is helpful to analyze how a person becomes a donor to an organization, and how, ideally, that person increases in loyalty to the group and expresses that increase in loyalty with a steady increase in giving.

A person goes through phases in moving from not giving at all to giving regularly several times a year. The first phase begins when a person hears or reads about a group working on issues that she or he is concerned about and decides on the spur of the moment to make a donation. That first gift is called an "impulse" gift. After the donor is thanked for that gift, he or she will be asked for another gift for a different aspect of the organization's work (see Chapter 6, Using Direct Mail, for how often to ask and what to ask for). We call a donor who has given three or four times over the course of one or two years a "habitual" donor. This person sees himself or herself as part of the organization, even though probably not a big part. Next, the habitual donor is asked personally for a larger gift; if he or she responds with a larger gift than he or she has given before, this donor becomes a "thoughtful" donor.

The process of moving people from non-donor to donor to habitual donor to thoughtful donor is the main focus in planning the annual fund. Every year, an organization needs to recruit a certain number of new donors, to upgrade a certain number of regular donors into major donors, and to give all their donors three or four chances during the year to give extra gifts.

A group can expect to retain about two-thirds of its individual donors every year, with the greatest proportion of the one-third who drop out being people who give once and not again. In planning fundraising strategies, then, you need to have a few strategies whose sole purpose is replacing lost donors. If you are losing less than one-third of your donor base, you do not have enough donors. If you are losing more, you are not doing enough to keep your donors and, in the case of most grassroots organizations, it usually means you are not asking donors for money often enough. You also need to have a few strategies designed to cultivate a group of habitual donors — people you can turn to every year, and sometimes several times a year, for gifts. And, finally, you need to have some strategies to get current donors to give more money — these are called upgrading strategies. A wide variety of fundraising strategies and their uses are discussed in Sections Two and Three.

Capital Fund

In addition to planning how much money your organization needs each year and what strategies will be used to raise that money, organizations occasionally need to raise extra money for capital improvements. Capital needs can range from getting new computers to buying and refurbishing an entire building. Most donors who give capital gifts have previously given thoughtfully to an annual fund. They know your organization, they believe in your cause, and they have the resources to help you with a special gift. These resources could be a computer they are not using, land they donate for a building, or a large monetary gift to build the building. These gifts are given by donors only a few times in the donor's lifetime, and are almost always requested in person.

Strategies for soliciting capital fund gifts are discussed in Chapter 17, Capital Campaigns.

Endowment Fund

An endowment fund is a glorified savings account in which an organization sets aside money that it does not spend. It uses only the interest from that money to augment its annual budget. Endowment funds are raised in many ways, but are most often funded by planned gifts such as bequests. A gift from a person's estate is in some ways the most thoughtful gift of all and usually reflects a deep and abiding commitment to an organization. It reflects the donor's belief that the organization will continue to exist and do important work long after the donor is dead. The idea of making an endowment gift can be introduced to donors in a variety of ways, but generally a person making such a gift has a personal relationship with the organization. Various planned giving vehicles are discussed in Chapter 18, Planned Giving.

Three Goals for Every Donor

An organization has three goals for every donor. The first goal is for that person to become a thoughtful annual donor — to give the biggest gift he or she can afford on a yearly basis. The source for an annual gift is the annual income of the donor. The second goal is for as many donors as possible to give capital or special gifts. These do not have to be connected to capital improvements, but are gifts that are unusual in some way and are only given a few times (or possibly only once) during the donor's lifetime. Capital gifts are usually given from the donor's assets such as savings, inheritance, or property. A donor cannot afford to give assets every year and so will only give these gifts for special purposes. The third goal is for every donor to remember the organization in his or her will or to make some kind of arrangement benefitting the organization from her or his estate. An estate gift is arranged during the donor's lifetime but wholly received by the organization only on the donor's death. Obviously, these gifts are made only once.

Most small organizations will do well if they can plan a broad range of strategies to acquire, maintain and upgrade annual gifts, but over time organizations need to think about capital and endowment gifts and learn to use fundraising strategies that will encourage such gifts. Grassroots organizations do receive bequests and gifts of property, art, appreciated

The Story of Gina Generous

To understand how a person might move from not giving at all to becoming a thoughtful donor to leaving the organization a bequest, consider the experience of Gina Generous.

Gina Generous comes home from work tired and frustrated. It's been a long day. She feeds her cats, kicks her shoes off and sits down to leaf through her mail. Most of it she characterizes as "junk" and throws away, but one piece of direct mail catches her eye. It's not fancy, but it is from a shelter for homeless women and Gina generally supports women's causes. She opens the letter, reads it quickly and decides to send a small gift. As she waits for her dinner to cook, she writes out a check for $15 and puts it in the return envelope that accompanied the appeal. She mails it the next day then soon forgets about the group.

This impulse gift does not represent Gina's true giving ability or say very much about her commitment to the shelter. Now the homeless shelter must try to move Gina to the level of habitual giver, and they do.

In a few days Gina again comes home tired, and again feeds her cats and reads her mail. In it, she has received a short personal thank-you note from the shelter. "Wow. How nice," she thinks. She again feels good about her gift and the name of the group is more firmly planted in her mind.

Over the next few months, Gina receives a copy of the shelter's newsletter and one day she drives by the shelter. About three months later, Gina receives another letter from the shelter. This letter thanks her again for her previous gift and asks if she can make a special extra gift to help buy some playground equipment for the children of the women at the shelter. Gina is touched by the request and sends $25. Again, she is thanked.

Three months later, she is asked again for a special extra gift — this one to help defray the costs of a job training program that will partially be funded by the city. While Gina thinks this is important, she has also had to replace two tires on her car, so sends nothing. Three months after this — now nine months since her first gift — she is invited to an open house at the shelter. She attends and is given a tour of the facility and meets the director and some board members. Everyone who attends the open house is asked to leave a check in a jar by the door if possible. Gina gives another $15.

By now, Gina has moved from being an impulse donor to being a habitual donor to the shelter. Whenever they ask, she gives unless she really can't afford to. She feels she is a part of this organization and may even mention it to friends from time to time.

After a year or two of giving small gifts two or three times a year, either by mail or at a special event, Gina receives a personal letter signed by a board member, asking her to consider upgrading her gift to $100. The letter thanks her for her past support, reviews how important the shelter is, and asks her not to make a decision until the board member calls her. Gina now has to think about the organization: How important is it to her? Can she afford it? Does she care enough to send $100 to this group? What will she want to find out from the board member to help make her decision?

Whatever her decision, Gina has moved to the next level, that of thoughtful donor. She may thoughtfully decide to give $100, or she may decide to give $50, or she may continue to give small gifts a few times a year, but she has had to think about her giving. She gives $100.

Over the course of the two years, Gina's relationship to the shelter went from impersonal giving by mail to a little more personal (attending events) to very personal (being solicited by a member of the board).

Over the next few years, Gina is asked to give again, and to give more until, after five years of being a regular donor to the shelter, she is giving $250 a year. That year, the shelter decides to buy a new building so that they can be a model shelter and be able to conduct their many programs on-site. The building will cost $350,000. They receive some state and federal funding for the purchase and $25,000 from a foundation; they must raise $100,000 from individuals. They launch a capital campaign to ask each of their donors for a capital gift in addition to their annual gift. Gina is asked to serve on the capital campaign committee because she has given so regularly and steadily for five years. She comes to events and is acquainted with several board members. Gina agrees to serve on the committee and to give $5,000 that she inherited from an aunt. She is happy to find a meaningful way to use this money that she did not expect to receive.

After the campaign is completed, Gina becomes a regular volunteer at the shelter and later serves on the board. When the shelter institutes a planned giving program, Gina changes her will so that the shelter is the beneficiary of the bulk of her estate.

The progression for Gina from impulse to habitual to thoughtful donor is natural and feels good to Gina. But for the shelter it is the result of careful planning and a strong commitment to developing relationships with donors.

stock and the like. Only by asking will you find out what your donors might be willing and able to do for your group.

Organization's needs	Donor helps using
Annual	Yearly income
Capital	Assets (savings, property, stocks)
Endowment	Estate

Three Types of Strategies

Because all strategies are directed toward building relationships with funding sources — whether these sources are individuals, as this book stresses, or foundations, corporations or government — it is important to understand the types of strategies that create and improve these relationships. There are three broad categories of strategies — acquisition, retention and upgrading — and they relate directly to the progression that donors follow — giving impulsively, giving habitually and giving thoughtfully.

1) Acquisition strategies. The main purpose of these strategies is to get people who have not given to your group before to give for the first time. Direct mail is probably the most common acquisition strategy. Acquisition strategies seek impulse donors, and the income from them is generally used for the organization's annual fund.

2) Retention strategies. These strategies seek to get donors to give a second time, a third time, and so on, until they are donors of habit. The income from retention strategies is also used for annual needs.

3) Upgrading strategies. These strategies aim to get donors to give more than they have previously — to give a bigger gift regularly, and later to give gifts of assets and a gift of their estate. Upgrading is done almost entirely through personal solicitation, although it can be augmented by mail or phone contact or through certain special events. Upgrading strategies seek to move habitual donors to thoughtful donors. The income from thoughtful donors is used for annual, capital and endowment needs, depending on the nature of the gift or the campaign for which the gift was sought.

As you plan, note beside each strategy you intend to use whether you are using it for acquiring, retaining or upgrading donors, and make sure it is the best strategy for that purpose.

House Parties Two Ways

An organization decides to hold some house parties to raise money. Seven out of 12 board members invite friends to their home and ask them for money for the group. The remaining five board members who don't want to have a party at their house help with invitations, food, clean-up and so on.

No thought is given to the purpose of these parties beyond the goal of raising money. No one thinks about whether these parties should be used for acquiring, keeping or upgrading donors. Consequently, each board member has a hodgepodge of people at the event — some are donors, some never heard of the group but came because a friend asked them, and some came because they are neighbors and it looked there would be free food. Many people are invited to more than one house party because there is no attempt to sort lists ahead of time.

The parties make about $6,000 so they are not a waste of time or effort, but some donors complain about being invited to so many events and many non-donors at the parties do not make a gift.

The following year, the organization decides to use the same strategy but to segment the parties and be more thoughtful in their approach. First, they compile a master list of everyone to be invited to ensure that no one is invited to more than one party unless that person would give at more than one party. Then they designate some parties as being only for people who have not given before, with a sprinkling of current donors to encourage the non-donors to give.

Next, they decide on the fundraising method for each party. One board member wants to charge people $25 to come to his party so that every person who is there will have made a donation, and he does not do another pitch at the party. Another feels that her friends will give more if she gives a pitch at the party; she aims for first gifts of $50 to $100 from most of the guests. Another board member who has a particularly fancy house has an elegant party for current donors. This party is used specifically as an upgrade strategy; the donors who are invited are capable of giving more than they currently do. At the party, the guests are introduced to members of the board and given an opportunity to discuss a political issue related to the group and make recommendations for action. The party is limited to 15 people. In a personal follow-up solicitation, the hosting board member asks each person for $500.

By determining which parties are for which purpose, the organization now increases its earnings from these parties fourfold to $24,000. It also acquires 40 new donors, upgrades 15 donors, and does not receive any complaints. As an unexpected side benefit, three donors offer to give their own house parties.

You Can't Save Time

For small organizations, the ultimate reason to be thoughtful about fundraising strategies is to work smarter, not harder. The group noted in the house party example in the sidebar raised 400 percent more money in their second year of houseparties by spending a little more time to think about the strategy more thoroughly. There is a Buddhist saying, "We have so little time that we must proceed very slowly." This applies to fundraising and especially to small organizations with tight budgets that have little room to make errors due to carelessness and lack of thought.

It is clear to me from years of working with nonprofit organizations that you cannot save time. You can put time in on the front end, planning, thinking things through and doing things right, or you can "save time" on the front end and put it in at the back end, clearing up the mess, handling disgruntled donors, and having to do more fundraising because what you have done did not raise the money you need. This book will help you be a front-end time user!

4.

Making a Case for Your Organization

The previous chapters discussed the framework for fundraising, the logic of the fundraising process, and the fact that the organization will ultimately be supported not so much by money itself as by relationships with individual donors who give money because of their increasing commitment to the group.

The next logical step an organization must take, then, is to examine why it exists and what it does. This is the bedrock on which a fundraising plan is built.

The first task in fundraising is to develop a written document that describes in some detail the need an organization was set up to meet, the way the organization will meet that need, and the capacity of the organization to meet that need. This document is called a "case statement." It is an internal document for use by staff, board and key volunteers. It is not a secret document, but it is too long and cumbersome for use in approaching the general public. Parts of it will be used in brochures, proposals, direct mail letters and the like, and nothing that is produced by the organization will contradict the information in the case statement. Hank Rosso, author of *Achieving Excellence in Fundraising*, compares the case statement to a "copy platform" used by advertisers. A "copy platform" delineates the features, the uses and the need for the product. The advertisers will use this information in creating commercials, slogans and ads, and they will not add any features that are not true of the product.

The Contents of the Case Statement

The case statement includes the following elements:

1. A statement of mission that tells the world why the group exists.

2. A description of goals that tells what the organization hopes to accomplish over the long term — in other words, what the organization intends to do about why it exists.

3. A list of objectives — specific, measurable and time-limited — that tell how the goals will be met.

4. A summary of the organization's history that shows that the organization is competent and can accomplish its goals.

5. A description of the structure of the organization including board and staff roles and what kinds of people are involved in the group (such as clients, activists, business people, clergy).

6. A fundraising plan.

7. A financial statement for the previous fiscal year and a budget for the current fiscal year.

Having this information in one document, with copies to key people in the organization, saves a great deal of time and helps guarantee that information and philosophies that are presented by board members, staff or volunteers in their personal fundraising letters, in speeches, or in conversations with funders and donors are consistent. Parts of the case statement change every year, and the entire document should be reviewed regularly to ensure that everyone is still in agreement with its premises and that the words used still accurately describe what the organization is doing. Let's take a look at each of the elements of a case statement.

The Mission Statement

The statement of mission, sometimes called the "Statement of Purpose" or the "Preamble to the Principles of Unity," answers the question, "Why does your organization need to exist?" People in an organization will often claim, "We know why we exist," and then describe their programs, but it may not be clear to a listener that the programs meet any particular need or that there is a problem to be solved. For example, an organization that buys run-down or abandoned apartment buildings and then fixes up and rents each unit well below market rates to elderly poor people has this mission statement: "A fundamental implication of the constitutional guarantee of the right to life, liberty and pursuit of happiness is housing. Decent housing should be a right and not a privilege, yet thousands of seniors have inadequate or substandard housing, and an increasing number have no homes at all. Housing For Seniors seeks to rectify this problem." At this time, their goal is to buy buildings and convert them. However, that mission statement would allow them to have a wide variety of goals, such as advocating with the city to provide housing, helping seniors keep their existing homes, educating the public about the housing shortage, or providing loans to seniors for housing.

In another example, an education organization that focusses on helping teenagers and adults understand how the economy works has this lofty mission: "Authentic human freedom begins with every person living free of any unnecessary economic compulsion. Understanding how economic forces work and how they can be changed is fundamental to this freedom." Their goals include teaching people how unsafe workplaces, wage discrimination, toxic dumping, substandard housing and poverty itself are not necessary for an economy to be healthy and how society could be restructured to eliminate these injustices.

The mission statement is generally not very long, and it does not tell people very much about what an organization does. One of the functions of a mission statement is to make the person hearing or reading it want to ask for more information: "Well, that's very nice, but how are you going to accomplish that mission?" This question allows the organization to describe its goals.

A hint about writing a mission statement: missions often start with "Because" or "Whereas" or with a noun, "People," "Rights," "The future." Avoid using any infinitive verbs such as to do, to provide, to help. Infinitive language is goal language.

Goals

Goal statements tell what your organization is going to do about the problem and indicate the organization's philosophy, which may be expanded in the section on history. The goals are what really distinguish one organization from another, since there are cases where very different groups have similar missions. For example, two organizations whose missions concerned the health of children, emphasizing how children are our future and their health is in our hands, both dealt with the issue of child immunization, but with opposite goals. One group documented the large number of children who were not immunized, particularly poor children and children of undocumented workers. Despite the fact that free immunization was available in their state, many parents did not trust the clinics where the inoculations were provided or did not understand the immunization process. This group worked to have inoculations administered in schools by a nurse to ensure that all children were immunized. The other group was organized by a woman whose child suffered brain damage resulting from a reaction to an immunization (this happens in one in 20,000 cases). She organized a group opposed to immunizations, saying that diseases such as diphtheria are so rare in the United States that the risk from immunization was higher than the risk from the disease. Two organizations with the same concern about children's health, with many goodhearted and thoughtful people working for them, and with opposite agendas. The goals were the defining factor.

Goal statements almost always start with infinitives: "to provide," "to ensure," "to monitor," "to educate."

Objectives

Objectives are statements of specific, measurable, verifiable, easy-to-evaluate actions of how the group intends to accomplish its goals. Objectives are evaluated yearly or in whatever time frame is specified in the objective. "In this calendar year, we will refurbish 14 units of housing and provide homes for 20 seniors." "We will teach four classes a month for nine months and estimate that 10 students will attend each class. A pre-test and post-test will be administered to evaluate our teaching methods and at the end of the year the curriculum will be modified accordingly."

History

The history section summarizes when the group was formed and by whom. If the group has gone through major program changes, some discussion of these changes is useful. This is also the section to provide further documentation of the need for your group. Two examples: "In 1989, Ourtown was shocked by an outbreak of smallpox. Ten children developed the disease and three died. This is when we discovered that children can be admitted to school without proof of immunization." "Homes for Seniors originally focussed on providing living accommodations for homeless seniors until we discovered that hundreds of seniors live in substandard housing, often without electricity or running water. From 1990-1992, we refurbished 20 units that were already inhabited and expanded our program to include upgrading substandard housing."

There are no set rules for the length of the historical piece. Again, common sense would dictate that you strike a balance between telling the whole story and risking boredom from too many details.

The Structure

The structure shows that the way a group is organized is consistent with its overall mission. This section discusses staff and board size, composition and governance. Some examples: "We have four staff who work collectively," or "Our board of 11 members is entirely composed of clients and former clients so that all decisions about the organization are made by people most knowledgeable and most affected by them."

This section can be long if an organization has a complicated or non-traditional structure, or it can be short if the organizational structure is fairly straightforward. The way an organization is structured is a key to its accountability. For example, an organization that claims it is committed to full participation of all members of the community but only has men on the board raises questions about their understanding of community. More and more, donors request information on structural issues to help determine if the group understands the implications of its mission and goals.

This section can also include brief biographical sketches of board members, resumes of staff, and numbers of members, volunteers, and chapters, if applicable.

A Fundraising Plan

The fundraising plan shows whether the organization has a diversity of funding sources and an understanding of the fundraising process. The fundraising plan shows all the sources of income and describes in a narrative fashion how this income will be raised or how these goals will be reached. In a similar way to the structure, the fundraising plan will also show whether the organization is consistent with its mission. For example, an environmental organization primarily supported by oil or timber corporations, or an organization working in the poverty pockets of the inner city with only major donor fundraising strategies both raise questions about how their financing can be consistent with their mission.

A Financial Statement and a Budget

A financial statement provides proof that the organization spends money wisely and monitors its spending, not only in total amount but by category. This would include an annual report, an audited financial report if available or a balance sheet if not. The budget is an estimate of expenses and income for the current fiscal year and should include a description of how finances are monitored — for example, "The finance committee of the board reviews reports monthly, and the full board reviews reports quarterly." (For how to create a budget, see Chapter 31, Developing a Budget.)

Developing the Case Statement

A case statement is usually developed by a small committee, but the board, staff and key volunteers must all agree on the case statement, particularly on the statement of mission and the group's future plans. If the people who must carry out the plans don't like them or don't believe they are possible, they will not do good work for the group. Therefore it is worth spending a good amount of time on developing the case statement. Hurrying a statement of mission or a set of goals through the board process to save time or get on with the job will come back to haunt you in the form of commitments not kept and half-hearted fundraising efforts.

Elements of the Case Statement

Section on	Establishes
Mission	Why the organization exists
Goals	What it will do about why it exists
Objectives	How it will accomplish the goals
History	A track record, showing which objectives have been accomplished already
Structure	Consistency of composition and governance with regard to the goals
Fundraising plan, financial statement, and budget	That the organization intends to exist into the future and is planning and managing its finances appropriately. Also shows that salaries, benefits, rent, and other costs are consistent with the mission

5.

The Board of Directors

The broad purpose of a board of directors is to run the organization effectively. To qualify for tax-exempt status an organization must file a list of names of people who have agreed to fulfill the legal requirements of board membership. The board members are bound to insure that the organization:

- Operates within state and federal laws
- Earns its money honestly and spends it responsibly
- Adopts programs and procedures most conducive to carrying out its mission.

The best summary of a board member's responsibility is contained in the state of New York's Not-for-profit Corporation Law (the language of which has since been adopted by many other states). According to this law, board members must act "in good faith and with a degree of diligence, care and skill which ordinarily prudent men [sic] would exercise under similar circumstances and in like positions."

Board members, in effect, own the organization. They are the final policy makers and they employ the staff. They are chosen because of their commitment to the organization and long-term vision. As the Council of Better Business Bureaus points out, "Being part of the official governing body of a nonprofit, soliciting organization is a serious responsibility, and should never be undertaken with the thought that this is an easy way to perform a public service."

The responsibilities of board members fall into several broad categories. How any specific organization chooses to have board members carry out these responsibilities will depend on the number of board members, the number of paid staff, the sources of funding, and the history of the organization. There are few right or wrong ways to manage an organization, but there are ways that work better in some groups than in others.

With that in mind, let's look at board member responsibilities.

Responsibilities of the Board

Board members are responsible for the following:

1. Ensuring organizational continuity. The board must develop leadership within both board and staff to maintain a mix of old and new people in both spheres.

2. Setting organizational policy, reviewing and evaluating organizational plans. The board ensures that the organization's programs are always in keeping with its statement of mission, and that the statement of mission continues to reflect a true need.

3. Carrying out long-range planning. The board should set aside a time, usually at an annual retreat, in which long-range plans are discussed and formed with reference to the case statement. Where does the organization want to be in two years, five years, 10 years? How big does the organization want to become? If it is a local group, does it want to become regional or national? What are the implications of world events for the group's work, and what is its response? How can the group become more pro-active, rather than reactive? These and other questions can be answered during the long-range planning retreat. Some organizations find it helpful to have a board-level long-range planning committee. This committee can raise and research appropriate questions and bring recommendations to the board for discussion and decision.

4. Ensuring fiscal accountability. The board approves and closely monitors the organization's expenses and income. The board makes certain that all the organization's resources, including the time of volunteers and staff as well as money, are used wisely.

5. Managing personnel. The board sets and reviews personnel policies, hires, evaluates and, when necessary, fires staff. These tasks are often delegated to the executive director. She or he then takes the place of the board in personnel matters. The board hires the executive director and evaluates his or her performance regularly. The board is also the final arbiter of internal staff disputes and grievances and should pay close attention to maintaining good staff-board relationships.

6. Funding the organization. The board is responsible for the continued funding and financial health of the organization. From the point of view of fundraising, board members have two responsibilities: give money and raise money.

Board Structure and Size

There is no evidence that any particular board structure works better than another. Each structure will have its strengths and weaknesses. The structure your organization chooses will probably stem from past history and the desires of the present board members. Some groups work best with a collective structure, including open meetings, informal discussion and decision by consensus. Other groups do better with a hierarchical structure, a parliamentarian who will help the group follow Robert's Rules of Order, and a formal method of discussion and decision making. The only rule of thumb is that the simpler you can keep your structure, the better.

The size of the board also depends on the group, but there is evidence that the ideal size is between 11 and 21 members. A board of fewer than 11 members will probably have too much work, and one of more than 21 members is likely to be unwieldy, with work unevenly divided. If you already have a large board, work can be most effectively accomplished through small committees, keeping full board meetings to a monthly or less frequent schedule. A small board can also be divided into committees, which can be fleshed out with non-board representatives.

Statement of Agreement

For a board to operate successfully, each member must understand and respect the structure and decision-making process as well as the mission of the organization, and must feel that she or he can fully participate in it. Achieving this understanding is difficult if these things are not clearly described to prospective board members before they agree to serve. One technique that many groups have found helpful is to develop a statement of agreement for board members. This statement serves as a job description and clarifies board responsibilities and authority. On the next page is a generic example of such a statement.

This kind of agreement defines understandings that may never before have been verbalized; it also helps channel board members' motivation to serve the organization.

Once a board has developed this type of contract it can be read at regular intervals to remind people of their commitments. It can also be used for internal evaluation and to recruit new board members.

Such an agreement also improves relations between board and staff. Staff know board limits and will not make demands that exceed those

STATEMENT OF AGREEMENT

As a board member of _____, I understand that my duties and responsibilities include the following:

1. I am fiscally responsible, with the other board members, for this organization. It is my duty to know what our budget is and to take an active part in planning the budget and the fundraising to meet it.

2. I am legally responsible, along with the other board members, for this organization. I am responsible to know and approve all policies and programs and to oversee the implementation of policies and programs. I know that if I fail in my tasks, and if the organization becomes the subject of a suit by a private person or of the federal or state government, I may be held personally liable for the debts incurred.

3. I am morally responsible for the health and well-being of this organization. As a member of the board, I have pledged myself to carry out its mission. I am fully committed and dedicated to this mission.

4. I will give what is for me a significant financial donation. I may give this as a one-time donation each year, or I may pledge to give a certain amount several times during the year.

5. I will actively engage in fundraising for this organization in whatever ways are best suited to me. These may include individual solicitation, undertaking special events, writing mail appeals and the like. There is no set amount of money that I must raise because I am making a good faith agreement to do my best and to bring in as much money as I can.

6. I will attend (#) _____ board meetings every year and be available for phone consultation. I understand that commitment to this board will involve a good deal of time and will probably not involve less than _____ hours per month.

7. I understand that no quotas have been set, that no rigid standards of measurement and achievement have been formed. Every board member is making a statement of faith about every other board member. We are trusting each other to carry out the above agreements to the best of our ability, each in our own way, with knowledge, approval and support of all. I know that if I fail to act in good faith I must resign, or someone from the board may ask me to resign.

In its turn, this organization is responsible to me in a number of ways:

1. I will be sent, without request, quarterly financial reports that allow me to meet the "prudent person" section of the law.

2. I can call on the staff to discuss programs and policies, goals and objectives.

3. Board members and staff will respond in a straightforward and thorough fashion to any questions I have that I feel are necessary to carry out my fiscal, legal and moral responsibilities to this organization.

limits. Board members know when they can say, "No, this is not my responsibility."

The Board and Fundraising

The reluctance of board members to take responsibility for fundraising can usually be traced to two sources: 1) board members don't understand the importance of taking a leadership role in fundraising, and 2) they are afraid of asking for money. Board members cannot give themselves wholeheartedly to the process of fundraising unless these two problems are resolved.

The reason that board members must take a leadership role in fundraising is simple: they own the organization. They are responsible for the well-being of the organization and for its successes. Furthermore, their supporters and potential supporters see board members as the people most committed and dedicated to the organization. If they, who care the most about the group, will not take a lead role in fundraising, why should anyone else? When the board does take the lead its members and the staff can go to individuals, corporations, and foundations and say, "We have 100 percent commitment from our board. All board members give money and raise money." This position strengthens their fundraising case a great deal. More and more, sophisticated individuals and foundations are asking organizations about the role of the board in fundraising and taking a more positive look at groups whose board plays an active part.

Board members are often reluctant to participate in fundraising activities because they fear they will be required to ask people for money. It's true that many fundraising strategies require board members to make face-to-face solicitations. This is a skill and thus can be learned, and all board members should have the opportunity to attend a training session on asking for money (see Chapter 12, Personal Solicitation).

In a diversified fundraising plan, however, some board members can participate in fundraising strategies that do not require directly asking for money. While some can solicit large gifts, others can plan special events, write mail appeals, market products for sale, write thank you notes, stuff envelopes, enter information into a data base, etc. Every one's interests and skills can be used. Board members inexperienced in fundraising can start with an easy assignment ("Sell these 20 raffle tickets") and then move on to more difficult fundraising assignments ("Ask this person for $1,000"). Some fundraising strategies will use all the board members (selling tickets to the dance), whereas others will require the work of only one or two people (speaking to service clubs or writing mail appeals).

Often people who join a board bring two myths with them that hamper their participation in fundraising. First, they feel that since they give time they should not be called on to give money. "Time is money," they will argue. Second, if an organization has paid staff, board members may feel that it is the staff's job to do the fundraising. Let us quickly dispel both of these myths.

While a person's time is valuable to them, it is not the same as money. You cannot go to the telephone company and offer to run their switchboard in order to pay your phone bill. You cannot pay your staff or buy your office supplies with your time. Further, everyone has the same amount of time in a day, but people have vastly unequal amounts of money. Finally, people are rarely nervous to ask someone for their time, but are very reluctant to ask someone for their money, even though time is a non-renewable resource, whereas money is not.

In training, I often use this example: "If a board member is assigned to call three people and tell them about a meeting on Wednesday night, he or she will do it. If two people can come to the meeting and one can't, the board member does not take this personally and feel like a failure. However, if this same board member is assigned to ask these same three people for $100, he or she will probably be very uncomfortable without training in how to ask for money." I have conducted thousands of trainings in how to ask for money but I have never been asked to lead a training in how to ask for time. Comparing time and money is like comparing apples and asphalt. Board members must understand that contributions of time and money are very different, although equally important, parts of their role.

Paid staff have specific roles in fundraising. These are to help plan fundraising strategies, coordinate fundraising activities, keep records, take care of routine fundraising tasks such as renewal appeals, and assist board members by writing letters for them, form fundraising plans with them and accompany them to solicitation meetings (see Chapter 29, Hiring a Development Director). Fundraising staff provide all the backup needed for effective fundraising. It is clearly impossible, however, for one person or even several people to do all the work necessary in a diversified fundraising plan. Just as it is foolish for an organization to depend on one or two sources of funding, it is equally unwise for it to depend on one or two people to do fundraising.

The final reason for all board members to participate in fundraising is to ensure that the work is evenly shared. Fundraising is rarely anyone's favorite task, so it is important that each board member knows that the other members are doing their share. If some members do all the fundraising while others make policy, resentments are bound to arise. The same resentments will surface if some board members give money and others don't. Those who give may feel that their donation "buys" them out of some work or that their money entitles them to more power. Those who do not give money may feel that they do all the work or that those who give money have more power. When board members know that everyone is giving their best effort to fundraising according to their abilities, the board will function most smoothly and members will be more willing to take on fundraising tasks.

Common Board Problems and Suggested Solutions

While each board of directors will have its own problems and tensions to be resolved, many boards have a number of problems in common. These are discussed here, along with some solutions.

1. Board members are overworked — too much is expected of them. Nonprofit organizations use all of their volunteers to augment paid staff. The smaller the organization, the more responsibility volunteers will have, becoming more and more like paid staff. To a certain point this is fine. But there comes a time when board members are taking on much more work than they had agreed to. Overload can result when board members are given new work by staff or because board work takes longer than originally planned. When board members find themselves attending three or four meetings each month and spending hours on the telephone, they begin to dread calls and meetings and to count the days until their term is up.

This dynamic can be changed or averted altogether by adhering to the following principles:

a) Board members should feel they can say "no" to tasks that go beyond their original commitment.

b) Staff and board members should ensure that tasks given to the board have a clear beginning and end. Thus, when additional work is essential, board members should be assured that extra meetings will last no more than a month or two and that once that task is accomplished they will not be asked to do more than the minimum for a few months.

c) A careful eye should be kept on what the whole board does with its time. Board members (particularly the executive or steering committee) should ask, "Are all these meetings necessary? Can one person do what two have been assigned to do? Or two people what four have committed to do?"

d) Boards should not be asked to make decisions for which they are unqualified. Sometimes consultants need to be asked for recommendations, or the board needs to be trained to handle tasks of management and fundraising.

2. Individual board members were uninformed about the amount of work. This problem can arise either because the person was given little impression of the amount of work involved beyond attending regular board meetings, or because she or he already serves on the boards of other organizations and is thus overcommitted. In the latter case he or she cannot fulfill the expectations of any of the organizations and feels overworked even while not doing very much for any one organization.

A clear and precise statement of agreement (as discussed earlier in this chapter) will help with this problem. The statement can be used to screen out people who are overextended and to call current board members into accountability.

3. The board avoids making decisions. In this instance the board constantly refers items back to committees or to staff for further discussion and research. The whole board never seems to have enough information to commit themselves to a course of action. This problem is generally the result of inadequate board leadership. The board chair or president must set an example of decisiveness. He or she needs to point out that the board can never know all the factors surrounding a decision and yet must act despite factors changing on a daily or weekly basis.

The person facilitating a meeting should always establish time limits for each item on the agenda and push for a decision within the allocated discussion time. This can be done at the beginning of the meeting. Close to the end of the time allotted for an item, the chair should say, "We are almost at the end of time for discussion on this item. What are the suggestions for a decision?" If the chair or facilitator of the meeting does not take this role, individual board members should take it upon themselves to call for a time limit on discussion and a deadline for a decision.

Very few decisions are irrevocable. Decisions can be modified, expanded, or scrapped altogether once they are made and put into action.

4. The board makes decisions, notes them in the minutes, and then forgets about them. As a result of this process the board both fails to implement their decisions and usually has to decide the same issue again in a few months or years. Further, board members feel that they are not taking themselves seriously and that their work is for nothing. Three methods can be used to avoid this problem. One method is to appoint a member to keep track of decisions and remind the board of them. The secretary of the board can serve this function, or someone designated as "historian." A second, complementary, method is for decisions from board meetings (as distinct from meeting minutes) to be written up and kept in a notebook that is available at every board meeting. The notebook can be indexed so that decisions can be easily found. The chair and executive committee should familiarize themselves with this book. Finally, each board member should read and keep a copy of the minutes of every meeting. Then, each member can help remind the whole of decisions made.

5. A few board members do all or most of the work. When this happens, those who do the work resent those who are not carrying their share. Those who don't work resent those who do because they imagine them to have all the power. Inevitably, some people will work harder than others and some will work better. Nonetheless, the board should plan for work to be evenly shared and for everyone to take an active role, assuming that all members will work equally hard and equally effectively. Above all, board members must value everyone's contribution. The person who stuffs envelopes is as valuable as the person whose friend gives $5,000. People rise to the standards set for them. Mediocre work should not be accepted.

6. Staff members don't really want the board to have power, or some board members don't want to share the power evenly. Sometimes people take and keep power because they enjoy having power and building empires. More often, though, they take power because they are afraid to let go — afraid that others will not do as well as they have. This is particularly true when some board members have served for many years or when a person on staff has seen the board turn over several times. Whoever perceives that someone is hoarding power or refusing to delegate tasks (either staff or board) should address their concerns to the appropriate committee. That person should name specific instances to the committee in which they think that happened so that people can have a clear sense of what they are doing wrong and change their behavior accordingly. Generally, people will share power in the organization as others prove reliable.

All of the dynamics described above, as well as others including personality conflicts, deep political disagreements, or staff-board conflicts can be serious enough to immobilize an organization. The board and staff may not be able to resolve the problem themselves. Sometimes they can't even figure out what the problem is. Board or staff members should not hesitate to seek help in that case. A consultant in organizational development or a mediator can help the group articulate and solve its problems. Although for a board to find itself in such an extreme situation is unfortunate, it is usually no one person's fault. To not ask for help in getting out of the situation, however, constitutes a failure of board or staff members to be fully responsible.

Some conflict can be creative, and board members and staff should not shun difficult discussions or disagreements. There is built-in tension between program and finance committees, new and old board members, and staff and board personnel. As Karl Mathiasen, a veteran board member and consultant to organizations for social change, states in *Confessions of a Board Member*, "My own feeling is that if you go to a Board meeting and never during that meeting have a time during which you are tense and your heart beats faster and you know that something is at stake — if you lack that feeling two or three meetings in a row, there is something wrong with the organization."

Recruiting and Involving New Board Members

Once an organization has a clear sense of the board's roles and responsibilities, defined the type of structure it wants (collective, hierarchy, etc.) and developed a statement of understanding or similar agreement, it can begin the formal process of recruiting additional board members. Two key tenets of board composition are: 1) while sharing a sense of commitment to the organization's mission and goals, board members also need to represent a diversity of opinion and skill; 2) ideally, the combination of all the people on the board will provide all the skills required to run the organization.

To recruit board members, the current board should appoint two or three people to form a "nominating committee." In some organizations this becomes a standing committee on the board. This small group will assess the present board's strengths and decide what skills or qualities are needed to overcome the board's weaknesses. The following chart is an example of a way to evaluate the current board and quickly spot the gaps. Each group should fill it in with the board membership criteria it has established.

Skill	Name of Board Member			
	Reilly	*Stedman*	*Burger*	*McHenry*
Budgetting	x			
Personnel Issues		x		
Fundraising		x		
From individuals	x	x		
Special events			x	
Marketing			x	
Planned giving			x	
Membership				x
Program Planning	x	x		
Evaluation		x		
Publicity				x
Client	x			
Former client			x	
Diversity requirements				

Note: Each group should decide what types of people should be represented on the board in terms of race, sex, sexual orientation, age and so forth. It is also important to note that no one person can speak for an entire constituency.

Some of the unmet criteria could probably be satisfied by one or two people. In other areas you may need several people to develop the balance you want. For example, most community organizations will want several community activists who also embody a range of other qualifications, but may only want or need one attorney or business person.

There is a common belief that a board should have "movers and shakers" on it. Bank presidents, successful business people, politicians, corporate executives and the like are thought to be people with power and connections, making them ideal board members. This is definitely not necessary. There are hundreds of successful organizations whose board members are neither rich nor college-educated and who have no access to and little desire to know the movers and shakers of their community. Other qualifications and the ability to commit time to the work of making the organization successful are of far greater importance.

First and foremost, board members and new recruits must understand, appreciate and desire to further the goals and objectives of the organization. Enthusiasm, commitment and a willingness to work are the primary qualifications. Everything else required of a board member can be learned, and the skills needed can be brought by a wide variety of people and taught to others on the board.

In assessing what skills and qualifications your board lacks, then, don't just go for the obvious recruits. For example, suppose that no one on your board understands budgeting. An obvious solution would be to recruit an accountant or corporate executive to meet this need. If you know someone in one of these areas who shares the commitments and ideals of your group, then certainly invite her or him to be a board member. But if you don't know anyone whose profession involves budgeting, use your imagination to see what other kind of person might have those skills. In one organization, a self-described housewife does all the budgeting and evaluation of financial reports. Her experience of managing a large family has taught her all the basics of financial management; she is completely self-taught. Anyone who has to keep within a budget may have excellent budgeting skills: ministers, directors of other nonprofit organizations, small businesspersons, homemakers.

Another example: If the gap on your board is in getting publicity, an obvious choice would be someone who works in the media or has a job in public relations. However, as many groups know, anyone willing to tell his or her personal story or who is articulate about the issues can get media attention if a staff person lays the groundwork. A staff member can arrange an interview, send a press release and put together a press packet. A volunteer can then do the follow-up required to get the media coverage.

The Recruitment

Prospective board members are found among friends and acquaintances of current board members, staff members, former board and staff members, and current donors and clients. Ideally, a prospective board member is someone who already gives time and money to the organization.

The chair of the board should send a letter to each prospective board member asking the person if he or she is interested in serving on the board and giving a few details of what that would mean. The letter should state that someone will call in a few days to make an appointment to discuss the invitation in detail. Even if the prospect is a friend of a board or staff member, or a long-time volunteer, a formal invitation will convey that being on this board is an important responsibility and a serious commitment, and that it is a privilege to be invited. Whoever knows the board prospect can follow up the letter by talking to the person about being on the board. If no one knows the prospect, two people from the board should see the person. If the prospective board member does not have time to meet and discuss the board commitment, this is a clue that he or she will not have time to serve and should not be on the list of prospects.

Whoever meets with the prospective board member should go over the board's statement of understanding point by point. The current members should share their experiences in fulfilling their commitment and discuss what others have done to fulfill theirs. It is particularly important to discuss the amount of time board participation requires as well as the area of fundraising. Do not make the board commitment sound easier than it is. It is better for a person to join the board and discover that it is not as much work as was originally thought than to find that it is much more work and resent having had the commitment misrepresented.

The contact person should feel free to ask the prospective board member how he or she feels about the group or what experience he or she has in working with people of other classes, races, sexual orientation, and so on, depending on the composition of your board. Asking someone to be on the board is as serious as inviting someone to be a partner in a business, finding a new roommate, or interviewing staff. Do not expect people to change once they are on the board. What you see is what you get.

Tell the person why you are asking him or her to be on the board. Let him or her know that the nominating committee has given a great deal of thought to this choice. Give the person a few days to think it over. Ask him or her to call for more information or with further questions. Let this be an informed and considered choice. It is better for 10 people to turn you down than to get 10 half-hearted new board members.

Orienting the New Board Member

After a person has accepted nomination to the board and been elected, a current board member should be assigned to act as the new person's "buddy." The current board member should bring the new board member to the first meeting, meet with him or her (perhaps for lunch or dinner) once a month for the first two or three months, and be available for discussion. New board members have many questions that they are too embarrassed or shy to ask at the full board meeting. They will be incorporated into the life of the organization much faster if they can easily get the answers they need.

At their first meeting, the new board members should receive a packet of information including copies of the signed statement of understanding, the organization's by-laws, the case statement, and anything else that would be helpful to their understanding of the organization: an organizational chart, the current annual budget, brochures and other promotional information, and the names addresses, phone numbers, and profiles of the other board members and of staff members.

Board members work best when they feel both needed and accountable. They will be more likely to keep their commitments when they know that keeping commitments is expected, and that others are doing so. When this tone is established at the beginning, the board will function smoothly.

A Note on Advisory Boards

In addition to a board of directors, small organizations often find it helpful to form "advisory boards" made up of people who can help with various parts of the organization's program, including fundraising. Having an advisory board can be a helpful strategy, although it involves a good deal of work and does not take the place of a board of directors.

In some ways an advisory board is an administrative fiction. Unlike a board of directors, an advisory board has no legal requirements, no length of time to exist, and no purposes that must be filled. Such a board can consist of one person or 200.

Advisory boards are variously named depending on their functions. They may be called community boards, auxiliaries, task forces, committees, or advisory councils. Some advisory boards meet frequently; others, never. Sometimes advisory board members serve the group by allowing the organization to use their names on the organization's letterhead. In at least one case an organization's advisory board was called together, met, and disbanded all in the same day.

You can form an advisory board for the sole purpose of fundraising. Since this board has no final responsibility for the overall management of the organization, its members can be recruited from anywhere. Furthermore, the advisory board can be completely homogeneous — something a group tries to avoid in its board of directors.

People like to be on advisory boards. It gives them a role in an organization without the full legal and fiscal responsibilities of a member of the board of directors.

Is an Advisory Board Right for Your Organization?

Organizations sometimes see an advisory board as a "quick fix" to their fundraising problems. They may reason, "Next year our group has to raise three times as much money as it did this year. Our board can't do it alone and we don't want to add new board members. So, we'll just ask 10 rich people to be on a fundraising advisory board and they'll raise the extra money we need."

There are several problems here. First, finding "10 rich people" is not that simple. If it were, the group would already have a successful major gifts program. Second, a wealthy person doesn't necessarily have an easier time asking for and getting money than someone who is not wealthy. Nor will he or she necessarily be more willing to give your group money than a "not rich" person.

These are the conditions under which an advisory board is a solution to a fundraising need:

1. **Although the board of directors is already doing as much fundraising as it can, it is not enough.** An advisory board works best when it is augmenting the work of an active and involved board of directors.

2. **An organization has a specific and time-limited project that needs its own additional funding.** This can be a capital campaign, an endowment project, or a time-limited program requiring extra staff and other expenses. The advisory board commits to raise a certain amount of money overall or a certain amount every year for usually not more than three years.

3. **An organization needs help to run a small business or put on a large special event every year.** This type of advisory board is usually called an "auxiliary."

4. **An organization wants help in raising money from a particular part of the private sector, such as corporations, businesses, service clubs, or churches.** The advisory board, composed of repre-

sentatives from these particular sectors, plans the campaign and the members solicit their own colleagues.

Forming the Advisory Board

If you decide that an advisory board is a good tool for your group, be sure to write out clearly what you want in this group. Use the same specificity and thoroughness here as in drawing up a statement of understanding for your board of directors. In terms of fundraising, set an amount that you want the group to raise as a goal, the number of hours you expect them to work (per month, per event, etc.), and the number of meetings they need to attend. Also suggest ways for them to raise money. Sometimes you won't know what to suggest, which may be why you are forming this board. In that case, be clear that there is no staff expertise to guide advisory board members.

Be straightforward with prospects for your advisory board. Tell them your goals and choose people who can work to meet those goals.

Use the same priorities in choosing members as when forming a board of directors. Of primary importance is the members' commitment to your organization. They must of course be willing to express that commitment by fundraising.

Once you have formed an advisory board the staff of the organization must provide back-up as needed and guide the board as much as necessary. The chair or designated representative of the board of directors should receive reports from the advisory board and frequently call or write the chair of the advisory board to express the organization's appreciation for the advisory board's work. Advisory board members should receive minutes of every meeting, be phoned frequently, and generally treated like major donors to the organization (which they are).

Allow the advisory board to develop a direction. The first few months may be slow, but once an advisory board begins to work well and carry out its commitments, its members can raise a substantial amount of money every year.

SECTION 2
Strategies to Acquire and Keep Donors

INTRODUCTION

The vast majority of fundraising time is spent getting people to give once and then getting them to give again. The strategies that form the backbone of this effort are the ones we are most familiar with: direct mail, special events, and solicitation by phone or in person. People in my workshops sometimes ask if there aren't easier ways to raise money than these. I am tempted to answer, "Yes, but the 'Easy Ways To Raise Money' workshop is much more expensive than 'Hard Ways To Raise Money,' which is what you are attending." But I restrain myself because I know that these tried-and-true methods are labor intensive, require extensive attention to detail, and don't always pay off the way we plan.

The following seven chapters will help you to use these strategies properly and, I hope, give you a number of ideas of variations on the theme. The concluding chapter of this section is on writing thank-you notes. I devote an entire chapter to it because thank-you notes can also be varied and interesting and because thanking people for what they do for your organization is both the simplest and most important thing you can do, besides running your organization soundly and honestly, to get a donor to give again.

6.

Using Direct Mail

Direct mail fundraising is the term used to describe impersonal fundraising letters sent by bulk mail. Letters that are addressed to an individual — "Dear Mrs. Smith" — or letters sent first class are not technically direct mail pieces, although these more personalized letters may borrow from direct mail principles in their look or style of writing and the body of the letter may be identical to letters going to dozens — or thousands — of recipients. Direct mail letters are sent in minimum quantities of 200, pre-sorted by zip code for the post office; at the post office they receive bottom priority for processing.

Direct mail solicitation (often derisively called "junk mail") is a relatively recent strategy on the fundraising scene. It was first used on a mass scale in 1968 for the Barry Goldwater for President campaign. For the next ten years direct mail fundraising became a popular method and many organizations derived the bulk of their income from it. Over time, its effectiveness has decreased; the market has been saturated with it and people have become accustomed to it, making letters from groups one never heard of no longer as interesting to open.

According to researcher Woody Igou writing for *In These Times*, in 1988 the postal service delivered 63 billion pieces of unsolicited mail. This figure has certainly not decreased in the past several years. To place this huge number in a context, Igou noted that 40 percent of the total mail in the world is domestic mail in the U.S., and 40 percent of that mail is direct mail from both commercial and nonprofit sources. This means that about one out of every six pieces of mail worldwide is direct mail. For many Americans far more than one out of six pieces coming through their mail slots is an unsolicited fundraising letter.

Some fundraising professionals (and probably thousands of consumers) have questioned the continued use of direct mail as an effective fundraising strategy. Despite all the bad publicity it gets, however, direct mail remains the least expensive way an organization can reach the most people with a message that they can hold in their hands and examine at their leisure. A well-designed and well-written direct mail piece sent to a good list (more on all of this later) has consistently yielded a 1 percent response — though small, this is far greater than any other way of reaching large numbers of people who do not know about your group. Many groups also use direct mail letters to communicate with current donors and ask for additional gifts. As a strategy, direct mail is here to stay and grassroots organizations can and should use it effectively.

Two Functions of Direct Mail

Direct mail soliciting has two functions — donor acquisition and retention. Along with special events, it is one of the most versatile strategies an organization can use to develop closer and closer relationships with its donors. The two functions overlap with the first two steps in the sequence of the donor-organization relationship discussed in Chapter 3, Fundraising Needs and Strategies. The third step, upgrading, is done more through personalized mail and personal contact.

Donor Acquisition

Donor acquisition — getting someone to give for the first time — is the primary purpose of direct mail, and direct mail does it better than any other strategy. Here's how. Organization A trades 2000 names of their donors for 2000 names of donors to a similar group. Organization A sends a direct mail appeal to the other group's names; 1 percent — or 20 people (the expected response) — become donors. Suppose it costs 40 cents for each piece of mail (including postage, printing, paper and the use of a mail house to send it) or $800 total. Suppose most of the 20 donors give $30, which is the suggested donation. Some give more and some give less; Organization A grosses $600 on the mailing. Subtracting net from gross, they lost $200. But, in fact, they spent $200 to acquire 20 donors, who will now be moved to the next stage.

A note on numbers: 2000 names is considered by most experts to be an appropriate test sample size. The idea is that if you get a 1 percent or better response from a sample of 2000 names, you should send the appeal to the whole list. If the response is less than 1 percent, you can change the appeal or abandon the list. To take advantage of direct mail rates, you only need 200 names, but 200 is not considered statistically significant for predicting future response on that list or a similar list. However, read on to find out how to make acquisition by direct mail within the reach of most small nonprofits.

Retention

Once a person becomes a donor, the organization has to try to ensure that the donor maintains a loyalty to their group and gives routinely. The best way to increase retention of donors — that is, to get donors to repeat their gift — is to ask them for money more than once a year. Small organizations should ask their current donors for money at least two or three times a year, either through the mail or with a combination of mail and phone solicitations and special events. This frequency of asking will not offend people and will keep the name of your group in your donors' consciousness. It also enables you to take advantage of the ups and downs of each donor's cash flow. Every time you ask your donors for an extra gift by mail, you can expect that about 10 percent of them will respond. In this phase you make back the money you spent acquiring these people. You will probably even show a profit.

To be considered an active donor (as opposed to a lapsed donor), a person must make a contribution at least once a year. Most organizations have a renewal rate of about 66 percent — enough to generate a nice profit.

The following chart shows one organization's direct mail plan and its results. Note that the renewal mailing is what makes direct mail acquisition a profitable strategy.

Acquisition and Renewal through Direct Mail: One Organization's Results

Income

Acquisition mailings

5 mailings of 2000 pieces each; 1% response @ $25 (100 donors acquired from these mailings)	$2,500
Three more mailings to those who gave asking for extra gifts	
10% response from 100 donors at various amounts (30 extra gifts from the 100 acquired donors)	$ 750
One renewal mailing to these 100 donors; 66% at $25	$1,650
Total income	**$4,900**

Expenses

Acquisition mailings (renting or exchanging lists, printing postage, etc) 10,000 pieces at .35	$3,500

Three more mailings to 100 donors

   3 X 100 X .40 $ 120

Renewal mailings (one to everyone and a second
to those who do not respond to the first)

   150 letters total X .40 $ 60

Total expenses   **$3,680**

Net gain, 66 donors $1,670

Note: Mailings to fewer than 200 donors at a time will require first class postage, thereby increasing the cost per piece for these mailings.

Large organizations that send frequent direct mail appeals often have a fund of $5,000 to $50,000 that they constantly reinvest in these appeals. Money coming in from one appeal is invested in the next until the fund is depleted. Organizations spending that kind of money often hire direct mail consultants to design their appeals and to handle all the details of writing, printing and mailing them.

If you have read this far, you are probably thinking, "Well, that counts my group out. We don't have the front money, we don't have the lists, and we can't wait a year or two for the repeat gifts and renewals to come in to start making money on this scheme."

Don't despair. There is a way for even small groups to use mail appeals effectively. To do so, they must decrease the risk by decreasing the amount of money spent on each mailing. At the same time, they must try to increase the response rate, so that they at least break even on first-time mailings to a list and with luck, make money.

These goals are achieved in two ways: 1) by writing to more carefully selected lists and 2) by mailing to fewer people at one time. In the example above we used the conventional estimate of 1 percent response from a new list, which, to be safe, is what you should use in making predictions and planning costs. However, with smaller, targeted mailings, a response rate of two percent or even three percent is not unusual.

Let's look at the scenario above on a much smaller scale with much more targeted lists.

Direct Mail Acquisition and Renewal: A Smaller Scale

Income

5 acquisition mailings X 200 pieces each;

   2% response @ $25 (20 new donors) $500

Two requests for extra gifts to 20 people X 10% = 4 gifts $100

Renewal mailing to 20 people at 66% response X $25	$250
Total income	**$850**

Expenses

1000 pieces of mail X .40	$400
40 letters asking for extra gifts X .40	$ 16
Renewal mailing to 30 people (includes second mailing to those not responding) X .40	$ 16
Total expenses	**$432**
Net gain, 13 donors	$318

Developing Lists for Direct Mail

The main ingredient for the success of any mail appeal is the list of people it is sent to. Compile or choose lists carefully. Make sure that each person's name is spelled correctly and that the address and zip code are correct. People tend to be miffed when their name is misspelled, and a wrong zip code will mean the letter won't be delivered.

Lists are divided into three categories relating to the likelihood of people on that list making a donation. These categories are hot, warm and cold.

◆ **A hot list** consists of people who have already made some kind of commitment to your organization. In order of decreasing heat, these people are your current donors (from whom can you expect a 10-66 percent response); lapsed donors from the past two years (5-10 percent response); volunteers and board members who are not yet donors (various response rates depending on the group, but probably not lower than 5 percent and possibly as high as 100 percent); and finally, the close friends and associates of all of the above people who are not yet donors (2-5 percent response).

◆ **A warm list** consists of people who have either used or heard of your services or are donors to organizations similar to yours but have not heard of your group. These lists should yield a 1-3 percent response.

◆ **A cold list** is any list that is more than a year old, or any list of people about whom you know little or nothing. The phone book is an example of a cold list.

Hot Lists

The hottest list of people for any organization is its list of current donors. The second-hottest list includes friends of current donors, because most people are friends with people who share their values and commitments. Therefore, to find new hot names to send appeals to, send current donors an annual mailing asking them to send the names and addresses of friends they think would be interested in your organization. Some people will send only one or two names, and most people will not send any, but others will send in dozens of names. With a mailing list of 1000 donors, you can be assured of getting at least 200 names from this type of appeal. Many organizations regularly remind their current donors to send in names of potential contributors by including a coupon in their newsletter and a request for names in other appeals.

Friends of board members, volunteers and staff are also hot prospects. On a yearly basis these people should also be asked to provide a list of names, which can be compared to the current mailing list; anyone who is not already a donor can be solicited. Of course, any board member, staff person, or volunteer who isn't already a donor is a hot prospect as well.

Some statisticians claim that every person knows 250 people — relatives, school friends, colleagues, neighbors and so on. Of this number perhaps only 10 to 20 will be suitable prospects. Nevertheless, with each volunteer or member contributing some names, you will soon have the 200 needed for a bulk mailing.

Warm Lists

If your organization gives people advice, referrals or other service over the phone or through the mail, create a system to gather the names of people served. A notebook to log the needed information can be kept by each phone. When people call, respond to their request and then ask if you can send them more information about your organization. People who don't want an appeal will decline to give their name. Names from information requests that come through the mail can be transferred directly onto carrier envelopes; every time you have acquired 200 names you can send an appeal by bulk mail. Some groups prefer to send appeals by first class mail as the names come in. This ensures a hotter prospect, but the postage cost makes it more expensive.

People who buy any of your organization's products, such as booklets, educational materials, T-shirts, etc., are prospects for a mail appeal.

Certainly, their names should be kept to advertise any new items you produce, and some of them will become members of your organization. The same is true of people who attend conferences, seminars, or public meetings that you sponsor.

People who attend special events who are not donors should receive an appeal soon after the event. Pass out a sign-up sheet, or conduct a door prize drawing to get names and addresses. People who previously gave your organization money but no longer do constitute a warm list if you have correct addresses for them.

Renting and Trading

The other type of warm list are lists of people who belong to organizations similar to yours. To get these names requires renting or trading mailing lists. No one actually buys a mailing list. They rent it; that is, they acquire the right to use the list one time. Many organizations with large mailing lists (5,000 or more names) use the rental of their lists as a fundraising device. You may have noticed that if you give money to one organization, within a few weeks you will receive appeals from several similar organizations. Your name has been rented because you are a proven "buyer" through direct mail.

You rent mailing lists either from a mailing list broker or from another organization. Professional mailing list brokers have a wide variety of lists available, which are used by both nonprofit organizations and businesses. Most brokers will send you a free catalogue of the categories of names available and the number of names in each category. The variety is astounding. A quick glance through one catalogue shows these possible offerings: sports medicine doctors, corporate secretaries in corporations with budgets over $250,000, earthquake research engineers, season ticket-holders to dance performances, donors to animal shelters, women in the press, or even the fascinating category, "super-wealthy women" (236,000 nationally).

These lists come to you on labels in zip-code order. Most lists cost about $75-100 per thousand names, with a minimum rental of 2,000 names. For a small additional fee you can have lists crossed with each other, yielding the names, for example, of all the super-wealthy women who are donors to animal shelters or of earthquake engineers who are donors to historic preservation projects.

To find mailing list brokers, look in the Yellow Pages under Mailing Houses, Mailing List Brokers, or Fundraising Services and Consultants.

Also, ask organizations that use direct mail services for their recommendations.

Many low-budget organizations trade mailing lists with other organizations for a one-time use. Usually, lists are traded on a name-for-name basis: 200 names for 200 names and on up. A group can also trade names for as many names as they have and rent the rest. If your organization has 500 donors and you want another group's list of 2,000 donors, trade your 500 and pay for the remaining 1,500. Depending on your relationship with the other organization, it may rent the list to you simply for the cost of producing the list on labels or the cost plus handling, or it may seek to make some profit.

If you almost never rent your list, each of your names may be worth two and up to five names of an organization that rents their list more often. If you have a little-used mailing list of 200 names, you may be able to trade for a list of 1,000.

Dos and Don'ts of Sharing Lists

Do share your list with others. Organizations often feel reluctant to share their donor lists with other organizations. Some fear that their donors will prefer the other groups and stop giving or give less to their group. Studies of donors show that this is not true. In fact, donor loyalty to the first group they give to in a series of organizations with related goals is increased as they learn of similar organizations.

In other words, if a person gives to an environmental organization and then is solicited by several others he or she may think, "I already support a group that does good work on the environment," or "I've been concerned about environmental degradation for a long time, and it's good that a lot of groups are working on it."

Furthermore, most people who give to charity give to between five and eleven charities. Usually most of the charities are similar: they may all be arts organizations or environmental groups, or they may be civil rights and civil liberties causes, but there will be some similar theme in most of them. People change one or two charities each year, dropping one and taking on a new one. You are going to lose some donors every year, but you will not lose donors simply by sharing your list.

Sometimes organizations fear that their donors will take offense at being solicited by so many groups. To ensure that this does not happen, simply include a line in your newsletter that says, "From time to time we make our mailing list available to other organizations that we feel would be of interest to our members. If you would rather we did not include your name, please drop us a line and we will make sure that you do not receive any of these mailings." You can publish this announcement in every issue of the newsletter to be sure that every donor sees it. Very few people will actually write in with this request. Most people like to get mail. When a survey queried people in the San Francisco Bay Area about their favorite part of the day, 71 percent said, "Opening my mail."

Do not steal mailing lists or use mailing lists that are marked "members only." Because mailing lists are fairly easy to compile and acquire, once you have the systems in place there is no need to be underhanded with others' lists. Further, your group's reputation may suffer. Almost all mailing lists, particularly those rented from commercial firms, have a certain number of "dummy" names, that is, names that are placed to identify the use of that list. The letter addressed to a "dummy" name goes to the source of the list. Suppose you have "liberated" the list of members of a service club that has given your organization a donation. John Q. Jones is on that list. "Q" is his code for service club, and when he gets a letter using that initial, he knows it came from the service club list. He is also in position to know or discover that no one gave your group permission to use the list. The situation can then become unpleasant and counter-productive to your fundraising efforts, especially if Jones announces at the next meeting of the club that members should not join your group.

A final rule about list acquisition and development: **Do not save mailing lists.** In any list that is more than three months old seven percent of the addresses will be inaccurate. After you have used a list twice (if you have not been given a once-only arrangement), you have gotten 90 percent of the response you are going to get from that list. Throw away the names of people who have not responded. Concentrate your efforts on getting new names and refine your systems so that the names are as "hot" as possible. The quality of the list is pivotal to your direct mail success.

The Direct Mail Package

More than a letter in an envelope, a direct mail appeal needs to be conceived as a package. The appeal is "wrapped" in a certain way to entice the donor to open the letter, then to read the letter, then to fill out a check and put it in the return envelope. This is a lot of pressure on a few pieces of paper with no power of their own. The work of your organization is only one variable in determining the success of your appeal.

The standard package has four parts: the "carrier" or outside envelope, the letter itself, the reply device and the return envelope. Each part of the package is complementary to the others, and all the elements work as a unit to have the maximum effect on the person receiving the appeal. We will examine each element separately and then discuss putting the elements together.

The Carrier (Outside) Envelope

Many mail appeals fail because, although much attention has been spent on writing an effective letter, it is enclosed in an envelope that no one opens. First class personal and business mail can be sent in a plain envelope with great security that the person receiving the letter will open it. In the case of first class mail, the envelope is simply a convenient way to carry the message.

In a fundraising appeal sent by bulk mail, however, the outside envelope has an entirely different purpose. It must grab the prospect's attention and then intrigue them enough that they want to open it and see what's inside. The envelope in this case is like gift wrapping. Everyone wants to know what's inside a present. In fact, gift-wrapping works so well that even when you may know what the gift is, there is still a thrill in opening the wrapping.

That thrill and that curiosity — from the low level if you know what is inside to the high level if you don't, is what you should strive for with mail appeals. Make the prospect want to know what is inside the envelope.

Get Personal

The main idea is to make the envelope look as though it contains a personal letter. There are two ways to do that: 1) make the envelope look as if it were sent by first class mail, or 2) make it different from other mail appeals the prospect will be receiving.

The methods you choose to accomplish this purpose will depend on how many volunteers you have to help with the mailing, your judgment about whether this is the best use of their volunteer time, how many pieces you are actually sending, and your goal for the mailing.

Look First Class

The best way to make a mail appeal look as though it was sent first class is for the address to be handwritten. If your appeal is going to fewer than 750 names, this is not too arduous a task. The addresses can also be typed (rather than word-processed) for a similar effect.

In addition to or instead of writing or typing the address, you can use a precancelled bulk-mail stamp in place of the more common postal indicia. These stamps may be purchased at the post office where you bring your bulk mail. The rules for sorting and handling mail with these stamps are the same as for any other bulk mailing.

Consider the rest of the envelope. If you are in a major metropolitan area where a lot of mail appeals originate, don't put your name and return address in the upper left-hand corner. Either use only your address without your organization's name in the upper left-hand corner or put the information on the back flap of the envelope. In either case, the prospect asks, "Who is this from?" and opens the envelope to find out.

On the other hand, if you are in a rural area, it is likely that the people receiving your appeal will open all letters that originate in their county or small town. In that case, you want your return address to be fairly prominent on the front of the envelope.

Look Different

Most mail appeals are sent in standard business-size envelopes (called No. 10). Your appeal will stand out if it arrives in a smaller or an odd-size envelope. Personal letters are not generally sent in business-size envelopes, so to make your appeal look more personal, send it in a No. 6¾ or No. 7¾, or in an invitation-style (A-2 or A-4) envelope. One word of caution: if you use small envelopes, make sure your return envelope is smaller yet, so that it will fit into the carrier envelope without needing to be folded.

The least effective strategy is to use "teaser copy." However, it should not be totally disregarded. Teaser copy involves writing, drawing or using a photograph on the envelope itself which intrigues the reader or causes some emotional response that will make the recipient open the envelope. So many direct mail appeals use this technique that it will not make your envelope stand out unless yours is very unusual.

You may wish to experiment with various styles of outside envelopes to find which methods work best for your organization. Save mail appeals from other groups that you open and figure out what about the envelope caused you to open it. The more creative you can be in designing the outside envelope, the greater chance you will have of the prospect reading your appeal.

The Letter

Because of the cost and volume of direct mail, it has been studied very carefully for more than 20 years. A few simple principles have emerged about what makes a direct mail letter effective. I discuss these shortly. But to appreciate the principles, you must keep two general ideas in mind. The first is that a direct mail appeal is not literature. Because of this fact, many good writers are not good writers of direct mail letters. The direct mail letter is not designed to be lasting, or to be filed away, or to be read several times with new insights emerging from each reading. It is disposable, part of a culture increasingly acclimated to disposable goods of all kinds — from diapers to cameras to contact lenses. The function of the fundraising letter is simply to catch the reader's attention and hold it long enough for the person to decide to give. The recipients of fundraising letters most often read these letters on their own time. It is not their job to read the letter, and if the letter has its intended result, they will wind up paying money for having read it.

Second is the "So what — Now what" continuum. Adults, when reading, watching TV or a movie, listening to a lecture, or even to a lesser extent, listening to someone they care about, subconsciously go back and forth between these two questions. If the first question, "So what?" is answered satisfactorily, they move to the next question, "Now what?" Seesawing between these two questions provides is a strong screening device for filtering out trivia, boring details and rhetoric. To be sure, what is trivial and boring to one person may be profound or lifesaving to another, so the answers to these questions will vary from person to person. However, details about when your organization was founded or the permutations of your organizational structure will not pass the "So what?" test, and the myriad problems that led to your current budget deficit will only bring on a fit of "Now what?" questioning.

As you write your letter, then, imagine the reader asking at the end of each sentence, "So what? What does this have to do with me, people I care about or things I believe in?" If the sentence stands up under that scrutiny, then read the next sentence while asking, "Now what?" Does this sentence offer a solution, provide more information, create confidence in the group?

Using the "So what — Now what" spectrum as the foundation, build your letter on the following principles:

1) People have very short attention spans. A person should be able to read every sentence in your letter in six to fifteen seconds. Each sentence must be informative or provocative enough to merit using up the next six to fifteen seconds reading the next sentence.

2) People love to read about themselves. Partly this is a result of the "So what — Now what" question, but it also reflects a desire to be treated personally. The reader of the letter wonders, "Do you know or care anything about me?" "Will giving your group money make me happier, give me status or relieve my guilt?" "Did you notice that I helped before?" Therefore, the letter should refer to the reader at least twice as often and up to four times as often as it refers to the organization sending it. To do this requires drawing the reader into the cause by saying, "You may have read," "I'm sure you join me in feeling," "If you are like me, you care deeply about . . ."

When writing to solicit another gift or a renewal from someone who is already a donor, use even more references to what they have done. "You have helped us in the past," "Your gift of $50 meant a great deal last year," "I want you to know that we rely on people like you — you are the backbone of our organization." Using the word "You" makes your letter speak to the reader rather than at him or her.

3) People must find the letter easy to look at. The page should contain a lot of white space, including wide margins, and be in a clear and simple typeface. Break up paragraphs so that each is no more than two or three sentences long, even if such breaks are not absolutely dictated by the content. Use contractions (won't, you're, can't, we're) and write in an informal style. This is a letter, not a term paper. Do not use jargon or long complex words.

4) People read the letter in a certain order. First, they read the salutation and the opening paragraph, but then, no matter how long the letter is, they read the closing paragraph and then the postscript. Sometimes people read the P.S. before the closing paragraph. Up to 60 percent of readers decide whether or not to give based on these three paragraphs and will not read the rest of the letter. The other 40 percent will read selective parts of the rest of the letter, usually parts that are easy to look at, such as facts set off in bullets or underlined phrases. Only a small number of people will read the entire letter.

Length of the Letter

There has been much debate about the length of a direct mail letter. Many people claim that they never read a long letter and object to groups wasting trees to print them. Direct mail consultants, on the other hand, advise their clients to send four- to six-page letters. In fact, the evidence is overwhelming that a two-page letter will get a better response than a one-page one and that four pages will often get a better response than two pages. It is also true that consumers don't read these long letters — in fact, most of them only read the three parts of the letter already discussed.

So why do longer letters work when people don't read them? Because a longer letter makes it look as though your organization has more to say, and therefore more substance to its work. It says to the reader, "We know you are not some slouch that will give to just anything, so we will explain ourselves." And it allows the organization to take the space it needs to make a case for itself without jamming words onto the page.

The Opening

Use the opening paragraph to tell a story, either about someone your group has helped or some situation your group has helped to rectify or about the reader of the letter. There is a saying in fundraising: "People buy with their hearts first, and then their heads." Programs and outcomes need to be described in "people" terms (or animals, if that is your constituency). Remember that Americans have been told a lot of stories and are increasingly skeptical of stories, so make sure that your story is true (even if facts have been changed to protect someone) and that it is credible and typical. You don't want someone saying, "What a sad story, but that could only happen once, so I'm not going to give." Finally, have the story resolve itself positively because of the work of your organization. Here are some examples.

Someone the group has helped:

"Tony and her two children, ages three and five, have been homeless for two years, moving in and out of shelters. Tony has had work off and on, but has not been able to save enough to pay the security deposit on an apartment because of the cost of childcare. This week, because of Homes Now, Tony and her children will move into a two-bedroom apartment. Monday morning Tony will start a full-time job and her children will be cared for at our daycare program."

The paragraph ends here. The body of the letter goes on to explain how many working people are homeless and how this group helps homeless people with housing, job training and daycare.

A situation the group helped to change:

"To some people it looked like a vacant lot, full of weeds, old tires and paper trash. So when Dreck Development proposed paving it over for a parking lot, few objected. After all, it is a poor neighborhood and a parking lot would be useful to commuters who work in the Industrial Park a few blocks away. To Joe Camereno, the lot looked like a park. He called Inner City Greenspace and asked us how to go about protecting this vacant lot. Today it is Camereno Park. How did this come about?"

The opening ends here. The rest of the letter lets people know how Inner City Greenspace can help them transform vacant lots, treeless streets and abandoned buildings into more livable community spaces.

Where the reader is part of the story:

"As a resident of Rio del Vista, you were probably as shocked as I was to learn of the toxic waste dump proposed for Del Vista Lake last year. Working together we were able to save the lake, but now the dump is proposed for Del Vista Canyon. We've got another fight on our hands."

The letter goes on to explain why Rio Del Vista is often targeted for these projects and what can be done about it.

Any of these styles can be effective openings. The one you use will depend on your list and available stories, or what the role of the reader is in the situation described.

The Closing Paragraph

The next paragraph people read, which is the last paragraph of the letter, suggests the action you want the reader to take. It is specific and straightforward:

"Send your gift of $25, $50 $75 or whatever you can afford. Use the enclosed envelope and do it today."

"A gift of $25 will help us reach 200 people."

"For your gift of $25, we will send you our quarterly newsletter, 'Community Views,' which will keep you posted on our progress. Your gift is a critical part of our efforts to provide health care to uninsured people."

If your group has several different membership levels, only the simplest description is used in the letter. This last paragraph is a short paragraph, with the full details of benefits explained on the reply device.

The P.S.

This is the final sentence people read and, in a small but significant percentage of cases, the only sentence.

The P.S. is most commonly used to suggest action:
"Don't put this letter aside. Send your check today."

Sometimes it offers an additional incentive for acting immediately:
"Every gift we receive before April 15 will be matched by Nofreelunch Foundation," or

"We have a limited supply of Important Book by Important Author. Send your gift of $50 or more as soon as possible to insure that you get one."

The P.S. can be used to tell a story:
"P.S. An independent study showed that the quality of our schools has improved because of Community Concern. It also showed that we have a long way to go. For the sake of the children, please make your donation today."

Or to make the reader part of the story:
"You cared enough to come to our community meeting last week. We hope you will join us in our critical work by making a donation now."

The Rest

The rest of the letter tells more of your history, discusses your plans, tells more stories, gives statistics and lists accomplishments. Use devices other than straight paragraphs to break up the text. These devices might include **bullets:**

"Because of us:

+ In 1990, a city ordinance banning the distribution of birth control to teenagers was repealed as unconstitutional
+ All teenagers in this community receive sex education as a part of their biology courses
+ We remain the only independent clinic providing referrals and birth control to anyone who needs it, regardless of their ability to pay."

Or **underlining**

"When it got up to 10 drive-by killings in one month with half of the victims children, the neighborhood association had enough!"

Who signs the letter is not critically important. If a famous person can be found to sign the letter, then the letter should be from that person. "I am happy to take time out of my busy movie schedule to tell you about Feisty Group." Otherwise, the chair of the board or the executive director can sign. The letter should be signed, however, and it should not be signed by more than two people or it begins to look like a petition. The person who signs the letter should have a readable, straightforward signature.

The Reply Device

Many years ago when fundraising was in its infancy the reply device was called "the little card that people send in with their check." This has been shortened to "The reply device" but means the same thing. The reply device is probably the most overlooked component of the direct mail appeal, but as consumers become more accustomed to direct mail, this little element is more and more important.

In the letter, the organization refers to the reader using the word, "You." The reader reads about her or himself. In the reply device, the reader responds to the organization while continuing to read about him or herself. The reader is asked to respond by saying, "Count me in" or "I agree" or "I'm with you."

More and more, when people open mail from groups they have heard of or causes they believe in, they move right to the bottom line — how much will it cost to join? If the reply device holds their attention, they may return to the letter, or they may just give without referring to the letter at all.

The reply device can be the one piece of paper the donor keeps from the mail appeal, as happens when someone reads an appeal letter, decides to give, then puts the return envelope and reply device into their "Bills to be Paid" file and throws the letter away. Two weeks later, the reply device must rekindle the excitement that the letter originally sparked, using a fraction of the space.

Therefore, the design of the reply device is crucial. The reply device is usually on card stock and is cut smaller than a return envelope so it fits easily with a check into the return envelope. Make sure when you design your reply device that it fits into the return envelope! Some organizations prefer the "wallet flap" style of envelope in which the reply device is on the back flap of the envelope itself (see illustration). There is no reason to think that one style is preferable to another.

If possible, the reply device should display the logo of the group and have a catch phrase to remind prospects of what the group stands for, or its mission. Some organizations actually put a brief description of their group or their project on the back of the card.

Probably the trickiest part is using few words to let people know how much it costs to join and the benefits. Many organizations display a simple series of boxes showing a range of gift amounts, with the benefits the same for any amount of money donated. If you have more elaborate benefits of membership or incentives for giving, put the amount first, then describe the incentive. Naming your membership categories is not worth that much, unless you have really clever names, or really good incentives. "Patron," "Benefactor," "Friend," all have little or no meaning, and inevitably reflect a hierarchy of giving that is just as well avoided.

The rest of the card must have room for the name, address and phone number of the donor, or a place for a label, and a statement about how to make out the check.

People will read your suggested donation range until they find a number they are comfortable with but, all else being equal, people will generally choose the second option in a line of numbers. So given a choice such as:

____$15   ____$25   ____$50   ____$100

most people will choose $25. Put the amount of money or the membership option that you want most people to choose, and that makes the most sense, in the second slot and build your categories around that. Sometimes your numbers will not be in order of ascending value, as in:

____$35   ____$25   ____$50   ____$100   ____other

You may wonder why not start with high numbers or put a large number in that second slot? Because people will not pay more than they can afford, and you don't want to scare them off. A group with this sequence:

____$100   ____$50   ____$35   ____$500   ____other

may wind up giving a message that small gifts are not encouraged.

On the other hand, do not suggest an amount you would rather not receive, such as $5. If someone wants to or needs to send that much, they can check "other." By suggesting it, you will get it from people who could have given a lot more.

The Return Envelope

There are two styles of return envelopes: business reply envelopes (called BREs) and plain self-addressed envelopes. With a BRE, the organization pays the cost of the postage, which is about twice as much as that of a first class stamp, but is only paid on those envelopes that are returned. With a plain self-addressed envelope, the donor affixes a stamp.

For low-budget organizations, BREs are not necessary. In fact, organizations have ceased using them as consumers have become aware of the cost. Unless you are working with a sizzling hot list of current donors, do not put a first class stamp on the return envelope. On the other hand, do not try to save money by not including an envelope. Your percentage of response will decline significantly if you do not use a self-addressed envelope of some kind.

Other Enclosures

The letter, reply device and return envelope are all that is necessary to make an excellent mail appeal. There are some additions you can use if you wish. Whether they will increase your response rate depends on many other variables, but they might.

♦ **The lift-out note.** A small note equivalent to the notes in commercial direct mail packages that say, "Read this only if you have decided not to buy our tires." This note is usually handwritten, or at least done in a different typeface than the letter. It is from someone other than the person who signed the letter and provides another compelling reason to give. For example, a letter signed by Judy Blacetti, director of an organization concerned with police brutality, had this lift-out note,

> "Emmett Smith, whom Judy writes about in the enclosed letter, is my son. I had often told Emmett, 'A policeman is your friend.' I still believe that should be true. Join us, please. Don't let there be another Emmett Smith." The note is signed "Lois Smith."

Of course, most people will read the lift-out note first, even though it reads as though you would read it after the letter. People's curiosity is aroused and they now read about Emmett Smith in the letter.

♦ **A newspaper article.** If your organization has received positive press, reprint the article. If possible, reprint it on newspaper-quality paper so that it looks as though you cut the article out of the paper. People tend to think that if something was in the newspaper it is more true than if you said it yourself.

♦ **An internal memorandum.** Similar in theory to a lift-out note, these organizational documents give readers the impression that they are learning something they normally would not be privy to. For example, an organization working to feed starving people in the Sudan used this internal memo:

To: Joe (the director, who signed the letter)
FR: Fred Smythe, Comptroller
RE: Recent food shipment
Joe, we can't continue to send this much food without a lot more money. I'm way over budget already and getting more and more requests from the field. There is no way we can send medical supplies as well. You have got to cut back.

Joe then scrawls on the memo, "I received this memo just as I was about to send out this letter. Please help with as much as you can as soon as you can. Lives hang in the balance."

♦ **Fact Sheet.** A well-designed, easy-to-read fact sheet highlighting exciting facts about your organization can take the place of one page of your letter. Many organizations are now using a fact sheet with a two-page letter and finding their results are just as good as using a longer letter. Even though the number of pages are the same, a fact sheet is handy because the same one can be used with several different letters. A fact sheet should be on your organization's stationary. It should include the "facts" that you depend on donations from individuals, and with what minimum donation a person can become a member of your organization. This reinforces the message of the letter, reaches those people who only read the fact sheet and not the letter, and allows you to use the fact sheet in other kinds of mailings or give it away by itself at rallies or house parties.

♦ **Brochure.** Surprisingly, using a brochure in a direct mail appeal will almost always decrease your response. Brochures are more complicated to look at than fact sheets or newspaper articles and hold the reader's attention longer, which could be good except that a brochure does not generally emphasize giving, so it winds up holding attention and not achieving the purpose of the mailing. Brochures are designed to be included with foundation proposals, to be given away at special events or to people writing for more information, and to be sent with personal letters asking for money.

Putting the Package Together

Be sure that your letter and enclosures are free of typographical errors. One typo can change the meaning of a sentence or, more often, render it meaningless. And typos give a bad impression of your group's work. Although your letter should look as though it was typed and be in "regular" — that is, typewriter — typeface, the carrier envelope, reply device and return envelope generally should be typeset or done in a fancier computer font if you have that choice. Remember, the only impression that donors recruited by mail will have of your group will be from what they get in the mail.

Be sure that the envelope color and the paper stock for your letter do not clash. Avoid strong colors such as bright yellows or reds or any dark colored paper. People with vision problems have a difficult time reading off of dark colored paper, and you don't want to lose a prospect because he or she couldn't read the letter. Use sharp contrast in your type and paper color so that the words are easy to read.

Do a spot-check of all the printed materials. Sometimes a printer's mistake will leave the middle 25 letters smeared or blank. While you can't look at every piece individually, you may be able to stop a mistake from being sent out.

Be sure that your reply device fits into your return envelope. The card should not have to be folded to fit into the envelope.

Put your return address on everything: the reply device, the letter, and the return envelope. That way if someone loses the return envelope, she or he can still find you.

Fold the letter so that the opening paragraph appears on the outside rather than on the inside, as would be the case with a normal letter. A person pulling the letter out from the envelope should be able to begin reading it without having to open it or turn it around.

Make sure the response you want is obvious and easy to comply with: note on your reply device to whom to make the check payable, where to send it, and whether or not the contribution is tax-deductible.

Some communities have laws that require you to send a copy of your appeal to a government agency for approval before sending it out or to list your federal identification number on everything you send. Be sure to investigate and comply with these laws.

A Note on Time of Year

There is a saying among direct mail consultants that the best time of year to send an appeal is when it is ready. There is much truth in this saying because there are no really bad times of year and no really excellent ones; the best time will always be when the appeal is fresh and exciting. However, all things being equal, there are some months when donors may be more responsive than others. In order of effectiveness, they are:

January-February

September-November 15

November 15-December (If your program feeds the hungry, houses the homeless, or is a religious organization, these may be your best months.)

March

May

June (This is a particularly bad month for people with children in school because their attention is on end-of-year school functions and their own and their children's summer vacations.)

April (Again, Christian religious organizations may do very well here, but most everyone has their mind on taxes.)

August

Every organization needs to adjust the timing of its direct mail appeals according to its constituency. Farmers have very different schedules from schoolteachers. Your constituency's religion and how fervently they practice it will affect some timing; elections will affect timing; even what other organizations your constituents belong to and what they are up to may have an impact.

Renewals

The final use of direct mail is to renew gifts on an annual basis. There are many ways to set up renewal programs, but the simplest one is best for low-budget organizations. First, code your donors into small, mid-range and major givers. (See Chapter 12, Personal Soliciation, and Chapter 28, Record Keeping, for full details about setting up donor records.) For some groups, a small gift will be any gift under $50, but for most groups it will be any gift under $35. Mid-range donations are $1 over the top of your small gift range up to $1 less than major donations. For most groups, this will be $36-100, or $51-250. Everyone giving above that level is a major donor.

At renewal time, all donors of small gifts should receive a form letter asking them to renew their gift, all donors of mid-range gifts should receive a personalized word-processed letter, and major donors should receive a personal letter followed by a visit or phone call. (If you have a donor base of 100 or fewer people, you may want to personalize all your renewals.) Your donors are now coded S (small), MR (mid-range) and MD (major donor).

Direct mail renewals are used only with the S list. The S list is then sub-coded into four categories according to the quarter in which the donor gave: those who gave in the spring, summer, autumn and winter. Once each quarter, the appropriate group is pulled up from the computer or your paper record keeping system, their names are put on labels, and they are sent a simple renewal letter with a return form and return envelope. This is much easier than trying to write to people on the anniversary date of their gift, and much more effective in terms of renewal rates and cash flow than writing to everyone once a year regardless of when they gave.

The renewal letter follows the format of direct mail appeals. It should start with a sentence about the donor, affirming his or her importance to the group, tell a few accomplishments and ask for a renewal gift, with an upgrade if possible. This letter can be done on one page, but, again, do not jam the letter on the page, and don't try to say so little that your letter winds up being cryptic.

Design a renewal reply device that you will use with all renewals. The cards must then be coded with the season they are sent, so you can find the donor's file when a response comes in. Many donors hold renewal notices until they think their year is up or until they get around to responding. A special, coded response card will make it easy to distinguish a renewal from a new gift. As the renewals come in and are entered into the computer (or on 5" by 7" cards, if you are on a paper system), make sure the donors are thanked promptly. After six to eight weeks, pull up the name of anyone who hasn't renewed yet and send them another letter. This letter is firmer and shorter: "We need to hear from you soon. Please send your renewal contribution as soon as possible."

If you are a membership organization and/or you send donors a newsletter as a benefit, you will probably find it effective to send a total of three renewal notices to non-renewing donors. If you send a third renewal, it says, "Your subscription/membership has expired. Before we take you off the list, we want to make sure that we haven't made a mistake, or that you haven't accidently set our other reminders aside. Please use the enclosed note to either renew your subscription or tell us why you are not renewing."

Most social change organizations allow people to be members or receive the newsletter without paying if the person is interested in the group but can't afford to join or subscribe. This is certainly appropriate;

however, you don't want to keep people on your list whom you never hear from. They are not necessarily too poor to send in a gift. More likely, they do not read your newsletter or your appeals and do not remember how they got on your list. One woman told me that her husband belonged to a certain group and gave regularly. At some point, her husband left her for another woman but did not send the group a change-of-address notice. The group's appeal letters and newsletter kept arriving at the ex-wife's house. "Every time I saw that newsletter, I thought of what a creep my husband was. I kept thinking they would take him off the list. But no. Month after month, I got that newsletter. Finally, I wrote to them and several more months went by before it finally stopped coming."

The general rule for renewals is that everyone who wants to stay on your list should reaffirm that desire at least every 12 to 18 months. A quarterly renewal system for small donors will help you keep your mailing list up-to-date.

In Chapter 2, I noted that the normal renewal rate for donors is 66 percent — that is, 66 percent of people giving you a gift in one year can be expected to give you a gift in the following year. The remaining 34 percent will not renew. No matter how often you appeal to people and how wonderful your organization is, some people will only give once and not again, or will give two or three times and not again. This probably has little to do with you and more to do with them changing jobs, having children, moving, divorcing, marrying, etc. This means you must attract enough new donors every year to replace 34 percent of your donor base.

If your renewal rate is less than 66 percent, you are probably not doing enough to keep your donors. Examine your program to ensure:

- You are writing to donors more than once a year asking for money
- You are thanking donors promptly with a personal note
- You are sending at least two renewal notices
- Your records are accurate and up to date.

If your renewal rate is more than 66 percent, your organization does not have enough donors. Any organization can have an 80-90 percent renewal rate if they are only working with 100 donors or so. A 66 percent renewal rate is a sign of health. It means enough people are being fed into the system. The donor pyramid gets smaller as you move up from first-time donors to habitual donors to major donors. There are fewer and fewer people at each stage. In order for there to be an adequate number at the top, there must be an adequate number at the bottom.

What To Do With the Responses

There are few things as thrilling as receiving gifts from a successful mail appeal. When you go to your mail box and pull out all these return envelopes that you know have checks in them, it is tempting to just cash the checks, spend the money and go home early. But receiving the checks brings on a whole new set of tasks.

First, all donors must be thanked, preferably within 48 hours of the group receiving their gift, and certainly within seven days. Sometimes you will not be able to meet this time frame, so remember that a late thank you is always better than no thank you (see also Chapter 13, The Thank-You Note).

The gift must also be recorded (for additional detail, see Chapter 28, Record Keeping). Use the following steps:

- ◆ Photocopy the check before cashing it. This is a book-keeping basic, but also helps with fundraising, as a lot of information is on a check.
- ◆ Be sure to note the day the check arrived, what appeal it was responding to, and when the thank-you note was sent out.
- ◆ Be sure to cash the check as soon as possible.

Evaluating Your Appeal

In order to know if your appeal has been effective and which of your appeals are the most effective and why, you must "track" and evaluate them. Without evaluation all fundraising is simply shooting in the dark. To get maximum benefit from a mail appeal program, evaluation is essential. The process of tracking is simple: you want to find out how many people responded to a particular appeal and how much money it brought in.

The reply devices of each appeal must be "coded" in some way. If you have access to free or inexpensive printing, you could print them in different colors or change them in some way. If you don't, a cheap and easy method is to use a colored marker to put a dot on each reply card. Make a note of which color you are using for which mailing. Then, as they come back, note each response on a tally sheet. Simply mark each response under the week or month that it came in. The heaviest response will come during the first four weeks after you could reasonably expect most people to have received the mailing (always send one to your organization in order to get a sense of how long it takes to arrive). Ninety-five percent of the responses will be in by the end of two months.

At that time, add up the responses and the money earned and evaluate the appeal in these categories:

- Total number of gifts received and total amount given
- Number of donors by category (under $15, $15-35, $36-100, $100 +)
- Percent of response (divide the number of responses by the number of pieces mailed)
- Mode gift (the gift received most often)
- Cost of mailing
- Ratio of income to expense (divide the amount of money you received by the money you spent)
- Any narrative comments

The percent of response and the mode gift are the most important aspects of the evaluation. The percent of response tells you much more important information than the amount you earned. For example, one organization's appeal to 1,000 names generated only two responses (.002%); one response was for $10 but the other was for $1,500! The board was told that the mail appeal had generated $1,510 but not the percent of response. They decided to do more mailings to similar lists and quickly spent all their profit because the lists were virtually worthless to them.

Similarly, the mode gift gives you useable information, whereas the average gift, which many groups spend time figuring out, is a virtually meaningless number. For example, if you received 25 replies to a mail appeal and 24 were for $25, but one was for $1,000 (given by the mother of the board chair), your average gift would be $64. That doesn't tell you anything. But knowing that the mode gift is $25 tells you this is a good amount to ask for and the majority of people responding from that list feel comfortable with it.

After you finish your evaluation, take the mail appeal with all its components and the evaluation and place it in a file folder. If you decide to repeat the mailing, you will have all the information you need in one place.

After several mailings, you can pull out all the evaluation forms and see what they have in common. Do some types of lists seem to respond better than others? Did the mailing with a premium offered do better than the mailings without? Does one set of facts or one particular story seem to stir more people to give? Remember to test only one variable at a time. You cannot find if more people respond to a one premium or another in a mailing that is testing a lift-out note and a letter against a letter alone. Also, you must use portions of only one list to test responses. You cannot test one variable on a list to a service club and another variable on a list to a group of health activists.

If you have mailed fewer than 2,000 pieces, you will not have a statistically significant evaluation. However, using your instinct and what information you are able to garner, you should be able to make some educated guesses about what is working and why.

7.

Variations on the Mail Appeal Package

The last chapter discussed in detail the purposes of direct mail and how to put an effective direct mail package together. This chapter presents a number of variations on the direct mail appeal to make your mail appeal package not look like a mail appeal at all. It also discusses the use of promotional items, benefits and premiums, and a number of types of mail appeals you might want to try with your mailing lists or members.

These six variations on the basic mail appeal package will not work for every organization, and not all possible variations are explored here. The point is to suggest a number of options for using the principles of direct mail fundraising. Some of these may inspire you to create other variations on the theme.

A Gift Catalogue

A gift catalogue is a mail appeal in which the organization lists items it needs and their costs. People then either donate an item or, more usually, the money to purchase an item for the group. In the latter instance the donor's gift is "earmarked" for a particular item. (Note: There is an important difference between the words "earmark" and "designate" in giving. An "earmarked" gift is to be used for the purpose indicated until that need is filled; after that, it can be used at the organization's discretion. A "designated" gift can only be used for the purpose for which it is designated, even if that need has been filled. Organizations are advised to stay away from the term "designated.")

Gift catalogues work particularly well for groups such as shelters, land preservation organizations, clinics and other health services and the like, whose shopping list can inspire donations more readily than can those of organizations that simply need office supplies.

A land trust, for example, successfully uses the gift catalogue in their efforts to preserve ecologically significant land. A sampling of the items contained in their catalogue includes:

- Binoculars: four pairs, $200; one pair, $50
- Classroom visits: 10 visits, $400
- Scholarships for docent trainees: cost per docent, $50
- Gates for fences: one gate, $100
- Hand lenses: 25 hand lenses, $32
- Refrigerators for houses on the preserves: two propane refrigerators, $800
- Research grants for various projects (which are described)
- Weather-monitoring equipment: complete cost, $450

The budget of the organization using a gift catalogue must be easily broken down into gift categories, which are described in the catalogue. The catalogue itself may be only a few pages long. It should include an "order form" that is a variation on the reply form. People can then "order" more than one item.

Some organizations have used this concept to raise money for intangible program components, such as client care or provision of services. A nonprofit therapy collective listed these items in their gift catalogue:

- Scholarship for one family session: $60
- Complete six-week program: $360
- Parent effectiveness training: Full scholarship: $200 Partial scholarship: $50
- Day care for children of parents in therapy: $8/hr. = $____ (indicate number of hours you wish to donate)

The actual gift catalogue can be fancy or plain. It can include illustrations of needed items or photographs of people using the services. It can be laid out like a regular mail order catalogue or can simply list the needed items on a sheet of paper. Using your imagination in layout and adding drawings and illustrations will make your catalogue more effective. Laying it out in the form of a newsletter or booklet will give it the air of a catalogue and make it stand out from regular mail appeals.

Using Your Newsletter as a Mail Appeal

If you have a newsletter or magazine that contains articles or information that people want and find useful and cannot easily obtain elsewhere, use your publication as an advertisement for your organization. Show people who are not familiar with your publication what they will get for their money by sending them a sample issue with information on how to subscribe.

You can have a special cover made for one issue of your publication or create a special issue used only for promotional purposes. If your newsletter is long (12 pages or more) and expensive to produce, consider making up a special short edition. This piece might be four to eight pages and contain one or two excellent articles — the best of your previous issues plus a listing of articles and information that people would receive by subscribing. In this variation, the cover becomes the mail appeal. The cover includes a return form to be torn off, which is essentially a subscription form. A return envelope stapled into the newsletter will increase your returns. This appeal is not sent in an envelope.

Make sure it is clear that this issue is complimentary and tell people where to look for information about subscribing. Some groups have found it effective simply to stamp "Complimentary copy — please subscribe" on a number of their newsletters each time and send these complimentary copies to people whose names they have acquired. These can go with the regular mailing of the newsletter or as a separate mailing. If the newsletter is good enough, that simple message can be enough to generate donations.

The Brief Message

Organizations working on issues that are familiar to most people, or whose mission is totally self-evident, can use the brief message format. Your appeal and return form are all on the same piece of paper, and a return envelope is enclosed.

The brief message conveys the following: "I am not going to use a whole sheet of paper and precious minutes of your time. You know who we are. You read the paper and hear the news. Join us. We need you."

Brief messages are effective when the group or the group's work is well known and requires little explanation. The brief message must use the word "you" effectively. Groups working on specific health issues such as arthritis, cancer, asthma, or groups providing easy-to-understand programs such as homeless shelters or stop smoking clinics can avail themselves of this method.

An excellent example of the use of the brief message is an appeal from the United Negro College Fund, which pictures a handsome African

American man looking depressed and contains this brief message: "His math got him into college. Economics may keep him out. Give to the United Negro College Fund." The reader is pulled in quickly and asked to decide almost before there is time to think about it.

Phantom Event

In a phantom event people are invited to a special event that is not going to happen. The event is described in detail, and the prospects are invited to stay home and miss it. The appeal is sent in the style of an invitation, with an RSVP used as the return form.

Phantom events work because they catch people off guard, they amuse people, and because, in fact, they appeal to the many people who don't enjoy large social events.

The Board of Directors of Californians for Action invites you to their first annual gala nonevent. The City Council, Robert Redford, Tom Hayden and other notables will not be there. In fact, no one will be there. You will not have to mingle with people you barely recognize. You will not have to eat soggy hors d'oeuvres, buy a fancy outfit to appear in, or travel after dark.

Please join us in staying home

Time: 6-10:30 pm

Date: June 14

Cost: $58.95. Send us the $50 and keep the $8.95 to buy a bottle of wine to share with a loved one.

We look forward to not seeing you.

RSVP by June 1, using the enclosed card.

Pictures

Organizations that serve animals or people in distress can often express their message more poignantly through photographs or drawings than with words. A picture can take the place of many pages of text. Pictures can be part of a letter or a separate enclosure. For pictures to be effective they must be real and they must not be sentimental, maudlin or patronizing. Photographs must not demean the people or animals in them.

Sometimes photographs are used to jar people's sensibilities. This can be effective when done carefully. Showing an animal caught in a leg-hold trap, for example, is far more moving than a wordy description of the trap and its effect. A picture of the bodies of people killed by death squads provides vivid evidence of a situation that many people find hard to believe.

Drawings, such as an artist's rendering of a new building in an appeal for a capital campaign, are usually used to augment the text of a letter. Again, the drawing must depict something real and be well done. It does not generally replace as many words as a photograph.

Promotional Items

Many long-established organizations use promotional items to draw in donors. The method works because people open the envelope to get what's inside — stamps, bumper stickers, pencils, address labels, seeds, etc. It also works by generating a feeling of obligation to reciprocate with a donation. Because these items are expensive it is generally better to use them as part of a thank-you package, if it all. With the exception of groups that have always used these items, they do not seem to increase the rate of response relative to their cost.

Use of Benefits and Premiums

An organization that intends to have a large base of donors who repeatedly give small gifts must establish a workable benefits program. The purpose of a benefits program is to give donors something tangible for their donation. Benefits are important for the simple reason that Americans are consumers. We are accustomed to getting things for our money, and even nonprofit organizations compete for the consumer dollar on this level.

The psychology of a benefit is this: the donor sends a gift and your organization, in gratitude for the gift, sends a *free* benefit. The donor is not buying the benefit, which costs much less than his or her donation.

Although supporting the work of the group gives the donor a feeling of good will, this feeling lasts only a little while, and the donor needs a reminder of the gift and of the work of the group. A thank-you note is the first reminder. It should go out within 48 hours of receipt of the gift. The second reminder is the item or items that the group will send the donor regularly.

In setting up a benefits program, the organization must define what relationship their donors will have to the organization. If you decide that you want your donors to have a feeling of ownership and involvement in your organization, you should consider establishing a membership. Each donor is then called a member. If your by-laws already specify the rights of members, and if you do not wish to give donors voting or other rights specified by your by-laws, simply amend your by-laws to include a class of nonvoting members, number unlimited. If you do not wish to have members, you might establish giving categories such as "friend," "supporter," "benefactor," and the like.

After you decide what to call your donors, you must decide what you are going to give them and whether donors who give more money will get more attention. Most organizations find it useful to have three donor categories, each reflecting a greater contribution amount and each with incentives to join at that rate. The categories might be:

- **Basic:** $25-49 — includes basic benefits package
- **Larger:** $50-$500 — includes basic package plus a book, T-shirt, or other incentive
- **Major Donor:** $500 and up — includes the above, plus regular reports on the progress of the organization and individual attention.

Generally, you will be seeking smaller gifts through the mail. A major donor requires face-to-face soliciting.

The Basic Benefits Package

The most common benefit is a newsletter. Appropriately, this benefit regularly reminds donors of your group, raises their level of awareness about your group's work, and provides information not available elsewhere or a point of view not generally expressed in the mass media. Other possible basic benefits include a T-shirt, bumper sticker, membership card (which doesn't have to entitle the member to anything), discounts to special events, or other educational materials.

There are two guidelines for choosing benefits for donors: 1) the fulfillment costs (that is, how much it costs your organization to produce and send the item you promised) should never be more than one-fifth of the lowest membership category, and 2) while you can always add benefits, you cannot take them away.

In deciding on a benefits package, then, start with small benefits that you know your organization can continue to afford, and that you have the staff or volunteers to provide. The difference between a bimonthly newsletter and a quarterly one will not be nearly as important to the donor as it will be to your budget and staff and volunteer time.

If you decide to have incentives for larger donations, try to find something that promotes your organization. A book about the work you do or that is related to a topic you address is good. Books can usually be purchased directly from the publisher in quantities of 100 or more for 40 percent off the cover price. Paperback volumes are fine. The problem with books is that it may not be easy to find a new book every year.

Paperweights, tote bags, bookmarks, bumper stickers, T-shirts and the like are all acceptable as well. Specialty merchandising firms can send you catalogues of available items on which they can print your logo or message at low cost.

Premiums

Premiums are additional thank-you gifts for donating within a specified time period. Announcement of a premium is often included in the mail appeal letter at the postscript, whose main purpose is to move the donor to act: "P.S. Send your gift by December 1 and we will send you a special edition of a calendar created by a local artist for our group." Or, "P.S. We have a limited number of signed lithographs that we will send to the first fifty donors. Join today." You don't want the renewing donor to put your appeal in the pile of bills to be paid later or to lose the appeal, so you offer them a premium for acting promptly.

Premiums are particularly useful in securing renewal gifts. The majority of these donors are probably going to give anyway; the premium simply encourages them to give sooner rather than later, or more if the premium calls for that ("gifts of $40 or more get two free tickets to the spring concert").

The best premiums from your organization's point of view are ones that you already have. For example, suppose you are doing a concert and ticket sales are slow. Offer renewing donors a free ticket for renewing by a certain date. Or suppose you have had too many calendars printed and cannot possibly sell them all before the beginning of the new year. Offer them as a premium.

In using premiums for acquiring new donors, remember to add the cost of the premium when figuring the cost of the mail appeal. This will lower your net income, but if you gain even one or two percentage points in response, the cost will be offset. You can also use premiums when you don't wish to commit yourself to a regular benefit — just send the premium item when you have it.

Appealing to Current Donors

Once your organization has acquired donors, it should appeal to them several times a year. Too often, appeals to current donors are overlooked. Years of testing have proven that some donors will respond every time they are asked, another group will give less automatically but more than once a year, and that renewal rates for all donors (even those who do not respond to extra appeals) are higher when they receive several appeals a year.

Many groups have discovered that with repeated appeals they can raise enough money from their current donors to be able to scale down their recruitment of new donors. Many large organizations appeal to their donors eight to 12 times a year, which tends to have a saturating, and in the case of many donors, alienating, effect. For small, low-budget groups, two to four appeals a year will raise more money without irritating your donors. In fact, two to four appeals a year will barely make a ripple in the volume of mail most of your donors are receiving.

Repeated appeals are successful for a number of reasons. First, a person's cash flow can vary greatly from month to month. A person receiving an appeal from a group he or she supports may have just paid car insurance and so throws the appeal away. If the organization were to ask again in two months the person might have more money available and make a donation.

Second, different people respond to different types of appeals. Sending only one or two appeals a year does not allow for the variety of choices donors want. Organizations often discover that donors who regularly give $25 a year will give $50, $100, or more when appealed to for a special project. People who respond to specific project appeals are often called "bricks-and-mortar" people. They "buy" things for an organization: media spots, food for someone for a week, a job training program, a new building.

We rarely know why people don't respond to appeals. Despite this lack of knowledge many people are willing to make the assumption that the donor doesn't want to give, when any of the following might be true:

◆ The donor has been on vacation and mail has piled up, so anything that is not a bill or a personal letter, including your appeal, gets tossed.

◆ The donor is having personal problems and cannot think of anything else right now, even though he or she might be quite committed to your group.

◆ The appeal is lost in the mail, or the donor meant to give but the appeal got lost or accidentally thrown away before it could be acted on.

Donors do not feel "dunned to death" by multiple appeals. On the contrary, they get a sense that a lot is happening in the organization. Their loyalty is developed when they know that their continuing donations are also needed. Most important, they have an opportunity to express their own interests when a particular appeal matches their concerns.

Once an organization has accepted the idea of sending appeals throughout the year, they often wonder what they are going to say in each one. The following section contains 12 ideas to help you choose some approaches. Some of these appeals are taken from or modeled on specific groups' letters. Some will suit one organization better than another, but almost any organization should be able to find one or two ideas that they could modify and use for their group.

Seasonal Appeals

End-of-year: "As you close your books for this year, please remember (organization). This is your last chance to make a tax-deductible donation to our group and count it for this year's taxes."

Beginning-of-year: (written as a testimonial). "One of my New Year's resolutions was to give more money this year to (organization). I realized that, like many of my resolutions, this one could fade if I didn't act now. So I sent an extra $25 on January 5. I imagine that many of our members made a similar resolution. Perhaps you did. If you are like me, time may pass without action. So join me, and send that extra donation now."

Holiday Appeals

Lincoln's Birthday: "President Lincoln was only one of the more famous people to be killed with a handgun. I know you want to end this senseless outrage. An extra donation from you, sent today, will give us the extra funds we need to work on (special program) against handguns/crime in the street/to strengthen our community organization activities/or escort people who are alone across campus."

Valentine's Day: "Do you often think of important people on Valentine's Day? Do you remember them with flowers, candy, or cards? I know I do. This year, I thought of other important people in my life — the people at (organization). They really depend on us, their members, for the financial support they need. Will you join me in sending an extra donation? You can send flowers or candy as well. Simply use the enclosed card."

Labor Day: "A time to take the day off. But what about all the people who want to work — the part of the population that is unemployed? For them Labor Day is another reminder of their joblessness. Our organization is providing training to thousands of people so that they can get good jobs in areas needing workers. Remember the unemployed this Labor Day with a gift to (organization)."

Columbus Day: "Columbus discovered America. This is one part of American history almost everyone knows. The problem is that this is only a half-truth: Columbus discovered America for white people. There were already people here — our people. We are Americans. Yet our history since Columbus has been one of genocide, displacements, and oppression. At Native American Organization, we are determined to reclaim Columbus Day. You have helped us in the past. Will you help us, on this holiday, to continue our vital work?"

Thanksgiving Day: "We would like to make Thanksgiving Day a little brighter for hundreds of people in our city who cannot afford to buy food. With your donation of $14.50 we will provide a family with a turkey and all the trimmings. Please give whatever you can."

Christmas/Hanukkah/Kwanzaa/End of year: "We are just $400 short of our goal to buy a new furnace for our runaway house/send our staff person to the state capitol to press for the bill we have been working so hard on/distribute thousands of leaflets telling seniors how to get their homes insulated for free. Can you help us meet our goal with a special end-of-year donation?"

Old Stand-bys

Anniversary: "Our organization is now entering its third/fifth/fiftieth anniversary of service to the community. Celebrate with us by sending 1 dollar/10 dollars/100 dollars for each year of our existence. For your gift we will be pleased to send you a special anniversary parchment, suitable for framing. In addition, for those donating $1,000 or more, there will be a special reception honoring (famous person), who has been so helpful to our cause."

Famous Person: "I'm _____. You may have seen me on television. In my personal life, I am very concerned about birth control/tenants' rights/public education. I believe that (organization) defends our rights in this area. Please join me in supporting them." (Famous person can be truly famous, such as a movie star, or someone well known only in your community and widely respected there.)

Another member: "My name is _____. I have been a member of (organization) for five years. In that time, I have witnessed the continuing erosion of our rights and the seemingly malicious efforts of our leaders to take what little we have left. All that stands between them and us is (organization). In the past five years, our organization has succeeded in _____ and _____. That's why I am giving a little extra this year. Twenty dollars is not a lot, but it really helps, and if everyone gave just $10, $20, or $35, it would really add up. Will you join me?"

Urgent need: "We have an urgent need to raise $2,000 to alert the public to the hazards of chemical dumping currently being proposed for the east side of town. This little-known bill, which has the support of our supervisors, will bring unwarranted health hazards to more than 1,000 people. The town council is trying to slide this bill through without our knowledge, and thus our protest. Help us stop this outrage now, with an extra donation of $25, $35, or whatever you can send."

8.

How to Conduct Special Events

Special events are social gatherings of many sorts that expand the reputation of the organization, giving those attending an amusing, interesting, or moving time, and that may make money for the organization sponsoring the event. The variety of special events is practically limitless, as are the possibilities for money earned or lost, amount of work put in, number of people participating, and so on.

Because of their variety and flexibility, special events are excellent strategies for acquiring, retaining or upgrading donors, although they work best for acquisition. Special events are both the most common fundraising device used by small organizations and the most misunderstood. They can do things for an organization that no other fundraising strategy can do as well, yet what they can best do is often the last thing that is expected or wanted.

Special events should have two goals:

◆ To raise the visibility of the organization.

◆ To bring in (new) money.

Enhancing visibility raises the overall profile of the organization in the community. The visibility of your group can be assessed by asking this question: Of all the people who should know about you, what percentage do? Visibility is the cumulative effect of publicity and word-of-mouth reporting. Events are excellent publicity-generating tools because they give the media a "hook" around which to focus attention on the group. A newspaper or radio station may be interested in discussing the actual event — an auction, self-defense class, or concert — and will mention the sponsoring group's name; they may even do a longer profile of the sponsoring nonprofit, thus raising visibility. With each successive event, and in combination with other fundraising and organizing efforts, the organization will become known to more and more people.

Eventually the organization will become known to all who should know about it.

Raising money is a secondary goal for a special event because there are many faster and easier ways to raise money than this one. An organization that simply needs money (perhaps from being in a cash flow bind, or having an unexpected expense) will find that the slowest ways to raise that money are by writing a proposal or having an event. On the other hand, an organization that wants to raise its profile, bring in new people, and perhaps make some money immediately will find a special event an ideal strategy. In many cases special events can lose money or barely break even and still be successful because of the publicity and visibility they produced.

Types of People Who Attend Special Events

Two categories of people attend events: those who come because of the event itself and those who come both for the event and to support your group. In the first category are people who would come to a particular event no matter who sponsored it. These people attend flea markets, dances, movie benefits, decorator showcases, auctions, and the like. Many times these people will not even know the name of the group sponsoring the event.

In a similar vein are small businesses or corporations that will buy ads in an adbook, donate raffle prizes, buy tables at luncheons, or even underwrite an event, but would not give the organization money under any other circumstance. They want to take advantage of advertising inexpensively to a specific audience and the resulting good will. Raising money from a person or a business who would not give you money otherwise does not constitute "acquisition," but is a smart use of an event, even if these are one-time donors. For organizations in rural communities or serving a very small constituency, unable to build a large base of donors, events that draw strangers will be imperative.

The second group of people are both interested in the event and believe in your group's work. They may not have heard of your organization before learning of this event or they may already know of your organization and want to support it while getting something important to them. For example, women wanting to take a self-defense class may choose one sponsored by the local rape relief program rather than a commercial gym in order to support the program. After the classes, some of the participants may want to join the program as volunteers and paying members. People who buy all their holiday presents at a crafts fair put on by a local publicly supported radio or television station, or enter marathons sponsored by groups they believe in are good prospects for follow-up direct mail.

There are also people who appreciate your organization but can't afford or don't want to give more than a small amount. For them, buying a $1 raffle ticket or attending a $4 movie is a perfect way to show their support.

Choosing a Fundraising Event

Several criteria should be considered in choosing a fundraising event, including the appropriateness of the event, the image reflected on the organization by the event, the amount of volunteer energy required, the amount of front money needed, the repeatability and the timing of the event, and how the event fits into the overall fundraising plan.

Appropriateness of the Event

Appropriateness is a major factor that, if overlooked, can have damaging results. To decide if an event is appropriate, ask yourself, "If people knew nothing about our organization except that it had sponsored this event, what would their thoughts of our group be like?" If you think the answer is "neutral or good," then the event is appropriate. If you think that you would have to explain more about the group or counter what the event implies about it, you should think again.

Examples of inappropriate events abound. In the extreme, if you are the symphony you don't sponsor a pie-eating contest; if you run an alcohol recovery program you don't have a beer bash. Often, however, the question of appropriateness is more subtle than in those examples, as shown in the following two case studies.

A question of timing: A community center in a factory town of 25,000 people held a yearly luncheon attended by about 500 people at $50-100 a plate. The luncheon had been a successful fundraiser for three years. In 1990 the town's industry laid off half of its work force. Unemployment in the town rose from four to 25 percent. That year the community center still held its luncheon, and still 500 people came. By the end of 1992 the industry had shut down altogether. Unemployment was now up to 40 percent; many people lost their homes and exhausted their unemployment benefits. The town was gloomy; businesses were closing. The community center needed the money from the luncheon more than ever. Since there were at least 200 people who could still afford the price, they held the event. They were sharply criticized for doing so in light of the severe economic austerity that most of the towns-people were facing. The yearly luncheon had become inappropriate due to circumstances outside of the control of the community center.

A question of judgment: A women's health organization holding a raffle offered as a top prize a case of fine, expensive wine. During pro-motion of the raffle a number of studies were released showing a high rate of alcoholism among women. An internal debate ensued over whether it was appropriate for a group working to prevent dangerous drugs and devices from being given to women to offer alcohol — a potentially dangerous drug — as a raffle prize. Proponents argued that only 10 percent of the population is alcoholic and that alcohol does not harm most people who use it. The chance of an alcoholic winning that prize was slim compared to how many people would be attracted to the raffle because of the prize. However, opponents swayed the group by reasoning that they would not approve of a contraceptive that hurt "only" 10 percent of its users. The group withdrew the prize.

Image of the Organization

As far as possible, the special event should be in keeping with the image of the organization or should promote the image the organization wishes to project. Although considerations of appropriateness sometimes include those of image, image is also a distinct issue. Many events that are appropriate for a group do not necessarily promote a positive image of it. For example, a library would choose a book sale over a garage sale, even though both are appropriate. An environmental organization would raffle a white-water rafting trip rather than a weekend at Disney-land. An organization promoting awareness of the problem of high blood pressure might choose to hold a health fair rather than a dance.

Energy of Volunteers

Looking at the volunteer energy required involves several considera-tions. How many people are required to put on this event? What would these volunteers be doing if they were not working on this event? Do you have enough volunteers who have the time required to produce this event — not only to manage the event on the day of its occurrence but to be attentive to all the details that must be carried out beforehand?

Volunteer time is a resource to be cultivated, guided, and used appropriately. For example, don't use someone with connections to possible large donors to sell raffle tickets at a shopping mall on Saturday afternoon. Similarly, a friendly, outgoing person who loves to talk on the phone should be the phone-a-thon coordinator or the solicitor of auction items and not be asked to bake brownies for the food booth at the county fair. Obviously, what the volunteer wants to do should be of primary concern. People generally like to do what they are good at and be involved where they can be most useful.

Front Money

Most special events require that some money be spent before there is assurance that any money will be raised. The front money needed for an event should be an amount your organization could afford to lose if the event had to be cancelled. This money should already be available — you should not, for example, use funds from advance ticket sales to rent the place where the event will be held. If the event is cancelled many people will want their money back. Events that require a lot of front money can create a cash flow problem in the organization if the need for this money is not taken into account.

Repeatability

You need to consider whether the event can be repeated annually. The best event is one that becomes a tradition in your community, so that every year people look forward to the event that your group sponsors. Using this criterion can save you from discarding an event simply because the turnout was small the first time you did it. Perhaps you got too little publicity and only a handful of people came; if each of those people had a great time and you heard them saying things like, "I wish I had brought Juan," or "I wish Alice had known about this," then it may be worth having the event again next year. To decide if an event is repeatable, evaluate whether the same number of people working the same number of hours would raise more money producing this event again.

Timing

Find out what else is happening in your community at the time you want to hold your event. You don't want to conflict with the major fundraising event of a similar organization, nor do you want to be the tenth dance or auction in a row. If you are appealing to a particular constituency, you need to think of their timing. Farmers are mostly unavailable during planting and harvest; Jews will not appreciate being invited to a buffet on Yom Kippur; gay men and lesbians won't come to something scheduled during the Gay and Lesbian Pride Parade, and so on.

The Big Picture

The final consideration is the place of the event in your overall fundraising picture. If you find that the same people attend all your organization's events as well as give money by mail, you are "eating your own tail" and need to rethink how you are using events. If you cannot seem to get publicity for your events, or you are unable to find an event that reaches new constituencies, then maybe mounting special events is not the right approach. If, after analyzing your donor base you decide that your organization needs to increase its number of thoughtful donors, then you won't do as many events whose main purpose is acquisition. In other words, the results of special events (new names, publicity, new volunteers) must be fed into the overall effort to build a donor base or the effort put into the event will have mostly been wasted.

How to Plan a Special Event

Special events require more planning time than one would imagine. Because so much can go wrong, and because many things often hinge on one thing so that one mistake can throw off weeks of work, events must be planned with more attention to minute detail than almost any other fundraising strategy.

The Committee for Special Events

There must be a small committee of volunteers overseeing the work for the event. Using paid staff time to organize a special event is expensive and does not help to train or involve volunteers in substantive fundraising tasks.

The job of the committee is to plan and coordinate the event, not to do every task. After planning the event, most of the committee's work consists of delegating as many tasks as possible. Large committees can be unwieldy and counterproductive. With a larger committee planning the event, it is likely that some important element will be left out, that the planning process itself will take longer, that the committee meetings will be like special events themselves, and that the committee members will quickly burn out.

Each special event should have its own committee, although there can be overlap from one event to another. Special events are labor intensive, however, and people need to have a rest period between events and a chance not to participate in an event. The committee must have staff and board support, and everyone must agree that the chosen event is a good idea. There are three simple steps a special events committee should take to ensure the success of the event: detail a master task list, prepare a budget, and develop a time line.

1. Detail a master task list. On a piece of paper make four columns labelled "What," "When," "Who," and "Done." Under "What" list all the tasks that must be accomplished. Include everything, even those things you are sure no one would ever forget, such as "Pick up tickets at printer" or "Send invitations to the board." Every minute detail should be on this list. Under the column "When" note beside each task when it must be finished. Now put the list into chronological order so that you have a list of things that must be done and the order in which to do them. After completing steps two and three, complete the "Who," column, noting to whom the task is assigned. When the task is completed, note the date under "Done."

2. Prepare a budget. Create two sheets to work with: one for estimating and recording *expenses* and the other for estimating and recording *income*. On each, create columns for the item being priced and its estimated cost (or income) and actual cost (or income). The actual costs and income are filled in after the event.

List those tasks from the master task list that will cost money and estimate how much on the expense sheet. List those activities that will raise money on the income sheet with their estimated income. When you subtract your expense sheet total from your income sheet total, you have the projected "net," or financial goal, of the event. The budget should be simple but thorough, so that all costs are accounted for and planned on.

As you budget, remember that an estimate is not a guess. If someone says, "The estimate for food is . . ." or "The estimate for printing is . . ." it means he or she has called several vendors for prices, bargained, and is satisfied that the estimate will be the price or very close to the price you will pay. As costs are incurred they should be noted in the actual column. As much as possible, put off paying for anything until after the event and work in cancellation clauses for rentals or other contracts. For example, if a hall rents for $600 with $300 required as a deposit, try to reserve the right to get all or part of that $300 deposit back (if necessary) as close to the date of the event as possible.

Ideally, of course, you will aim to get as many things as possible donated, but don't budget to get anything for free. Always put a price in the budget. This will protect you in case you do have to pay for something you had planned to get donated, and also give you a cushion in case you have an unexpected expense.

3. Create a time line. To ensure that you have thought of everything that should be done and that you have allowed enough time to do it all, think "backwards" from the target date for your event. If you want to have a dance on August 10, what would you have to do on August 9? To do those things, what would you have to do in early August? What would have to be in place by July 15? And so on, back to the day you are starting from. By this "backward planning," the committee may find out that it is impossible to put on the event in the time allowed. In that case they must either modify the event or change the date. Thinking through each week's tasks for the time line is likely to reveal expenses or additional tasks you hadn't thought of. Add these to your task list and budget.

As you plan, remember to take into account that although there may be 90 days between now and the event, there may be only 60 "working" days because of schedule conflicts. For example, if a number of your volunteers have children, you should check a school calendar to make sure you don't need anything done on the first or last day of school, during spring vacation, or on commencement. Few organizations can have a New Year's Eve party as a fundraiser simply because they cannot get anyone to work during the two weeks preceding New Year's Day.

Establish "go/no-go" dates. On your time line, you will notice that there are periods of intense activity alternating with lulls throughout the time leading up to the event. The periods of intense activity, where several tasks must be accomplished and each is related to the other (such as design, layout, proofread, print and mail invitations) are called "task clusters." These groups of tasks must be accomplished as designated on your time line. The date by which each cluster must be accomplished is a "go/no-go" date. At those dates, evaluate your progress and decide if you are going to proceed with the event, or if you are too hopelessly behind or too many things have gone wrong and you should cancel or modify the event. Go/no-go dates can also include goals for how many tickets you should have sold or how many ads for the adbook, or how many underwriters are lined up to ensure that the event will be successful.

Once the committee has prepared the task list, the budget and the time line, they are ready to proceed in assigning tasks to other volunteers. When you ask volunteers or vendors to do things, give them a due date that is sooner than the one in the "When" column of your task list. That way, in the best case you will always be ahead of your schedule; in the worst case — if the task is not completed — you will have some time to get it done.

What Not to Forget

Here is a checklist of commonly forgotten items in planning an event:

♦ Liquor license.

♦ Insurance (on the hall, for the speaker, for participants). Contracts vary on this, but check it out. It often happens that a hall or auditorium is inexpensive because insurance is not included but is required of the renting organization. A one-night insurance policy or a rider on an existing policy can cost upwards of $1,500.

♦ Logistics of transporting food, drink, speakers, performers, sound equipment, and the like to the event.

♦ Lodging for performers or speaker.

♦ Parking: either a well-lighted lot or available on well-lighted streets.

♦ If there is going to be food: plates, utensils, and napkins. Are salt and pepper needed? Cream and sugar for coffee or tea?

♦ Heat or air conditioning: is it available, does it cost extra, will you need to bring your own fans or space heaters?

Here are some questions you need to ask before the event:

♦ Is the venue wheelchair accessible? Make sure that all rooms are accessible, especially both the men's and women's bathroom doors, stalls, toilet paper dispenser, sinks, etc. Sometimes a building will be labelled "wheelchair accessible" when only the front door and one area of seating are actually accessible.

- ◆ Where and how to dispose of trash? Are there clearly marked recycling bins and trash cans?
- ◆ Will you allow smoking? If so, where, and is that clearly marked?
- ◆ Does the invitation's reply card fit into the return envelope?
- ◆ Has everything been proofread by at least two people?
- ◆ Is the organization's address on the reply card, flier, poster, invitation, everything else?
- ◆ Are the price, date, time, place, and directions to the event on all advertising?
- ◆ Have you considered the necessity of child care or language translation?
- ◆ How safe is the neighborhood? Will women feel safe coming alone?
- ◆ Can you see and hear from every seat? (Sit in a number of seats to make sure.)
- ◆ Who will open the room or building for you? Do you need any keys?
- ◆ Do you know how the lights work?
- ◆ Where are the fire exits?

The Evaluation

The final step in planning a special event is evaluating how it went. Within a few days after the event the planning committee should meet a last time to fill out an evaluation form, as illustrated below. Save this evaluation along with copies of the advertising, the invitations, and any other information that would be useful for next year's planning committee.

The evaluation will allow you decide whether or not to do the event again and will also ensure that the same number of people working the same amount of time will raise more and more money every year. It should not be necessary to create the planning documents described above more than once. Once you have created them, every year a new committee can modify and add to them, but each committee is building on the knowledge and experience of previous committees.

SPECIAL EVENT REPORT

Approximately how much time did the committee spend on this event? In evaluating this, try to subtract time not really spent on the event (side discussions, eating) and be sure to count time members spent doing errands and making phone calls _____.
Comments:_____
Did this event bring in any new members? __ Yes __ No   How many? __
Can people who came to this event be invited to join the organization? __ Yes __ No
Did this event bring in new money? __ Yes __ No   How much? _____
Does this event have the capacity to grow every year? __ Yes __ No
Comments: _____
What would you do exactly the same next time?_____

What would you do differently? _____

List sources of free or low-cost items and who got them and indicate whether you think they will be available next year: _____

What kind of follow-up needs to be done? _____

Which committee members did what work?_____

Other comments: _____
Which committee members would be willing to work on this event next year? _____

9.

Three Special Event Strategies

his chapter covers a discussion of two events: a raffle and a house
party. It also covers an important component of many events —
producing an adbook. These three activities have been chosen
because they are relatively easy to organize, they require few up-front
costs, and taken as a whole, they demonstrate all the principles that have
been discussed in this book. The next chapter contains an annotated
glossary of special events — a quick look at 24 events, their possible net
income and the time it takes to organize them.

How To Do a House Party

One of the easiest special events, and sometimes one of the most
lucrative, is the common house party. In some ways, it seems ludicrous
to describe how to do a house party, since anyone who has ever had a
birthday party, school picnic, anniversary celebration, let alone a small
wedding or bat mitzvah already knows most of what there is to know
about putting on a house party. However, because sometimes the seemingly easy events are fraught with pitfalls, I want to describe the obvious
and not-so-obvious about giving a house party.

First the basic definition of a house party: A person or persons
involved in a nonprofit group invites his, her or their friends to a party at
their house. The purpose of the party is to educate those attending about
the work of the nonprofit group and ask them to make a contribution.

The party is also a place to meet people, see old friends and eat
good food, so it sets up a cordial atmosphere for the request. A house
party allows someone not familiar with the group to learn a lot about it,
ask questions, and get some personal attention without being obligated
to give. People can either give a very small gift or not give at all without

embarrassing themselves, and they can attend the house party without having to pay to get in.

A house party is a good way to raise consciousness about the issues your organization is addressing. House parties are best used to explain a complicated issue to many people at once, allowing them to ask questions and get the information they want. In the early days of the United Farmworkers movement, for example, house parties were used to explain the plight of migrant farmworkers and the concept of this union to middle-class, non-agricultural people who had the right sympathies and ability to give but little concrete information.

A second use of a house party is to enable a group of people to meet someone famous or important whose work is related to your cause, such as a candidate for office, a refugee from El Salvador, a member of the African National Congress, etc. This person gives a testimonial or asserts a particular viewpoint, and the host describes what people can do to respond (vote, give money, boycott, give money, demonstrate, give money).

No matter what else you ask people to do, ask them to give money. It is the only thing they can do right on the spot and, because it is usually the most passive action, it requires the least amount of work. The final use of a house party, which underlies all the other uses, is to expand the organization's donor base.

There are five steps to putting on a house party:

1. Find someone who is willing to host it at his or her house and take on other responsibilities related to the event.

2. Prepare the list of people to be invited.

3. Design the invitation.

4. Choreograph the event, particularly the pitch.

5. Follow up and evaluate.

The Host/s

The host of a house party has several responsibilities, the least of which is providing the house and the food. The host invites anyone he or she thinks might be interested in the organization or the topic being discussed. The host (or another person) gives an appropriate description of the organization and the issues and introduces the guest speaker, famous person or someone most familiar with the issue to be discussed. Finally, the host makes a pitch for money.

The host must be a donor who has contributed a gift, regardless of size, that was significant to her or him. The donor asks the guests to join him or her in making a significant gift of their own.

The ideal host is someone close enough to the organization to under-stand the importance of the group and to be willing to conquer their fear of asking friends for money, but not so close as to have all their friends already be donors. A major flaw of house parties is that the same people are invited to several house parties for the same organization.

Prepare the List of People to Be Invited

Once someone has volunteered to host the party, the organization's staff must help that person decide who should be invited. A house party can have any number of people, but it generally works best when there are at least 12 guests and not more than 40. Figure out how many peo-ple the house can comfortably accommodate. If you are planning a pre-sentation, you will need to make sure most of the people can sit down at that time. If there is no presentation and the pitch is to be short, then having enough seats will not be so important.

You need to invite three times as many people as you want to attend. There should be one person from the organization (such as a board member, volunteer, or staff) for every five to eight guests, so include them in the numbers.

Obviously, start with the host's friends. Don't forget neighbors. Sometimes, a house party is also a way to meet your neighbors. For example, a member of a solidarity group had a house party at his apart-ment. He invited the entire apartment building. A neighbor from another floor, whom he had never met, gave $5,000 that night. Think about peo-ple from church, synagogue, social clubs, work and relatives. Except for those people specifically invited to mingle and represent the organiza-tion, don't invite very many people who are already donors. If you invite donors and use this opportunity as an upgrade strategy, focus on those who could be asked to give more money than they currently do.

Design the Invitation

It is important to design the invitation specifically for the group being invited. The invitation does not have to be fancy, and it can be printed at an instant-print copy shop, so expense shouldn't be an issue. For groups with access to desktop publishing programs, good-looking invitations can be turned out very inexpensively.

The invitation should reflect something about the host and about the crowd being invited. This will make people want to attend. Whether your invitation is to be serious or light, educational or assuming knowledge on the part of the invitee, always include the following:

◆ An indication that people will be asked for money. "Bring your checkbook" is the most direct way to make this known. You might also say, "A chance to learn about, and contribute to this important work." Or, "As we enter our tenth year, your financial support is more important than ever."

◆ A way for people to give without coming to the party. On the invitation's return card include the option, "I can't come, but I want to help. Enclosed is my donation."

◆ Encourage people to bring friends. Require an RSVP so you will know how many people are coming.

◆ Give people clear directions to the house. If finding the place is at all confusing, draw a map. Include the phone number of the host under the directions.

Choreograph the Event

Where most parties fail is in not having thought through exactly how the event will go. To avoid this danger, imagine yourself a guest at the event and play over in your mind what will happen.

You walk or drive up to the house. Is it obvious where to park? (This can be important if you share a driveway with people not attending the party, if there is a hidden ditch near your house, or if your neighbors are the kind that are likely to call the police about a guest parked too near the crosswalk.) Is the house obvious? Is there a porch light? Is there a sign saying "The ____ house party here"? This is especially important in rural communities where homes can be hard to see, and in big apartment complexes where it may be confusing to find the right number.

You come in to the house or apartment. Is it obvious where to put your coat? If not, someone needs to be stationed at the door to provide that information. Ditto for the bathroom.

You look around for people you know and make your way to the food. Is there a traffic jam at the food table? Pull the table out from the wall so people can serve themselves from all sides of it. Put the drinks on a separate table removed from the food table to force people to move on from the food or from the drinks. If possible, have several small platters of food, rather than two or three large platters. Are the plates big enough? You don't want people to feel like they have to come back for five helpings to get enough, or stay hungry because they are too embarrassed to keep going back for more food. People returning to the food table creates a traffic jam, and people feeling hungry creates a non-money-giving atmosphere. If the house allows it, there can be several food tables in different rooms serving different kinds of food. Serve things that are easy to eat while standing up — finger food rather than things that need a fork and knife. Don't serve anything that would be a disaster if spilled (such as red wine on light-colored carpeting, chili on your couch).

Once you get your food, you look for a place to sit. Are there enough chairs? Make sure no chair is sitting alone or obstructing people coming in and out of the entrance. When you're done with your food, where will you put your empty dish? Make sure there are several trash cans around for disposable dishes and utensils and a table for things to be washed.

The Special Moment: The Pitch

Everything at the house party should be built around the pitch. Make arrangements ahead of time with at least two and not more than four people that when the host says, "I hope you will make a donation," they will pull out checkbooks, or hand over checks to members of the organization. They don't have to be ostentatious about it, but a few people have to set the tone that this is the time to give money.

Some people object to this practice, claiming that it imposes too much pressure. However, a little more thought will show that it is the considerate thing to do. Few people have the self-confidence to be the first to do anything. When the host asks for money, many people are prepared to give, but everyone has a brief attack of anxiety, "Perhaps this isn't when you give the money," or "Perhaps I am the only person in the room who believes in this cause," or "Perhaps everyone else already turned in their money and I will look odd if I give my money now."

Time the pitch so that the most people will be there when it is made. This is usually an hour into the party. The host calls for people's attention. The members of the organization discreetly get envelopes ready and the two to four "plants" space themselves around the room. The host introduces himself or herself and welcomes everyone. If there is a presentation, the host introduces the presenter. (If there is more than one host, such as a couple, or a group, they should take turns talking so it is clear that both or all are involved.)

After the presentation, the host must be the one who gives the pitch. If the presenter is a famous person or somehow special to the work of the group, that person can sometimes make a formal request for money, followed by the host saying, "I hope you will join me in helping this important cause." It doesn't matter if the host is nervous or doesn't like asking for money. Your proceeds will be cut by at least half without a pitch from the party sponsor.

Sometimes people argue that doing the party — loaning the house, fixing the food, giving the time — should indicate the host's interest. Indeed it does. It shows that the host helped save the group the cost of renting a conference room at a hotel. But, in order for the guests to give money, the host must also say that he or she gives money and wants anyone who agrees with him or her to do the same.

How the pitch is made determines how the money will be collected. This is also decided ahead of time. The best way to get the most money at the party is to pass around envelopes immediately after the host speaks. If you would prefer, the host can say, "Please put your donation in the basket over there," and point to a place. Or the host can say, "You can hand me your check, or give it to any of the people wearing a carnation." In any case, tell people how and when to give the money.

House parties often fail at the moment right after the pitch. For example, at one house party, the host said, "I hope you will all think about making a gift to this group, which is my favorite." Then, without missing a beat, he said, "Now that the fundraising part is over, eat up and drink up! Let's have fun." People did exactly as they were told. For a few seconds they thought about giving a gift, then headed for the food. No envelopes were present, and no method of collection was obvious.

At another party, the hosts showed a videotape about the group, then took the tape out of the TV monitor and went into the kitchen. People sat around chatting about the tape, then got up to get drinks and food. After a while, the hosts re-emerged and went on with the party. People could be heard asking: "Are we supposed to give money?" or, "What are you supposed to do with the money?" Perhaps out of fear of being rude, they did not ask the hosts.

In those cases, the parties raised almost no money and left people feeling that house parties are a waste of time. They are if not done properly. Following the pitch and a short period for people to write checks, the host should thank everyone for coming and encourage them to stay and have more to eat and drink and enjoy themselves.

Evaluate and Follow up

After each party, take some time to evaluate what went well and what could have been done better. Particularly if you have a regular presentation, think about the length, the relevance, how to get a discussion going and so on.

Be sure to write thank yous to everyone who gave money, and put their names on the organization's mailing list. If the host failed to make a pitch, then immediately send the guest list an appeal letter. If people gave, go over the list of donors with the host and if there are people missing from it who the host thinks would have given but didn't take the opportunity or forgot, he or she should call them. If the host does not want to call, perhaps he or she would send them a note; as a last resort, the organization should send them an appeal letter as soon as possible.

Like all fundraising strategies, house parties only work if someone actually asks for the money. Otherwise a house party is just a party — fun but no funds.

How to Do a Raffle

A common, easy and fun way to raise money is a raffle. Almost everyone is familiar with raffles, having bought tickets for them, perhaps even won a prize.

Because raffles are so common, most people don't realize that they can be complicated to organize. When you are organizing a raffle, you can make your life easier by paying attention to the myriad of details that a raffle involves.

The first fact to keep in mind is that selling raffle tickets is illegal in every state. It violates gambling laws. You can, however, make raffle tickets available for a donation. Clearly, laws about raffles are rarely enforced, but it is important to organize your raffle so that you are within the bounds of the law. In addition to federal and state laws, you need to find out the laws in your own community. Sometimes, you will need to register with the Sheriff's Department, and in some towns, laws against raffles are strictly enforced, and you simply will not be able to do one. We will discuss how to set up your raffle so that you will be within the laws of most states.

Raffles appeal to people's desire to get something for less than it is worth. Your organization gets some gifts donated that are used as the prizes. These gifts can vary from straight cash to services, such as child-care for an evening or having your windows washed, to more glamorous or valuable prizes such as a trip, microwave oven, VCR, and so forth. There are usually five to 10 prizes, one of which is a Grand Prize. Tickets are sold for a donation of between $.25 and $10.00 each. Many more tickets are sold than prizes available, so one person's chances of winning are small. At an appointed day and time, all the tickets are put into a barrel or other receptacle, stirred up, and an uninvolved person, such as a small child, draws out the winning tickets. The organization makes money from the number of tickets sold. There is no other source of income in a raffle. Because the costs can be kept low — ideally the only costs are those of printing the tickets and getting the prizes to the winners — most of the income is profit.

There are several steps to a successful raffle.

Step One: Get the Prizes

Bring together a small committee of two or three people to decide what the prizes are going to be. It is helpful if the prizes are built around a theme, such as "vacations" or "services" or "household items" or "restaurants." Make a list of all the vendors who might give you a prize and what specifically you want from each of them. Remember that small business people, particularly those with storefronts, are frequently asked to donate raffle prizes. They may have policies against doing it; they may already have five charities and are not taking on anymore; they may be having a hard time and not be inclined to give you anything. Have at least twice as many places from which to seek prizes as prizes needed.

The small committee then goes out and solicits the prizes. Be sure to stress to the merchant how many people will see the tickets, how much other publicity you are going to do, how you will not ask for another item this year, or whatever is true for you. Merchants must think about how giving your organization an item is good for their business, and you must help them in that thinking.

Step Two: Get the Workers

While you are soliciting prizes, start calling volunteers and finding out how many tickets they are willing to handle. Keep track of who agrees to distribute tickets. Some people hate raffles — don't push them into taking tickets; they will resent it and probably not sell their tickets. Give the tickets to people who work in large office buildings or unions, or who have large families or large circles of friends. Obviously, the more people you can find to sell tickets, the better.

Raffles are a good opportunity to get some peripheral people involved, so don't just go to your reliable volunteers who already do everything else. Ask each person if they know someone who would be good at "selling" tickets. People's spouses or lovers, neighbors, business partners, etc., can be recruited for this effort. Have a prize for the person who brings in the most money for the raffle.

Step Three: Get the Tickets

Once you have the prizes, the committee decides which prize will be the grand prize, which second and so on. They decide the date of the raffle drawing. Raffles should go on for at least one month and can go on for up to six months without losing momentum. The ideal length of time for selling raffle tickets is two to three months.

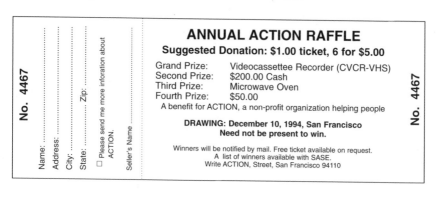

Printing the tickets requires attention to detail.

You must print on the ticket how a person can get a free ticket and that a list of winners will be available. This is to help ensure that the prizes were actually awarded. To increase sales, indicate "Need not be present at the drawing to win."

The tickets must be numbered. Although it costs more for the printer to number the tickets, it is worth it. Many organizations try to save money by not having numbered tickets or by numbering the tickets themselves. This is a foolish use of time. It is also critical that the ticket stub be perforated so it can be easily separated from the body of the ticket. Don't save money by printing cheap raffle tickets. Your volunteers will not distribute them as easily, and donors will be reluctant to give their money when the ticket does not appear properly done.

Not all printers can print raffle tickets because of the need for perforation and, usually, binding groups of 10 or 20 tickets into books. Find a printer who can, even if you cannot use your regular printer. Needless to say, seek to have the printing done for free, but don't scrimp on the tickets. They should be your only cost.

To know how many tickets to print, note how many tickets the volunteer workers are willing to take. Every volunteer ought to be able to sell a minimum of 25 tickets. Most people who live in a town or city can sell 50 tickets in two or three weeks with no difficulty. Some people will be able to sell 100 to 500 tickets in one or two months.

Always print at least 200 more tickets than your financial goal, because some tickets are bound to be lost or mutilated.

Notice in the illustration that the seller is asked to sign his or her name on the ticket stub. This is another incentive you can build in to your raffle: giving a prize to any person who sold winning tickets. You are obviously more likely to win such a prize if you have sold a lot of tickets.

To promote your organization, also offer people a chance to get more information about your work. If you do make such an offer, be sure you have planned to go through every ticket and pull out the people who indicated interest.

Step Four: Distribute and Keep Track of the Tickets

On your list of everyone selling tickets, note which numbers are on the tickets you send or give to each volunteer. Then keep track as the tickets are returned.

Create deadlines by having a couple of set dates for returns; this makes keeping track of the tickets easier. It is also easy to see who is selling the most tickets and who may need more tickets.

One final word concerning the law: many groups send raffle tickets through the mail to possible donors. This is against postal law and, if caught, your letters will be sent back. If you send the tickets by bulk mail, you risk having your bulk mail permit revoked.

In any case, raffles are not mail appeals. If you want to use the mail to raise money, do so, but do not combine raffles and mail appeals.

Step Five: Encourage the Workers

The job of the small committee is not to sell tickets, but to keep other people selling them. The organizing committee should call people at least once a week to see how they are doing with their tickets. Remind them of the deadlines and ask them to send in their stubs and cash. To encourage competition, tell them who is winning the "most sold" prize so far.

Step Six: Set Up the Drawing

Some organizations use the raffle drawing as a way to have another event, such as a dance or auction, at which more tickets can be sold right before the drawing, which is the highlight of the event. Certainly, adding another event onto your raffle may increase your profit, but it also doubles your work. If you don't want to have another event, just hold a small party for all the workers. Have food and drink and make the drawing a celebration and a reward for a job well done.

Step Seven: Round Up the Tickets

Surprisingly, most people find the most difficult task in a raffle lies not in getting the prizes and not in getting the workers, but in getting the tickets and the cash back.

Some workers will be careless with their ticket stubs, or return stubs and promise cash later, or claim to have sold tickets when they really haven't. If you have encouraged people to turn in money and stubs as they go along, you will have less difficulty than if you wait until just before the drawing. Stubs and cash should be due at least three days, and preferably five days before the drawing. That way, you can ensure that you have all the tickets accounted for well ahead of time. People should turn in unsold tickets as well, so that they can be passed on to more successful sales people and so that all numbers are accounted for.

The problem with a raffle is that all the transactions are in small amounts of cash. Someone sells three tickets to a co-worker, puts the stubs and dollar bills into his or her wallet, then goes to lunch and uses that cash on lunch without thinking. Later, he or she turns in more stubs than cash, and, without a careful record keeping system, this error might not be caught.

Another advantage of getting ticket stubs in well ahead of time is to make sure all the stubs are undamaged. Some people try to make their stub into the winning one by bending down a corner, sticking something on the back, or tearing it nearly in half and then taping it together. Workers will sometimes fold ticket stubs or spill stuff on them. These stubs cannot be used, and new stubs must be written. (This is, in part, the use of the 200 or so extra tickets.) During the drawing the stubs must be as uniform as possible.

Step Eight: Hold the Drawing

Get some kind of big box or barrel for the ticket stubs. Be sure to mix and re-mix the stubs thoroughly after each prize is drawn. Start with the bottom prize and work up to the Grand Prize. Have a blindfolded adult or small child do the actual drawing to guarantee neutrality. After the prizes are drawn, announce the prizes for top sales people and award these.

After the drawing, sort through the tickets for people who checked that they were interested in getting more information about your group. Many organizations also keep the ticket stubs and use them for a mail appeal later. It can be labor intensive to sort through the ticket stubs, getting rid of current members' names, and making sure that you only have one ticket stub for each person, even if they bought 20 tickets. However, for new groups, rural organizations, or small raffles, this is a good way to build a mailing list.

Step Nine: Send Out the Prizes, Thank Yous, and Evaluate

Arrange for the winners to get their prizes, either by picking them up at your office or receiving them in the mail.

Send thank-you notes to each person who sold tickets and to everyone who donated prizes.

Count your money. Note how many tickets were unsold, whether the problems were with the workers, the merchants, the tickets themselves, etc. Make a file with all the information about the raffle in it, including lists of winners, list of people donating items, timing, list of volunteers and your evaluation. Next year it will be much simpler to do the raffle if the new committee can pull out the file and not have to start from the beginning.

Adbooks

An adbook provides a way for your organization to raise money from businesses and corporations by selling them advertising space in a booklet, program, menu, or other printed item. The adbook is distributed to people who are coming to an event and who will be likely to patronize the businesses that advertised there. Businesses whose owners may not care about the issues you represent may still buy an ad because they know your constituents use their business or want them to do so.

Adbooks are a superb fundraising strategy if they are well done on a regular basis. Some organizations use this concept as a way to underwrite conventions, luncheons, concerts, or any special event where a program or printed agenda would be appropriate.

Adbooks are lucrative because the business buying the ad is paying many times more for the ad space than its actual printing cost. An adbook can be as simple as a folded sheet of paper with ads on all sides, or as complex as a full-scale booklet printed in color. An adbook can also include coupons.

One advantage of adbooks is that they train volunteers to ask for money face-to-face in a situation that gives the donor a concrete value for his or her money. Some volunteers who are reluctant to ask for monetary donations outright are willing to approach business people to buy ads. They know that business people want and need to advertise and that they are always looking for creative ways to reach more people. The advantage to the advertiser is that the cost of space in your adbook is almost always less than the cost of an ad of comparable size in a newspaper. Even though a newspaper reaches more people, the people your adbook reaches are "hotter" prospects for the advertiser if their goods or services are particularly useful to your audience.

What Will It Look Like?

Like all fundraising strategies, producing an adbook requires careful advance planning. The first step is to plan what shape and size your adbook will be. While the exact number of pages will be determined by the number of ads you sell, the size of the pages will determine the size of the ads and how much you can charge for them.

What the adbook will look like may also be affected by your distribution plan. You may choose a different size or design for an adbook that will only go to people attending an event than for one to be distributed more widely. For wider distribution, you will need to decide if you will send one to all your donors, put it in stores, hand it out in your neighborhood to people on the street, or use some other distribution strategy.

What Should Ads Cost?

There are no set formulas for determining how much ads should cost. Check with other groups in your area that have done successful adbooks and see what they have charged. The price of the ads will depend in large part on how fancy your adbook will be and therefore how much it will cost to produce. If it is to be printed in color on glossy paper the ads must be more expensive than if it were simply printed in black and white. There should be some variation in price between ads on the covers of the adbook and those on inside pages. Cover-page ads (including the back cover and the two inside covers) are usually at least twice the price of ads within the book because the exposure is so much better. Some groups charge more for ads in the centerfold as well, since they too will have more exposure.

The ads are sold either by dimension in inches ("display ad") or by the number of words ("classified ad"). A display ad is prepared by the

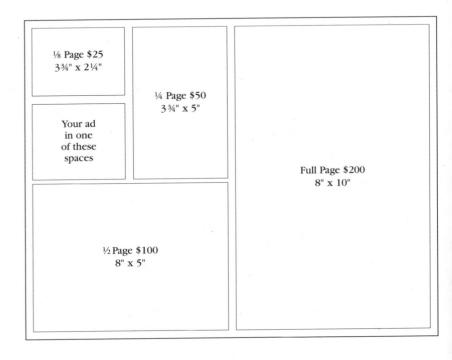

⅛ Page $25
3¾" x 2¼"

Your ad
in one
of these
spaces

¼ Page $50
3¾" x 5"

Full Page $200
8" x 10"

½ Page $100
8" x 5"

advertiser and sent to you "camera ready," that is, ready to go to the printer. For a classified ad, the advertiser sends the ad copy and you have the message typeset for inclusion in the book. Display ads are sold as full page, half page, one-third page, quarter page, and sometimes one-eighth page (depending on how big one-eighth of a page would be). Some groups choose only to have display ads so that they will not have to design classified sections.

It is a good idea to give businesses and individuals the option of buying a single line in your book and calling those advertisers "friends" or "sponsors." These listings are considerably less expensive. They do not advertise the person or business buying them, but they do show that the person or business is supportive of your organization.

Once you have designed your adbook and set prices for the ads, prepare sample pages to be given to volunteers in selling the ads. A sample layout for an 8 1/2 x 11" format is shown.

Time Line

The next step is to set a time line for ad sales. If the adbook is for an event, the event will be the distribution point and the deadline for final copy received must be at least one month ahead of the date of the event to allow for typesetting, paste-up, and printing of the book.

The time line can be prepared in the same way as for a special event, with a master task list and a budget. A large adbook will require about a six-week sales period. Two weeks before sales begin will be needed for planning, preparing materials and training the sales force. Four weeks at the end of the sales period will be needed for layout, typesetting, proofreading and printing. Thus, the total length of time to produce an adbook — from planning to delivery of the printed product — is 12 weeks.

Getting Ready to Sell

Make a list of businesses and individuals who might want to buy ads. Ask all volunteers, board members and staff to list all the businesses they patronize, companies they work for, companies their spouses and friends work for, and businesses that would serve a large cross section of your donors. (For example, a women's organization would be sure to include women's clothing stores, beauty salons, and women's bars.) To help people recall all the possible businesses they patronize, give them a list of suggestions, including banks, restaurants, vegetable stores, supermarkets, butchers, clothing stores, bakeries, liquor stores, and such people as doctor, mechanic, therapist, hairdresser, accountant, and plumber.

Place each name you receive on a 3" by 5" card with the address of the business and a contact person there, the name of the person who uses the business, and any other information that will be helpful to the sales person. (For example, Joe's Auto Supply, Joe Jones, owner, 512 Main St., board president's brother-in-law; also, Sally buys everything for her motorcycle there.)

Divide these cards among the volunteer sales people. If possible, volunteers should be assigned businesses and individuals they know, as they will have a better chance for success.

If you are a neighborhood or community group, it may be easier to have each volunteer simply approach every store on a square block of the neighborhood.

In addition to their prospect cards, the volunteers each need a supply of brochures describing the work of your organization, sample ad sheets with order forms to give each business, return envelopes in case the business owner wishes to mail in their ad or payment, and receipt books for payments received at the time of sale.

Prepare the volunteers for difficult questions they may encounter and provide possible answers, including convincing arguments. Each volunteer should stress how many good prospects the adbook will reach, how inexpensive the ad is, and how much members of your organization enjoy the business, store, or service where the volunteer is selling.

Selling the Ads

Depending on the type of business you are soliciting and the general style of your community, volunteers may first want to call the business owner or manager to make an appointment. In soliciting ads from corporations or large firms, sending a letter then following up with a phone call and visit will be imperative. When a business agrees to an ad, have them sign a form indicating what size ad they have taken and the cost.

Two or three volunteers should act as "team leaders" for the rest of the sales force. The team leaders play the same role as the planning committee for a special event. While they should also sell ads, their main function is to encourage people on their team and to make sure that volunteers are making their sales calls. Volunteers must understand that, more often than not, they will be turned down. It will take between five and eight solicitations to garner one sale. As is the case when soliciting major gifts, you rarely know exactly why you were turned down. Don't spend a great deal of time thinking about it; simply go on to the next prospect.

As sales are made a progress chart should be posted at the office, and progress reports should be given to sales people to encourage them. Once a week every sales person should be given a list of the businesses that have already bought ads. They can take this list with them on solicitations; business owners may be persuaded to buy an ad when they see the names of colleagues or competitors who have done so.

Thank businesses in writing immediately after they send in their ads and their money. When the adbook is produced send them a copy. Encourage your members to tell businesses they use if they saw the business in your adbook and to thank them for supporting your organization.

Some businesses will not send payment until the adbook is published. Careful records will show which bills remain outstanding and those businesses can be billed again after they receive a copy of the adbook. Because they have filled out and signed an agreement specifying the size and wording of the ad, it is extremely rare for business people not to pay.

Producing the Adbook

After all the ads are in and the sales period is over, the book must be produced. Groups usually find it helpful to have a second set of volunteers handle the production and distribution details. The sales force has done their task. A graphics designer or person with layout skills should be asked (or paid) to help ensure that the ads are laid out straight, that all the ads fit properly on each page, and that all the ads fit in the book. Layout can be done by hand or using a graphics program on a computer. Attention should be paid to putting ads that look nice together on the same page and to having some "white space" on each page so that the ads don't look crowded and unreadable. Great care should be taken to proofread all copy and to keep the display ads and all the copy clean. There must also be space, either throughout the adbook or in a specific section of it, for the conference agenda or program notes of the event, and there should also be information about your group and a membership form.

Once proofread, the final book is then ready for printing. Someone who knows about paper stock and the printing process should help select the paper and ink and deal with the printer.

The first year you produce an adbook is the most difficult. Businesses are taking a chance that you will do what you say in terms of quality and distribution of the book. If your adbook is successful and people patronize the businesses they have read about there, repeat sales will be easy to get. Be sure to save some copies of the adbook to use in next year's sales effort so businesses can see exactly what they will get for their money. If they like what they see, they will be more inclined to buy.

Adbooks can be lucrative both because the ads bring in much more money than the cost of printing them and because they are a repeatable commodity. They are good for training volunteers in fundraising techniques and for building community relations with businesses. They should only be done, however, when the group has the lead time, the number of volunteers required who can devote time to the adbook and are not also organizing the rest of the event, and access to the design and printing expertise required.

10.

A Potpourri of Special Events

The following 24 events are divided into three categories according to the time required to accomplish them: those that can be done in one month, those that can be done in three months, and those that require five or more months of preparation. Needless to say, some of the events that can be done in one month with several people working on them would take much longer if only one or two people were available, or could be much bigger if more time were taken. Conversely, some of the events requiring more preparation could be done in a considerably shortened time with the help of paid staff or more volunteers. Although, as has been repeatedly emphasized, special events should not be held primarily to raise funds, they do play an important part in the plans of low-budget, grassroots organizations as a fundraising strategy. Therefore, knowing a few general points about a number of special events will aid in choosing appropriate activities for your organization.

Each event listed is followed by a brief description of the event, the number of planners and other volunteers needed, and the principal costs of the event. All of these descriptions assume little or no involvement of paid staff. "Planners" are the volunteers in charge of the special event who then delegate as many tasks as possible to other volunteers.

Clearly, this is only a small sampling of all possible special events. However, they represent the major types of special events held by small nonprofit organizations; most other special events are variations on these.

Events That Can Be Done in One Month

Summertime Barbecue. Choose any weekend or holiday, find a park or beach, and invite as many people as you want to an "all-you-can-eat" barbecue. Volleyball, softball, and games for children round out this afternoon event.

Planners: 2 or 3. Tasks: Reserve a space for the barbecue, prepare and distribute advertising fliers or invitations. (City parks generally need to be reserved through City Hall or the park commissioner.)

Other Volunteers: 2 or 3. Tasks: Help with publicity, cook and clean up on the day of the barbecue.

Main Costs: Permits for the barbecue, plates and utensils, advertising fliers. Food can be an expense, but often a store or several stores will donate some or all of it if you will hang a large sign at the picnic noting their donation.

Charge: Adults, $12; children under 12, $6; under 5, free.

Dinner in a Private Home. A board member, staff person, or volunteers who lives in a nice or unusual home or setting and/or is a gourmet cook invites 10-25 people (depending on what the house will hold) to a sit-down dinner.

Planners: 1 or 2. The person doing the event may be the only planner. Tasks: Compile guest list; send the invitations; cook the food for the event.

Volunteers: 2 or 3. Tasks: Address invitations, tabulate RSVPs, help serve and clean up the night of the event.

Main Costs: Invitations, which need to be fancy or elegant, and postage. The person putting on the event usually donates some or all of the food and drink; if not, food and drink will be the only other large cost.

Charge: $35-50 per person/$50-80 per couple. Children are not generally included in such an event.

Garage Sale. On a small scale, garage sales are easy to organize and reasonably lucrative. Simply ask five to 10 people to clear out their closets and bookshelves and bring their donations to a garage or yard located on a street with a lot of foot traffic.

Planners: 1. Tasks: Call the donors (usually board or staff members), determine the location of the sale.

Volunteers: 4. Tasks: Prepare signs noting the place and time of the sale; help price the items for sale, staff the sale, collect money, refold clothes, answer questions of prospective buyers, and clean up, taking leftover items to Goodwill or other community thrift store.

Main Costs: None. Everything is free.

Charge: Price items well below their actual worth and attempt to sell everything that has been donated. Be prepared to bargain with buyers. In the last two hours of the sale, mark everything down 50 percent.

Pancake Breakfast. Serve an all-you-can-eat breakfast from 7:30-11 on a weekend morning at a public location, such as a church, service club, or community hall.

Planners: 2 or 3. Tasks: Finding a place, setting a date, preparing advertising.

Volunteers: 6. Tasks: Distribute fliers and help with any other invitations; cook and clean up.

Main Costs: Food, eating utensils, and advertising. The volunteers should seek donations or discounts on food.

Charge: Adults, $6; Children, $3. Try for volume of people, and make it affordable enough for a family to go out for breakfast.

Progressive Dinner. This event starts at one person's house for drinks and appetizers, moves to a second house for dinner, and a third house for dessert. Sometimes, two more stops are added, for soup and salad, and a final stop for coffee and liqueur after dessert. The houses need to be near each other, and the guests carpool or are transported from house to house, and then returned to the starting place.

Planners: 3. Tasks: Line up the homes; help plan the menu, solicit food donations or cooking services of local chefs. Generally, the three planners are also the people in whose homes the various parts of the dinner will take place.

Volunteers: 5. Tasks: One or two people to send invitations to all the people who are invited and then help to set up each house. Two or three people at each house to serve and clean up. Possibly one or two people to drive the guests from house to house, if they are not close enough together to walk.

Main Costs: Food, if the hosts do not wish to donate it; invitations and postage.

Charge: $25-50 per person; more if the food is very fancy or the homes very elegant or unusual, or if entertainment, such as music is offered at one or more of the homes.

Events That Can be Done in Three Months

Book Sale. The same idea as a garage sale, but having only books for sale.

Planners: 3 or 4. Tasks: Get the books, get a place for the sale and arrange publicity. Usually a mailing to all local donors asking for books will bring in a large number. Ask people to bring books to a central location, or offer to pick them up if you have people to do that.

Volunteers: 6 to 12, depending on the number of books. Tasks: Sort the books, staff the sale and clean up. Books should be sorted into hardbound and paperback and usually into broad categories such as fiction, travel, self-help, cookbooks, children's books, religion, philosophy, history, etc. It is a good idea to have someone familiar with books to pull out rare ones such as first editions, old books, and out-of-print books. These should be displayed on a separate table and assigned higher prices. Usually, a set price for paper and hardback books makes accounting easier and encourages sales. Set the price of non-rare books low so that you sell as many as possible. Volunteers also staff the book sale and clean up.

Main Costs: Advertising.

Charge: No admission charge, various prices for the books.

Cocktail Party. Hold an early evening event in an attractive setting and, if possible, with someone of note as the guest of honor.

Planners: 3 or 4. Tasks: Secure a place, find the person to honor, design the invitation.

Volunteers: 3 or 4. Tasks: Send the invitations, welcome people as they arrive, and, unless you have hired bartenders, serve the drinks.

Main Costs: Renting the place, if it is not someone's house, and the invitations, liquor, and finger food.

Charge: $15-25 per person. You can decide not to charge and to give a pitch at the event after the person of honor has given a moving speech. (See Chapter 9, Three Special Event Strategies, for a detailed description of how to put on a house party, which is a similar event.)

Crafts Fair. Give local artists a chance to display their wares while promoting yourselves to the public.

Planners: 3. Tasks: Identify a place to hold the fair, set the date, design the publicity. The place should be big enough for the number of crafts booths needed and in a highly trafficked area, preferably with its own parking lot. A church or community center is an excellent site.

Volunteers: 5. Tasks: Send out invitations to artists to display at the fair, advertise the fair to the general public, help set up the showroom, and clean up afterwards.

Main Costs: The place for the fair, the invitations, and publicity.

Charge: Varies, depending on how you decide to do it. Generally artists are charged a booth fee and there is a small admission charge for the general public. Artists can be asked to give a percentage of their sales for that day to the organization.

Haunted House. For Halloween convert a house, community center or church activity hall into a haunted house. Supply cardboard or plastic skeletons, plastic spiders, and the like, and set up lighting and sound systems for appropriate scary ambience. Some volunteers should dress up as mad scientists, vampires, witches, and so forth, and make occasional unannounced appearances to groups touring the house. Two or more volunteers must lead group tours of the house, telling a scary story, about the various parts of the house or objects in it.

Planners: 3 to 4. Tasks: Find a site, plan the publicity and the house setup.

Volunteers: 6 to 10: Tasks: Do advance publicity, setting up the house including lighting and sound, dressing in costume to lead groups through the house, collecting the entrance fees, and getting the house back to normal at the end of the day.

Main Cost: Publicity and sound and light systems, unless they can be hooked up to stereo and light fixtures already installed.

Charge: $1.00-2.00 per person, less for children under 7. The price should be low enough that children and their parents can take several tours through the house during the day.

Movie Benefit. A theater donates an afternoon or evening to your group.

Planners: 2 or 3. Tasks: Find the theater and work with its staff to select a movie, design publicity in cooperation with the theater.

Volunteers: 2 or 3. Tasks: Help get publicity out and, depending on your arrangement with the theater, collect tickets or work the concession stand.

Main Costs: Publicity.

Charge: The same price as the movie theater normally charges, or more. Bill it as a donation.

Open House. Invite donors and prospects to your office to meet the staff and board. An open house is not technically a fundraiser, but you can prominently display donation cans and sell your organization's products. You can also add a no-host bar.

Planners: 2. Tasks: Set the date, prepare the invitations.

Volunteers: 2 to 4. Tasks: Send the invitations, bring in the refreshments (usually finger foods, soft drinks, and wine), set up, welcome guests, sign up new members, and clean up before and after the event.

Main Costs: Food and publicity.

Charge: No charge at the door. Have things for sale (T-shirts, bumper stickers, etc.) and encourage people who are not already donors to join. Have a lot of membership information available and a person whose only task is to answer questions and enroll new members.

Tasting. An exotic, sophisticated or popular food or drink is offered in many guises or varieties for tasting. Wine, chocolate, liqueurs and cordials, fancy candy, and ethnic foods all lend themselves to this format.

Planners: 2 or 3. Tasks: Find a place, decide on a theme, and prepare advertising.

Volunteers: 4. Tasks: Get donations of the food or drinks to be tasted (manufacturers or distributors can gain a great deal of publicity through this event), distribute advertising, mail invitations, set up the place, collect money at the door.

Main Costs: Advertising. You may have to provide snacks at a wine tasting, or coffee and tea for a chocolate or candy tasting.

Charge: Varies depending on what you are serving, but usually at least $8 per person. Children are generally not encouraged to come to such an event.

Tour. A guided tour of a historic part of town or architecturally interesting buildings (houses, churches, or other places) or a nature walk.

Planners: 1 or 2. Tasks: Find someone to lead an appropriate tour, design the advertising.

Volunteers: 1 or 2. Tasks: Greet people as they arrive, provide refreshments at the end of the tour.

Main Costs: Advertising. Possibly an honorarium for the tour guide.

Charge: $5-15 a person, depending on how exotic the tour is or how knowledgeable the tour guide.

Workshop or Class. Offer a learning experience on almost any topic that people want to know about for which you have a qualified teacher. Topics might include organic gardening, sewing, knitting, fundraising, tennis, judo, computers, auto mechanics, aerobics, etc.

Planners: 1 or 2. Tasks: Find the teacher, get a place, and design publicity.

Volunteers: 1 or 2. Tasks: Help with publicity and registration, introduce the teacher at the start of the class, and clean up after the class.

Main Costs: The place and publicity. Try to get the teacher to donate his or her time and try to get a free place.

Charge: The going rate for similar classes; usually between $25 and $150 a person. Depends on the class and how well known or in demand the instructor is.

Events Requiring Five or More Months of Planning

Auction.

Planners: 3 to 5. Tasks: Find a place, secure an auctioneer, design publicity, help get prizes to auction.

Volunteers: 10 or more. Tasks: Get good items to be auctioned, getting adequate publicity, preparing a list of items to be auctioned to give to each participant, including value and minimum bid; the day of the auction providing food and drink at the event, setting up chairs, collecting money, arranging for delivery of auctioned items, cleaning up.

Main Costs: The place and the publicity. You may also have to pay a professional auctioneer, although usually a volunteer can be found.

Charge: Charge a nominal admission price and charge for food and drink. The bulk of the money is made from the auctioned items.

Bingo. You may be able to be a one-night beneficiary of an ongoing bingo game. Check with your community's laws to ensure compliance.

Planners: 1 to 4. Tasks: Set up the bingo game, which generally means renting out an evening of an ongoing bingo game, advertising, recruiting volunteers to manage the game. Some organizations prefer to pay the person running the game.

Volunteers: 2 or 3. Tasks: Run the bingo game, collect money, set up, and clean up. However, if you are the beneficiary of an ongoing game, you may only need volunteers to do publicity.

Main Costs and Charge: Varies from community to community. Check with other groups doing bingo as a fundraising device.

Concert. One of the most common fantasies of a low-budget group is the idea of having a concert with a famous or popular performer. This is one of the most difficult fundraising events to carry out successfully.

Planners: 5. Tasks: Find the performer (this can take months of research and cultivation) coordinate a time and place with the performer's schedule, prepare publicity.

Volunteers: Unlimited number. Tasks: Distribute publicity, sell tickets, set up food and drink at the performance hall (if allowed), etc. Many organizations choose to pay someone to handle the details of planning and implementing.

Main Costs: Rental of the performance space, publicity, and the performer's expenses (assuming that his/her/their fees are waived, you will still be charged for plane fare, local transportation, hotel, food, etc.).

Charge: Whatever is the going rate for similar performances, or more.

Conference. An expanded version of the workshop or class discussed earlier. A conference of one or more days is held on a particular topic and can include a series of speakers and workshops. Ideally, some continuing education credits should be offered.

Planners: 4 or 5. Tasks: Decide on the theme, arrange for a conference space, contact speakers and workshop leaders, plan publicity, create packets for conference attendees.

Volunteers: 12. Tasks: Advertise the conference, mail packets to conference participants, set up and clean up, pick up speakers at airport, bus station, etc., register attendees, answer questions, solve problems, and act as runners for any items needed at the last minute.

Main Costs: Advertising and conference materials, honoraria for speakers, rental of conference space.

Charge: Depends on the number of days and the type of conference. Charge the going rate for similar conferences. Do not undercharge.

Dance.

Planners: 3 or 4. Tasks: Decide on a theme, find a space, hire performers, and plan advertising.

Volunteers: 8-10. Tasks: Promote the dance, arrange for decorations, food and drink the night of the dance, get liquor licenses, take money at the door, staff the food and drink booths, set up and clean up.

Main Costs: The performers (unless donated), hall rental, security guard(s), publicity.

Charge: Depending on how popular the dance band is, charge at least $5 per person. Some groups charge $8-10 and include free munchies and one free drink. (This encourages people to buy more drinks, and is a lucrative strategy.)

Decorator Showcase. Each room of large, architecturally elegant or unusual house or one belonging to a famous person is decorated by a different interior designer. Charge people to come through the house.

Planners: 5 or 6. Tasks: Details seem almost infinite for this event. The main ones are to line up the house, the decorators, and plan publicity. There is a tremendous amount of work involved in coordinating the schedules and permission of the homeowners and the decorators and giving the decorators time to do their work with minimum inconvenience to the homeowners (who must have another home to use).

Volunteers: Unlimited numbers can be used. Tasks: promote the showcase, collect money, conduct the tours, arrange for parking for people coming to the showcase, and assist the planners in coordinating the whole thing.

Main Costs: Publicity.

Charge: $15-30 per person, depending on how fancy the house and the decorations are.

Dinner-Dance. An elegant affair usually held at a hotel, with a fancy dinner and excellent dance band.

Planners: 4-5. Tasks: As with the decorator showcase, details are everything here, and a comprehensive task list is imperative. Aside from the obvious details of renting the hotel, the band, etc., soliciting sponsors for the invitation is important. The invitation thus comes from 25 to 100 socially prominent people who join in inviting the rest of the community to a dinner-dance in honor of your organization.

Volunteers: Again, as many as possible to send out the invitations, collate the RSVPs, make a seating chart for the dinner, coordinate with the hotel's catering service, and oversee set up and clean up.

Main Costs: The room rental, food, invitations, and performer's fees. This is a costly event. Get as much underwritten or discounted as possible.

Charge: $50-250 per couple.

Fashion Show. Put on a traditional fashion show — models displaying the latest fashions — or for more fun, do a take-off on that idea. Variations abound, such as a "working woman's fashion show," which would show professional-looking but comfortable fashions for upwardly mobile working women, or an ethnic fashion show that would feature clothes from other countries, or a spoof on a fashion show, that might model clothing that is out of fashion, what never to wear in public, etc. The models can be professionals or, for fun, board and volunteers, or politicians and well-known people in the community.

Planners: 2 or 3. Tasks: Plan the theme, find appropriate models and clothing, find a place, plan publicity.

Volunteers: (not including models) 4 or 5. Tasks: Help with publicity, coordinate the show itself, write up descriptions of the fashions, announce the models and what they are wearing, set up and clean up. If food and drink are sold volunteers need to staff those booths.

Main Costs: Hall rental and publicity. If the models are paid that will be a main cost.

Charge: Depends on the theme of the fashion show and the intended audience; at least $10.

Tribute Luncheon. A fancy luncheon usually held at a hotel, honoring one or more people and featuring a well-known speaker.

Planners: 4 to 5. Tasks: Decide whom to honor and why, find an appropriate speaker, solicit a "committee" of 50 to 100 people whose names will be used on the invitation as joining in inviting the community to the luncheon, design the invitation.

Volunteers: Many. Tasks: Reserve the hotel room, arrange the food, send out invitations, collate responses, solicit corporations and businesses to reserve tables at the luncheon, arrange the seating, and see that things go smoothly the day of the luncheon. Many organizations produce an adbook as an additional source of funds.

Main Costs: The hotel, food and invitations, all of which are very expensive. Like others in this section, this event is heavy on front money and must be planned with great care.

Charge: $50-500 per person, depending on how fancy it is and who the audience is. Encourage corporations or wealthy donors to "buy" whole tables for a set price, which is usually more than just buying that number of seats. The idea is that a corporation gets more publicity for reserving a whole table and then all the people from that work place can sit together.

Walk-Jog-Bike-Rock-Read-a-Thon. Participants collect pledges for every mile they walk, jog, or bike, or every hour they rock in a rocking chair, or for some other measurement of endurance.

Planners: 2 or 3. Tasks: Plot the course of the marathon, get any required permission from the police department or City Hall for using the streets, design publicity.

Volunteers: 12 or more. Tasks: Help with publicity, monitor and mark pledge sheets of participants as they go by their checkpoints, collect money from participants (who must collect it from their pledges), provide first aid in case of injuries.

Main Costs: Publicity, permits, and prizes. Prizes are usually a T-shirt or certificate of participation.

Charge: There is usually no charge to enter, unless the 'thon is done as a race among participants, in which case an entry fee is charged.

Participants get whatever they can for each mile; usually a minimum pledge of 10-25 cents is suggested.

11.

Fundraising by Telephone

Imagine that you are sitting on your couch after a long day's work. You are sipping a delicious cup of hot tea, with your cat on your lap, watching TV or reading a good book when suddenly the phone rings. The cat flies off your lap. You think it could be important, curse yourself for not having a cordless phone, and get up to answer the call. A pleasant but slightly smarmy voice says, "Hello, is this Jane Smith?" and pauses for your answer. If affirmative, the voice continues, "Jane, how are you this evening? I hope you are well, because, Jane, did you know that there are 2,532 people in our community that are very, very sick tonight, and Jane, you can help them . . ."

This scenario is played out night after night in millions of homes in America. The fundraising phone call interrupts dinner, putting the kids to bed, or just relaxing. People complain about it incessantly and some states have even attempted to stop the use of the phone for sales or fundraising.

Yet, it works. Telemarketing continues to pull a greater percent of response than direct mail, and it is an excellent way of reaching a large number of people with a (somewhat) personal message. A basic fundraising axiom is that the closer you can get to the prospect, the more likely you are to get the gift. Phoning, as we all know, is "the next best thing to being there."

Like direct mail, telemarketing can be modified for small organizations in a way that allows them both to raise money and not offend donors. The two modifications small organizations will need are 1) to use very warm lists, such as lapsed donors, current donors, and friends of board, staff and current donors, or lists of donors to very similar organizations, and 2) to use only volunteers to do the calling. Even if a person is annoyed to be phoned during dinner, they will be less annoyed at a volunteer, who is giving her or his free time and doesn't sound as smooth or insistent as a boiler room professional.

When used by small groups and done by volunteers, telemarketing can more rightly be called a phone-a-thon.

Basic Technique of the Phone-a-thon

In its simplest terms, a phone-a-thon involves a group of volunteers calling people to ask them to support your organization with a donation. A phone-a-thon is an excellent way to involve volunteers in fundraising because it teaches them how to ask for money but is less intimidating to them than soliciting donations in face-to-face situations.

Phone-a-thons can be good money-makers. They are usually inexpensive to produce and have a high rate of return. From five to 10 percent of the people reached will contribute, and these percentages may be higher if you are calling lapsed donors. Compared to a direct mail campaign's response rate, which is often one to three percent from a warm list, a phone-a-thon has much greater potential for raising money. The costs involved include printing and postage, any toll call charges, and food and drinks for volunteers doing the calling.

A phone-a-thon can be organized by one or two people. It takes several hours of preparation followed by a five-hour time block for the event. Several people are needed to make all the calls. The following explanation of the steps to take will help you determine how many people will be required.

Preparation

To prepare for a phone-a-thon, the organizers take the following steps:

1. Prepare the list of people who will be called. These potential donors are people who have expressed an interest in your organization, have benefitted by something you have done for them, or are past or current supporters of your organization. People attending community meetings you have organized, alumnae or former clients, and members of and donors to other organizations are all prospects. Get their names and look up their phone numbers. (Organizations in small towns or rural communities or organizations that serve a specific neighborhood or geographic constituency may be able to use the phone book as their source of names, but generally this is too "cold" a list.)

List the names and phone numbers, with any code that is necessary (such as L = lapsed, CL = client, etc). Include columns noting what information you will want the telephone volunteer to record. A list of names might have the following headings at the top:

People To Be Called

Name and Address	Area Code and Phone Number	Response	Address verified?	More info sent?	Message left?	Thank you sent?	Other

Explain how to use the code when giving instructions to volunteers at the time of the phoning.

2. Set a date for the phone-a-thon. Pay attention to other events in your community — don't call, for example, on an evening when many people will be at a birthday party, community meeting or benefit auction for another group. Most people find that calling on a Tuesday, Wednesday, or Thursday night between 6:00 and 9:00 p.m. at the beginning of the month (near payday) works best. Some groups call on weekends with success, but calling on a sunny weekend afternoon may bring people racing in from their yard or interrupt them while entertaining and may irritate more people than necessary. No one is sitting in the sun on a Wednesday evening at 8:30. Pay attention to what's on television: Don't call during the Superbowl, on an election night or during the Academy Awards.

3. Write a script for volunteers to read as they phone. Generally volunteers can "ad lib" after the second or third call, but initially a script gives them a feeling of security. The script should be brief and to the point: "Hello, my name is _____ , and I am a volunteer with Good Organization. May I speak with you for a minute?" (PAUSE for answer.) "Thank you. Are you familiar with our work?" or, "Did you read about us in the Daily Blab?" or, "Did you receive our recent appeal?" (PAUSE for answer). If the answer indicates little familiarity with the organization's work say, "We are a group of concerned people working on . . ." and give a two-sentence or 15-second summary of your work. (PAUSE.) If there is no reaction or a positive reaction from the person being called, continue. "Our goal tonight is $___. We are asking people to help us with a gift of $15 or more. We will send you our quarterly newsletter (or other benefit). So far ___ people have pledged $___. Would you care to make a donation?" (PAUSE for answer.) If the answer is positive, continue: "We are trying to keep track of how much we have raised. What amount may I put you down for?" (PAUSE for answer.) "Thank you very much. I'll send an envelope for you to use. Let me just verify your address." (Read the address). "Thank you again. Good night."

In addition to the script, write up a list of questions that volunteers may be asked, with suggested answers. Include questions and statements such as, "Why haven't I heard of you before?" or, "I sent you guys money and never got anything."

4. Prepare three letters (samples of each are given below) and appropriate enclosures.

A letter for people who say yes:

> Dear___,
>
> Thank you so much for joining Good Organization with your gift of $___this evening.
>
> As you probably know, Good Organization is primarily supported by donations from people like you. Your gift will help us continue our work of_____. (Describe in two or three sentences.)
>
> Please fill out and return the enclosed card with your check in the envelope provided. You will begin receiving our newsletter in two weeks.
>
> > Sincerely,
> > Name of volunteer

Return card format:

> Name _____
> Address _____
>
> Enclosed is my pledge of $___. I look forward to receiving the newsletter and other benefits of membership.
>
> Make checks payable to: Good Organization.
> Mail to: Our Address
> (The return envelope should have a first-class stamp affixed.)

"Sorry we missed you" letter to people who weren't home or where an answering machine was reached:

> Dear___ ,
>
> Sorry we missed you this evening. We tried to call you because we wanted to ask you to join/renew/tell you more about Good Organization.
>
> Good Organization is _____ (brief summary of not more than three to five short sentences). We have been working on these issues since 19__. Our main program goal for this year is_____.
>
> I hope you will join us in our important work. For a gift of $___, we will be pleased to send you our quarterly newsletter, The Right-On Times. For a gift of $50 or more we will include a beautiful/important book/calendar/picture.

Please take a moment to read the enclosed brochure, then fill out the membership form and send it with your check today. Your gift sent now is more important than ever.

Sincerely,
Name of volunteer

Letter to people with questions about the organization:

Dear___,

Thanks for talking with me this evening.

I am enclosing the information we discussed, which I hope will answer your questions about Good Organization. Please feel free to contact our office to discuss any aspect of our organization's work further if you wish.

I hope you will decide to make a donation after reading this information. I am sure you know, as I do, how important our work is. Please do whatever you can.

An envelope and membership form are enclosed for your convenience. I look forward to hearing from you.

Sincerely,
Name of volunteer

If these letters go by bulk mail, each one must be exactly the same. In that case use the salutation "Dear Friend."

Enclosed with both the second and third examples is the same reply device used for everyone else, a fact sheet or brochure about your organization, and a return envelope. It is not necessary to stamp any of these envelopes.

To decide how many of each letter to have printed, count the number of people you will be calling and assume that half of them will answer. Of this number, from 5 to 10 percent will say yes and need the yes letter; another 10 to 15 percent will say, "Send me more information," and need the letter described in (c); the rest will say no. The other one-third will need the letter described in (b). Much depends on how good your list is, but this formula should give you enough letters without having lots left over. (You could also photocopy the letters as you go along, if you have or have access to a high quality copier. If you are working with a small list, you could print each letter off your computer.) If you do not date the letters and avoid using any reference to a month or day, you can use the same letters at other phone-a-thons throughout the year.

5. Determine how many phones and how many volunteers you will need. To do this, estimate that one person can make 30 phone calls in an hour and that people will work no more than three hours.

Therefore, one person can make 90 calls in an evening (including calls to people who aren't home) and fill out the appropriate follow-up letters.

To get by with fewer phones, people can work in teams of two to a phone. In this arrangement, as soon as one person has made a call and is filling in the appropriate letter, the other person begins a call. This way the phone is always in use. Sometimes a phone team agrees that one person will do all the talking and the other will do all the writing. Phone teams can make about 40 calls per hour per phone, or 20 per volunteer per hour. Since most people will not call for three hours straight, you will need one or two extra volunteers to make maximum use of the phones available.

Suppose you have 600 names to call. If one person made all the calls, at thirty calls an hour, it would take 20 hours. If each person has his or her own phone it will take seven volunteers with seven phones, each working three hours to get through the calls in one evening, plus one or two extra volunteers to relieve people.

In addition to the calling, allow two to three hours (or one or two extra volunteers) for stuffing envelopes, making sure information is recorded and cleaning up.

You may wish to conduct the phone-a-thon over two nights. This has two advantages: You can call more people or use fewer volunteers, and you can call people on the second night who weren't home on the first night.

Sometimes small organizations decide to conduct a phone-a-thon with each volunteer working from their home. While there is nothing wrong with this method and just as many calls can be made, having everyone in the same office is more fun and generates more momentum. That way, successful calls or rude responses can elicit immediate praise or sympathy, as appropriate. A group effort is also helpful in keeping track during the evening of how much is being pledged. (If you have to use individual homes, have at least two people at each home.)

For national or regional organizations, phoning can be done from different areas to save long distance costs.

6. Find a place. You will need one room or a suite of connected rooms with one or more telephones in each one. Depending on the number of telephones in your organization's office and the number of volunteers you have, you may have enough lines there. Real estate offices, travel agencies, law firms, large social service organizations, mail order businesses, and others with several desks with phones are good candidates to let you borrow their telephones for the evening. You will need to reassure the business that you will not disrupt or take anything, clean up before you leave, and in most cases pay for any long distance or toll calls.

7. Recruit volunteers. Use the phone-a-thon as an opportunity to bring in some new volunteers. Often people who have limited time or who cannot volunteer during the day can be recruited to work one evening on a phone-a-thon. It is a straightforward commitment with a clear beginning and ending and it does not require preparation or follow-up. Ask volunteers to meet for food and a training session 30 minutes before phoning begins.

The Night of the Phone-a-Thon

The committee planning the phone-a-thon should arrive at the phoning site 30 minutes early. Be sure that desk tops or tabletops where volunteers are to sit are cleared off so that your papers do not get mixed up with those of the person who uses that desk during the day. Put a stack of the three different letters, their enclosures, the return envelopes, the mailing envelopes, and a couple of pens on each desk. Put a list of names and a script by each phone.

Bring in juice, coffee, and snacks. Pizza, sandwiches, or other simple dinner food should be provided if volunteers are arriving at dinner time. The food should be kept in one part of the office, and volunteers should be discouraged from having food by their phones. Pay attention to details like bringing in napkins, plates, and eating utensils. In a borrowed space take out your own trash. Do not serve alcohol.

After all volunteers have arrived, been introduced to each other and had a chance to eat, go through the phoning process step by step. Go over the script and make sure people understand and feel comfortable with it. Review difficult questions they might receive and simulate a phone call from each of the categories: yes, maybe, no. Be sure people understand the different letters, know what to write on each, what enclosures go with them, and what information needs to be noted on the list of names.

You will need to decide whether volunteers are to leave a message on an answering machine or simply hang up. If you are going to send out a "Sorry we missed you" letter, the volunteer could leave a brief message to the effect that "I wanted to talk with you about our work, but will send you some information instead. I hope you will be able to help us." Be sure the message you leave is brief, since people only like to listen to long messages from new lovers or old friends.

Each volunteer or phone team goes to a desk. The committee that has planned the phone-a-thon begins calling immediately. When a few people are on the phone, shy volunteers will feel better about beginning to call. Try to avoid a situation where everyone in the room is listening to one person's phone call unless that person feels comfortable with that role.

A staff person or a phone-a-thon committee member acts as a "floater." He or she answers questions and fields difficult phone calls. The floater also continually tallies how much money has been pledged and announces the changing total to the group. The scripts are then changed to reflect new totals. The floater can also be preparing, "Sorry we missed you" letters for bulk mailing if that will be used.

Each individual should be encouraged to take breaks as they need to, but the group as a whole does not take any breaks.

At 9:00 p.m. stop the phoning. The first step in wrapping up is to finish addressing all envelopes and gather up the list of people phoned. If a bulk mailing is being done with the "Sorry we missed you" letters, try to do that quickly or do it the next day at the latest. Gather up any leftover forms, envelopes, letters, and cards. Tally the final amount pledged and let the volunteers know how successful the evening has been. If the amount pledged is below your goal, explain that you set your goal too high. Do not let the volunteers leave feeling discouraged.

The callers should be able to leave by 9:30 p.m., leaving the planning committee to do any final clean up.

After the Phone-a-Thon

Within two or three days, send all the volunteers a thank-you note for their participation. If you borrowed a space to conduct the phone-a-thon, write the owner or manager a thank-you note also. Thank everyone for whatever they did to make the event a success.

During the next two weeks you should collect about 90 percent of the pledges made. As each one comes in, a thank-you note should go out. At the end of two weeks go through your list and identify those who pledged but have not sent their money. Send them a gentle reminder. This is accompanied by a return envelope and a reply form. Most organizations do not find it worth the time and cost to remind people of their pledge more than once. You will generally lose about 7 percent of pledges. (Some people's way of saying no is to say yes and not follow through.)

Reminder letter:

> Dear___ ,
>
> This is just a note to remind you of your pledge to Good Organization made on the night of ____. In case you misplaced our letter and return envelope we enclose another. Thanks again for your pledge of $___.
>
> Sincerely,
> Name of volunteer

A month after the phone-a-thon, when almost all the pledges will have come in, tally up the final amounts received and write an evaluation of the event. The evaluation should note how many people were called, how many pledged, how many pledges were received, how many volunteers participated, where the phone-a-thon was held, how that space was arranged (if donated), and it should also include copies of all the letters and return forms used. File all this away so that the next time you do a phone-a-thon you won't have to start from scratch.

Getting Publicity for Your Phone-a-Thon

A phone-a-thon may be a good time to generate some publicity for your group. Publicity can make the community more aware of your group's work and can alert listeners or readers to the fact that many of them will be receiving phone calls from your organization on a specific day or evening. The organization's address and phone number can be included in all publicity so that people can call or send in a donation.

How much publicity a group is able to generate for a phone-a-thon will depend a great deal on the group's success in getting publicity for any of its work. Chances are that if an organization has never had any stories in the local newspaper or on radio or TV, they will not get coverage for their phone-a-thon. However, if the group does have a relationship with columnists, talk show producers, station managers, and so on, it may be able to use those contacts to get publicity for phone-a-thon.

Unless you are on very good terms with press people, the phone-a-thon alone will not be a newsworthy event. While a short press release or a public service announcement (PSA) describing the phone-a-thon may be used, an article or an interview will not come out of the phone-a-thon alone. It would be best, therefore, to use the occasion of the phone-a-thon to emphasize a new program, tell a human interest story, or have some other newsworthy reason to get press attention in which you mention the phone-a-thon.

All your publicity should emphasize the need for community support. Stress that your organization relies on the community for the bulk of its support or wants to rely on the community (if you don't now). Talk about what a gift of $25 to $35 will do for the group so that people have a sense that a small gift can make a difference.

Use a Public Figure

One way groups have interested the press is by having one or two famous people participating in their phone-a-thon. "Famous people" include not only national celebrities but also people well known only in your community, such as the mayor, city council members, well-respected community activists, the president of the community college, or a major corporate executive. The novelty that someone "famous" would help your organization lends credibility to your group. Also, almost everyone is flattered to be called by someone famous. If you decide to ask public figures to participate, be sure that they are well liked by your constituency.

Public figures can simply come for the first half hour of your phone-a-thon and make a few calls without making an enormous time commitment to the event. It is an easy way for both you and them to gain goodwill while they show their support of nonprofit organizations and of the work of your organization in particular.

Court the Media

If you can't get any publicity through your press contacts, simply send a letter to the editor of the local paper. Be sure you know how early to send it to receive publication before the event (particularly if you are a rural group dealing with a weekly or less frequently published paper). Many groups have found that letters to the editor are an effective way to get publicity for many issues. Again, give the address and phone number of your organization and the date of the phone-a-thon.

If you do get any publicity (even a simple press mention or public service announcement aired), write or call the press person with the results of the phone-a-thon and emphasize what a difference their publicity made. Include with your letter a press release or PSA announcing the success of the phone-a-thon and a statement of thanks to the community for being supportive. A letter to the editor can also follow up publicity. It is important to sound successful even if your phone-a-thon was not as successful as you had hoped.

There are drawbacks to extensive publicity that should be taken into account before seeking it. Publicity for a direct service organization may generate more clients than donors. One organization, whose purpose was to advocate for people with work-related injuries and to help them get the benefits they deserve, got a full-page interview about their work and their upcoming phone-a-thon in the local paper. The night of the phone-a-thon more calls came in than went out and they came from people needing the organizations' help. Volunteers were swamped; almost no outgoing calls were made, as all lines were full. The phone-a-thon was a financial failure but the experience certainly demonstrated the need for this group's work.

A second disadvantage of publicity is that phone calls may keep coming in long after the phone-a-thon is over. Your staff or daytime volunteers will need to respond to those calls in addition to doing their regular work. While handling the calls is not too time-consuming, making sure the right information goes out and keeping track of pledges and so forth can take a lot of time.

If you have taken all these contingencies into account, publicity may turn a good phone-a-thon into a giant fundraising success.

Other Uses of the Phone-a-Thon

There are three other common uses of the phone-a-thon technique: using the phone only to get prospects, following a mail appeal with a phone-a-thon, and using the phone-a-thon to renew lapsed donors.

Phoning for Prospects

This takeoff on a sales technique means phoning a large number of people, giving basic information about your organization and asking if the person would like to know more. If the person says yes, he or she turns into a prospect. There is no attempt to solicit a gift at the time of the phone call. The purpose of the call is to create a "hot" list for fundraising mail appeals.

During the telephone conversation the caller can determine the degree of interest by asking the prospect some open-ended questions about their knowledge of the organization and their philosophical support of its work. When interest is present the prospect will be sent more information about the organization and a list of ways that he or she can help, including giving money. Some groups use this opportunity to seek new volunteers, get support for or against a piece of legislation, ask for items that the program needs (for example, a shelter might ask for food or clothing), and so forth. A return envelope is included.

This strategy does not raise money per se. Instead it acquires prospects. The costs of phoning and of any mail and follow-up may well be only slightly less than the total amount received as gifts. Nevertheless, the organization now has a group of new donors who may give in response to appeals during the current year. Many of them will renew the following year.

This strategy is best for new groups that do not have an established constituency or for groups that have little name recognition even if they have existed for some time. It also works well for political organizations seeking to familiarize people with their candidate or their election issue.

This method differs from an ordinary phone-a-thon in the script and the training of volunteers for calling. The purpose of the call is only to determine interest and to get permission to send more information. Therefore, the script would read something like this:

> "Hello, I am Jane Smith, a volunteer with Shelter for the Homeless. I would like to talk to you for a minute, and I will not be asking you for money. Is this a good time?" (PAUSE) "Thank you. I'll try to be brief. Have you ever heard of our program?" (PAUSE) If the answer is "No" or "I don't know very much," continue: "Shelter for the Homeless is a 30-bed facility for homeless single people and families. It also provides job counseling and referral, meals and child care so that parents can look for work. Did you know that there are more than 2,000 homeless people in our community and more arriving every day?" (PAUSE) "Many people find our program excellent, but we know that others disagree with our approach or feel that some of the people using our services are freeloading. What do you think?"

Generally, the answers fall into three categories:

- ◆ People who are basically in favor of your work.
- ◆ People who like your program generally but have a specific objection to something about it.
- ◆ People who feel that everyone should help themselves and that your program is undermining the moral fabric of the country.

For answers in the first category the caller in this example might say: "I'm glad you feel that way. The shelter relies on community support for over three-fourths of its budget, and it is good to know that members of the community like what we are doing. I wonder if I could send you a brochure and some other information about our services and about different ways that citizens can help us. There is no obligation, and no one will call you afterwards, but you may find the information interesting." (PAUSE for answer.) If the answer is yes, then verify the name and address, thank the person for his or her time, and say good night.

If the answer falls in the second category, the specific objection in this case might be: "I support the ideals of your program, but the problem is that more people move to our community because you are here. We can't continue to absorb people this fast."

The caller needs to agree with the prospect in some way in order to acknowledge that the prospect's objection is valid. In this case, the caller could say: "It does seem that the more services that are provided the more people there are who need them, and that it is an endless cycle." (PAUSE) "But in our case it is interesting to know that no more people are moving here now than before we opened the shelter." Or, "Communities with no services for the homeless are experiencing as fast a growth rate of that category of people as our community. In fact, sometimes people call us from other states and we are able to discourage them from moving here because our economy is so tight right now. Then they don't have to come and learn the hard way."

When a person's objection is acknowledged as valid and then corrected or new information supplied, he or she generally becomes more receptive. If the person says something like "I didn't know that" or "I am glad to hear that," ask if you can send him or her more information, just as for prospects in category one.

In the case of answers in the last category, simply say "I appreciate your candidness. It helps us to know why people don't like our program. Thanks for your time. Good night."

The training of volunteers for this type of phone work is much more detailed. Volunteers must be able to listen, to deal with difficult questions, and to know when to give up. Each will take longer than calls in a fundraising phone-a-thon. Callers must be clear that they are only calling to determine interest, not to convert people.

Callers should practice with difficult questions and their answers in depth and familiarize themselves with many facts about the organization and the issues.

No list is needed for this phone-a-thon. The phone book can be used or you can do a random calling of any list of people. You can also use this strategy to determine the interest of donors to an organization doing work in an entirely different arena from yours, but where there could be a connection. For example, an AIDS-related service organization called a list of donors from several arts organizations to determine their interest in this service organization. They found a high level of interest and gained many new donors because the arts community has been hit hard by the AIDS epidemic.

Phoning After a Mail Appeal

This method is quite straightforward. A mail appeal is sent to a list of prospects. After two weeks all the prospects who have not sent money are called. The purpose of this method is to increase the return from the mail appeal.

The script is the only part that is slightly different from a regular fundraising phone-a-thon in that a sentence is added such as, "I am Joe Reilly from the Greenbelt Project. We recently sent you a letter about our work. Did you have a chance to read it?" Depending on the answer, the rest of the script is the same as that described in the first section of this chapter. If the person has read the letter and seems in favor of your goals, skip right to the question, "Will you be able to help us with a gift of $___?"

Generally, you will not indicate in the original letter that the prospects will be called. You want as many people as possible to send in their gift without being called. Some organizations have successfully tried a variation on this, by telling prospects in a letter that they will be called unless the organization hears from them by a certain date prior to the phone-a-thon.

Phoning for Renewals

In most organizations about one-third of all members do not renew their memberships from one year to the next. As a result, organizations spend most of their renewal budget trying to woo these recalcitrant members back into the fold. Usually an organization will send the member two or three renewal letters one month apart, each notice firmer than the one before. The third notice usually explains that the membership has or is about to lapse unless the member pays now. If there is still no response the organization removes the member's name from its mailing list.

The phone-a-thon can be used in place of either the second or third renewal notice. It is particularly useful for organizations with a large number of local members. Although it does not save the cost of printing and postage, it does provide a way to have much more personal contact with members than is generally possible.

Many organizations have renewal phone-a-thons twice a year. They find that while the response to a second or third renewal letter is two to five percent and sometimes less, the response to phoning is at least 10 percent and can be as high as 30 percent. This means that these organizations are cutting their member losses by 10 percent or more. This guarantees that the organization will have a 66 percent renewal rate, and not less, and they may be able to add another five percent on to that. A renewal phone-a-thon is almost exactly like a regular fundraising phone-a-thon.

First, identify from your mailing list all the people whose subscriptions have expired within the last six months, not including those who have had less than a month to renew. (Unless your organization is in a terrible financial bind and you really need the money, a person will feel harassed if you call too soon after your first renewal notice is sent.)

Next, prepare the letters to thank people for renewing and to contact people who weren't home when you called, as discussed in the first section of this chapter. Both of these letters are brief. The point is to remind the member of his or her commitment to give; there is no need to convince the person of the worthiness of your organization. Each letter is accompanied by a return envelope and a return form (pledge card).

When volunteers call the lapsed donors they will generally hear the following reasons for not renewing: People are out of work, forgot about it, thought they had renewed, or didn't receive the renewal letter. In some instances they were just about to renew and are glad you called.

It is important to believe whatever the member might say. For example, people who claim to have renewed but for whom you have no record could be asked to produce a cancelled check; however, it is easier and more productive in the long run simply to take their word for it and to reinstate them on the mailing list. Follow the adage, "the customer is always right."

When someone says that they no longer agree with the "course you are taking" or that they have a disagreement about a particular issue, ask them to explain. It may shed light on how the public perceives something you have done, or you may be able to clear up a misunderstanding.

At the end of the phone-a-thon make sure you have carefully sorted all the names into those who have renewed, those who requested to be taken off the mailing list, and those who were not home. Deal with complaints that same evening:

> Dear Mrs. Upset,
>
> We are sorry you have not received your newsletter for the past two years. Here are all the back copies you have missed. We will enter your name on our mailing list for the next year as a complimentary member. You past support means a lot to us, and again, we apologize.
>
> > Sincerely,
> > Name of Volunteer

As you can see, grassroots organizations can take advantage of fundraising by telephone. In addition to raising money, finding prospects, increasing renewal rates, and allowing an organization to have more personal contact with its donors, fundraising by telephone has an added advantage of teaching volunteers how to ask for money. The skills volunteers learn through phone-a-thons can be put to work in major donor campaigns.

12.

Personal Solicitation

Asking someone you know for money in person is the most effective way to raise funds. If you ask someone you know for a gift they could afford to a cause they like (a person fitting this description is called a "prospect") you have a 50 percent chance they will give something. Of the 50 percent that say "yes" to your request, half of them will give you the amount you asked for; the other half will give you less. This is a much higher response rate than you could ever get from direct mail or phoning. Further, the amounts you can ask for are much larger. It is ludicrous to ask for a $1,000 or $5,000 gift by mail or even over the phone. People need more personal attention for large gifts because they have to give them more thought.

If we were able to study how most fundraising happens, we would probably find that more than half of all fundraising requests are done in person — canvassing, Girl Scout cookie sales, raffle tickets, Salvation Army buckets, panhandling and so on all have a strong element of personal asking to say nothing of major gift, capital and endowment campaigns.

Despite these facts, personal solicitation is one of the most difficult strategies to implement. It requires personal involvement in an activity — asking for money — that most of us have been taught is rude, or worse, unthinkable. However, for organizations who are serious about fundraising, and particularly for those organizations that would like to increase the number of people in their donor base who give $50 or more, learning how to ask for money in person is imperative.

Why We're Afraid to Ask for Money

If the idea of asking for money fills you with anxiety, disgust, dread, or some combination of these feelings, you are among the majority of people. If asking for money does not cause you any distress, you have either let go of your fear about it or you are an unusual person.

To identify the sources of our fears we must look at both the role of money in American society and the attitudes about asking for anything

that have been generated by the strong puritan ethic tha.
heritage.

Most of us were taught that money, sex, religion and
taboo topics for discussion with anyone other than perhaps c
intimate friends. The taboo on talking about money and se..
stronger than that for discussing religion or politics. Many of us
taught to believe that inquiring about a person's salary or asking how
much he or she paid for a house or a car is rude. Even today it is not
unusual for wives not to know how much their husbands earn, for children not to know how much their parents earn, or for close friends not
to know each other's income. Many people know nothing about even
the rudiments of how the stock market works — for example, the difference between a bear and a bull market, or what the rising or falling of
the Dow Jones average means for the economy.

Many people, misquoting the New Testament, say, "Money is the
root of all evil." In fact, Paul's letter to the Philippians states, "Love of
money is the root of all evil." Money in itself has no good or evil qualities. It is a substance made of paper or metal. It has no constant value,
and it has no morality.

People will also say, "Money doesn't buy happiness," and describe
unhappy rich people they have known or read about, but most of them
are secretly thinking that they would be happy if they had more money.

Money is shrouded in mystery and tinged with fascination. Most people are curious about the salary levels of their friends, how much money
people have inherited, how the super-rich live. Consequently people
speculate a great deal about the place of money in other peoples' lives.
Money is like sex and sexuality in this regard: kept in secrecy and therefore fascinating. But just as much of what we learned as children and
teenagers about sexuality turned out to be untrue, so it is with money.
Our assumptions about it are for the most part based on speculation.

One major effect of money being a taboo topic is that only those
willing to learn about it can control it. In America an elite and fairly
secret class controls most of the nation's wealth, either by earning it,
having inherited it, or both. It serves the interest of this ruling class for
the rest of us not to know about who controls money and how to gain
control of it ourselves. As long as we do not understand basic economics, we will not control the means of production, we will not be able to
finance our nonprofits adequately, and we will not be able to create a
society in which wealth is more fairly and equally distributed, which is,
after all, the underlying goal of social justice movements.

Political activists and participants in social change must learn how to raise money effectively and ethically, how to manage it carefully, and how to spend it wisely.

The idea of asking for money raises another set of hindering attitudes, which are largely the inheritance of a predominantly Protestant culture. The puritan ethic inherited from our predecessors affects most Americans, including those who are not Protestants, and conveys a number of messages that guide our feelings and actions. If you are a good person and you work hard you will get what you deserve. If you have to ask for something, you have not worked hard enough and you probably don't deserve it. If you have to ask for something you are a weak person because strong people are self-sufficient.

With these very strong taboos operating against asking for money, it is a wonder that anyone ever does it! Understanding the source of our discomfort is the first step toward overcoming it. By looking at the effects of the taboos against both talking about money and asking for anything, we can decide to reject the assumptions on which they're built and therefore change our own attitudes and actions. The next step is to examine our fears of what will happen to us when we do ask for money. When people look at their fears rationally they often find that most of them disappear or at least become manageable.

Specific Fears

Fears about asking for money fall into three categories:

- Those that will almost never happen ("The person will hit me"; "I'll die of a heart attack during the solicitation")
- Those that could be avoided by training and preparation ("I won't know what to say"; "I won't know my facts, the person will think I am an idiot")
- Those that definitely will happen sometimes, maybe as much as half the time ("The person will say no").

In the last category — things that will happen — most people have three main fears.

1. "The person will say no." Rejection is the number one fear. Unfortunately it is also bound to happen to any solicitor, at least as often as acceptance does. Therefore, it is important to get to the point where you don't feel upset when some says no. You do this by realizing that when you ask someone for a gift you are seeing them at a single moment in their lives. A thousand things have happened to the person prior to your request, none of which has anything to do with you, but many of which will affect the person's receptiveness to your request. For example, the person may have recently found out that one of his or her children needs braces, that the car needs new tires, or that a client is not able to pay a bill on time. This news will certainly affect the prospect's perception of what size donation he or she can make. Events unrelated to money can also cause the prospect to say no: a divorce proceeding, a death in the family, a headache. As the solicitor, none of these things is your fault. Many of them you could not have known ahead of time and you may never learn them because the prospect keeps them private. If you feel personally rejected you have misinterpreted what happened and flattered yourself that you had something to do with the rejection.

As the asker, you have to remember that, above all, the person being asked has the right to say no to a request without offering a reason. Most of the time you will not know exactly why your request was turned down. Your job is not to worry about why this prospect said no, but to go on, undaunted, to the next prospect.

2. "Asking a friend for money will have a negative effect on our friendship." Many people feel that friendship is outside the realm of money. They feel that to bring money into a friendship is to complicate it and perhaps to ruin it. Friends are usually the best prospects, however, because they share our commitments and values. They are interested in our lives and wish us success and happiness. To many people's surprise, friends are more likely to be offended when they are not asked. They can't understand why you don't want to include them in your work. Further, if it is truly acceptable to you for a person to say no to your request, your friend will never feel put on the spot. Your friend will not feel pressured by your request, as if your whole friendship hung on the answer. When asking friends then, make clear that yes is the answer you are hoping for, but no is also acceptable.

3. "The person will say yes to my request, then turn around and ask me to give to their cause. I will be obligated to give whether I want to or not." This quid pro quo situation ("this for that") could happen. However, if someone you ask for money gives some to your organization, you are not obligated to that person, except to make sure that the organization uses the money wisely and for whatever it was solicited for. The obligation is fulfilled if the organization is honest. The solicitor does not materially benefit from a solicitation. They present the cause and the prospect is sympathetic and agrees to help support it. The cause was furthered. Beyond a thank-you note and a gracious attitude, the solicitor owes the donor nothing. If the donor then asks you to support his or her cause, you consider the request without reference to your request. You may wish to support the person or the cause, but you are not obligated to do so. If you think that someone is going to attach strings to a gift, don't ask that prospect. There are hundreds of prospects who will give freely.

Far from being a horrible thing to do, asking someone for money actually does them a favor. People who agree with your goals and respect the work of your group will want to be a part of it. Giving money is a simple and effective way to be involved, to be part of a cause larger than oneself.

Many volunteers find that it takes practice to overcome their fears about asking for money. To begin soliciting donations does not require being free of fear; it only requires having your fear under control. Ask yourself if what you believe in is bigger than what you are afraid of. An old fundraising saying is that if you are afraid to ask someone for a gift, "kick yourself out of the way and let your cause do the talking." The point is this: If you are committed to an organization you will do what is required to keep that organization going, including asking for money.

Prospect Identification

Once people feel somewhat relieved of their anxieties about asking for money, they have two more questions: Who shall I ask? and How shall I ask?

Ask A Prospect

Because personal solicitation is, by definition, done on a person-by-person basis, it takes more time than most strategies. For example, a direct mail appeal can reach dozens or hundreds or thousands of people with one letter, duplicated and stuffed into hundreds of envelopes. With direct mail, there should be an attempt to ensure that the list being used is one of people who are interested in a similar cause, but there is little attempt to go through the list name by name. The opposite is true in personal solicitation. It is done strictly name by name, person by person. As such, we are looking for people who are worth that much time.

The question that determines whether a person is a prospect could be phrased this way, "What evidence do I have that if I asked this person for 30 to 60 minutes of their time to meet with me, thus using up 30 to 60 minutes of my time also (plus preparation), this person would be likely to make a gift that is significantly bigger than they might have made if approached through a less time-consuming strategy?" Personal solicitation is generally used to ask for gifts of more than $100, but it works for all sizes of gifts. In this chapter, we will focus on identifying donors who could give a gift of $50 or more; for small organizations $50 is worth the time for a personal solicitation and opens the possibility of becoming a major donor to more people.

Three broad qualifications determine if someone is a prospect: Ability to make a gift of the size you are looking for. Belief in the cause or something similar. Contact with someone in the group who is either willing to ask this person or willing to allow their name to be used in the asking.

When you have positive, verifiable evidence of A, B and C, you have a prospect. If any one of the criteria is missing you have a potential prospect, usually called a "suspect," and if you are only sure of one of the criteria you have virtually a stranger. Let's look at each one of these in depth.

Contact

This is the most important of these three criteria and also the most overlooked. Do you know the prospect? Does anyone you know know the prospect? Without contact, you cannot proceed with a personal solicitation because there is no link between your organization and this person.

There are three ways for a person to have contact with your organization: 1) A board member, staff, or volunteer knows the person. 2) A board member, staff or volunteer knows someone who knows this person and is willing to either let you use their name in the approach ("Mary Jones suggested I call . . .") or, better yet, is willing to call on your behalf, ("Joe, this is Mary. I'm giving money to really amazing group and was hoping you would be willing to see a couple of their representatives and let them tell you about the group and ask you to join") 3) The person is currently a donor to your group, but no one close to the group knows the person. In that case, when you call you will say, "We don't know each other, but we share a commitment to . . . and I want to talk with you about an exciting project we are about to undertake."

Belief

In thinking through why someone might believe in your organization, return to your case statement (discussed in Chapter 4, Making a Case for Your Organization). What values does your group espouse? What organizations have similar values even if their goals are different? Be broad-minded and creative in assessing potential linkage. For example, people who give to children's organizations are often interested in environmental issues because they are concerned about what kind of world the children are growing up in and what kind of world it will be when today's children are adults. People giving to environmental groups are likely to be interested in health issues; people who give to libraries will support literacy programs, or creative educational projects: anything that helps people appreciate the value of reading.

In addition to looking for similar values, look for other things that might link a person to your group. Do you serve a neighborhood that the person's family comes from? If you have clients, do your clients patronize the prospect's business?

Try not to draw conclusions from facts about the person that could lead you to stereotype them. For example, many older people, particularly in the South, are Republicans because Abraham Lincoln was a Republican. Many American Catholics are pro-choice. Many donors to the arts also give to civil liberties organizations because of censorship issues.

Have staff, volunteers and board members write down all the values they hold dear and what beliefs tie them to your group. This should provide a broad list that you can then use to help screen potential prospects (see also Chapter 19, Using Donor Analysis).

Ability

Although first in the ABC order, ability is actually the least important factor in identifying prospects. An assumption can be made that if a person knows and respects someone in an organization and believes in the cause, they have the ability to make a gift. The question is, how much should they be asked for?

One of the biggest mistakes fundraisers make is assuming that how much a person can give will be related to how much money they have. Obviously, how much money a person has influences how much they can give, since no one can give more than they have. However, many wealthy people could afford to give much more than they do, while many poor people give a high proportion of what little they have.

Stockbrokers, bankers, and financial planners are interested in how much people have because they can help them have more. People are called "the haves" because of what they have, not because of what they give. Otherwise, they would be called "the gives." Fundraisers are interested in how much people give, and giving is the behavior to focus on, not having.

In terms of identifying how much a person could give, the best indicator is how much they give elsewhere. To figure out if a person gives away money, you could ask the contact what else the prospect supports, you could look on lists of donors from other organizations printed in their newsletters, annual reports, and programs. You can listen closely to what the person says. Do they complain about getting a lot of direct mail? ("I'm on everyone's list. Everyone writes to me.") This is probably a person who gives by mail. Do they complain about how many phone calls they receive? ("Just when we're sitting down to dinner, the phone rings, and its the disabled, or the whales, or the rainforest. The needs never end!") These calls are rarely random — they are made to people who give by phone. Is the person very busy? With what? Board meetings at the legal aid society? Organizing a special event for International Women's Day? The PTA? Being a docent at the art museum? Working for a political candidate?

Here are some guidelines for how to determine the size of a possible gift. To determine whether a person could give $50 to $500, you need to know little more about their ability than that they are employed in a job that pays more than minimum wage, that they are not supporting very many other people (children, partner, elderly relative) and that they have given in that range to some other group.

To determine if a person could give in the $500 to $2,500 range will require knowing that the person has a well-paying job or some other source of income (inheritance, investment, retirement, royalties), or is married to or living with someone who has a good job or inherited wealth or healthy retirement income and so is not the sole support of their household; that the household is not very large, and that the prospect is very committed to your group or to someone in your group.

To determine if a person could give more than $2500 will require more research, and more important, will usually require that the person is already a donor to your group and can be asked to upgrade their gift. No matter how wealthy and generous someone is, he or she will rarely start their giving to a small organization with such large gift. (I discuss these larger gifts in the section on upgrading).

Ultimately you will not know with any certainty how much a person could give because you can't know all their circumstances and because their perception of what they can afford can change from day to day. You make your best guess and you ask. People are rarely insulted to be asked for more money than they can afford; it's flattering to have people think you are that financially successful.

Steps in Creating a Prospect List

The people who are going to be involved in the personal solicitation strategy, seeking gifts of $50 to $500, need to meet and create a Master Prospect List. This is to ensure that no one gets asked by more than one person and that the right person does the asking in each case. Also, in a group setting people get more excited about the process and come up with more names and more enthusiasm for asking than they would on their own. More than one person in the group may know a prospect, so more information can be collected.

The first step is to have everyone in the meeting create a list of all the people they know or who would recognize them if they were to call and say their name. No one should censor themselves by saying, "He hates me," or "She's a tightwad," or "I can't ask them!" Just make the list. These are your contacts. Remember, contact is not necessarily the same as solicitor. You may not be the one who solicits the gift — you are simply the contact.

Now each person should take their list and beside each name note whether or not the person believes in your cause. If you don't know what they believe in, put a question mark. Cross off all the people who you know don't believe and put the people with question marks on a different piece of paper. Now, next to the people who are left — those whom you know and who believe in the cause — put what amount you think they could give in the $50 to $500 range. If you don't know, put a question mark. Each person then reads his/her list of prospects (or alternatively, writes them on a piece of butcher paper). If anyone else knows the prospects, they can agree or disagree or add other information. Each person reads their list with question marks concerning belief or ability to see if someone else can be helpful. If no one else knows the person, he or she is not a prospect.

Make a final master list of people whom you know, you know believe in the cause and you know could make this size of gift, and then you can decide who is going to ask each person.

PROSPECT RECORD

Date: _____

Name _____

Address (specify work or home) _____

Phone (work)_____ (home) _____

Contact(s) _____

Interest/involvement in nonprofits _____

Donations to nonprofits _____

Interest in our group _____

Occupation _____

Length of time in current occupation _____

Employer _____

Household composition _____

Does this person have any other source of income besides his/her salary (i.e. second income in the household, inheritance, investment, retirement, royalties,etc.)? _____

Other interests/hobbies _____

Suggested gift range _____

Suggested solicitor _____

Relationship to solicitor _____

Result _____

It is imperative for one or two people to take on the task of writing this information down and collecting it systematically. This is the job of development staff. If your organization does not have staff, one or two people from the board will take on this task. Try to make sure information is correct. It is also imperative that the information be kept confidential. You should never write down things that you only know from gossip or that are not helpful in seeking a gift ("had a affair with the Methodist minister" may be interesting, but is not prospect information). Some kinds of information will be more useful to some groups than to others. A group working with prisoners may wish to know if anyone in the prospect's family or the prospect himself or herself has spent time in prison. Otherwise, that would probably not be appropriate information. People working in historic preservation may want to know how long someone has lived in a community, whereas people working on animal welfare issues will not need to know that as much as whether the person has pets or livestock or likes animals.

People tend to know people who are in their own economic bracket, plus a few people who have more money and a few who have less. The few who have more know a few more who have more. Your friends who could afford $50 or $100 or $500 will know people who could also give that amount, so you can expand your list past your own contacts by asking other people for names.

On the previous page is a generic form for gathering information. You will want to design a form that works for your group. Keep in mind that you need to know less about someone if you are asking for $50 than if you are asking for $500.

How to Approach the Prospect

The first step in soliciting gifts from others is for the solicitor to give. The size of the gift is not important; what matters is that the gift is substantial for that person. When solicitors go out to ask for gifts, they must feel that they are not asking the prospect to do any more than they themselves have done.

After the solicitor has made his or her financial commitment, the prospects have been thoroughly researched, and the best prospects have been identified, the solicitor begins the process of asking for the gift.

The most formal approach involves three steps:

1. A letter describing the organization or the specific need, including a sentence or two indicating that you wish to ask the prospect for a gift and a request for a meeting to discuss it further, followed by

2. A phone call to set up a meeting, and then

3. The meeting itself in which the gift is actually solicited. Obviously, if you are approaching your spouse or your best friend you can skip the letter and perhaps even the phone call. In other cases the letter will be enough, and there will be no need for a phone call; in others the letter and a phone call will be enough, and there will be no need for a meeting.

Deciding whether to ask for a meeting will depend in large part on how much money you are requesting. Regardless of how generous, easy going, and committed a prospect is, he or she will almost always give more in a meeting than when asked over the phone. Because you are requesting a thoughtful gift — a gift that is big enough that the prospect needs to think about whether he or she can afford it, and whether he or she wishes to give your group a gift that big, you want sufficient time with the prospect to answer all questions and concerns. It takes about 30 minutes to have the conversation you need to have, and a 30-minute meeting sounds shorter than a 30-minute phone call.

The Letter

The letter should raise the prospect's interest, giving some information, but not enough for a truly informed decision. The letter should be brief, not more than one page. Its purpose is to get the prospect to be open to the idea of a meeting, which you will request to set up in your phone call. In other words, the letter introduces the fact that you will be asking for a large gift for your organization and that you want the prospect to be willing to give you a short amount of time to explain why you want this gift and why you think this prospect will be interested. No commitment to give or to be involved in any way is asked for in the letter — only a request for the prospect to discuss the proposition of a gift with the solicitor. The elements of the letter are shown below.

Ms. Concerned Activist with Good Paying Job
Professional Office Building
City, State ZIP

Dear Connie,

For several years you have heard me talk about Downtown Free Clinic. As you know, I have recently been elected to serve on their board of directors. At a recent meeting, we made a decision to launch a major gifts campaign, the main purpose of which is to help the clinic become financially self-sufficient. In the future, we want to depend on a broad base of donors rather than on foundations and government grants, which have proved most unreliable.

The goal of the campaign is $20,000 the first year. We need two lead gifts of $1,000 plus a number of gifts in the $250-500 range. The lead gift should be from someone of standing in the community, whose word carries weight. I am hoping you will consider being one of the leaders in the campaign because of your long-time activism in community health care.

(One more paragraph on the work of the organization.)

I know this is a big request, and I am hoping we can meet to talk about it. I'd also like to go over our fundraising plan and see what insights you can offer from your experience. I am very excited about the direction the organization is taking, and I can't really do it justice in this letter.

I'll call you next week to set up a time. Hope you are well. Enjoyed seeing you and your family at the baseball game last week.

Best always,

Annie
Another Concerned Activist

The letter is straightforward. Connie knows what the request will be, including the amount. She knows what the money is for. If giving to this organization is out of the question for her, she can decide that now. If giving a lead gift is out of the question, she has been given the option of giving a smaller gift in the sentence referring to "a number of $250-500" gifts. Her importance to the campaign has been stated. Yet there is nothing she needs to do at this point except wait for the phone call. No action has been requested — in fact, she has specifically been asked not to decide.

The Phone Call

If you say you are going to call you have to call. Rehearse the phone call beforehand to anticipate questions or objections the prospect may have. Be sure you know exactly what you are going to say from the very first hello. Many people find it useful to write down what they will say, in the same way that one writes a script for a phone-a-thon.

The phone call is the most difficult part of the solicitation. It is pivotal to getting the meeting; without the meeting you will probably not get as large a gift as you might have and you might not get a gift at all. However a phone call is always an interruption, even if the prospect really likes you. You can't tell if the prospect is frowning, smiling, in a hurry, or busy. You can't rely on how people sound on the phone. People who are perfectly happy to chat with you may sound brusque or harried on the phone. Many people simply do not like to talk on the phone, and their dislike of being on the phone may come across to you as a dislike of talking to you or a reluctance to discuss their gift.

To ensure that you have not caught the prospect at a bad time, ask, "Is this a good time to talk?" or "Do you have a couple of minutes right now?"

The purpose of the phone call is to get the meeting. Again, the prospect does not need to decide about his or her gift until the meeting. Rehearse with a friend the possible objections and difficult questions you can imagine coming up in your phone call and what you would say in each one.

If the prospect tries to put you off, do not assume that he or she is saying no. In fact, he or she may be trying to determine how serious you are about your organization. If you take the first put-off as a final no, it will appear to the prospect that you are either not serious about the group or about the prospect's gift.

Be sure not to read meaning into statements that can be taken at face value. For example, do not hear, "I don't want to give" in a statement such as "I'm very busy this month," or "I have to talk to my spouse before making any decision." Instead, respond as if the prospect is telling you the literal truth. For example, you could give this response to the first objection: "I can understand that. How about if I call you next month, when things might have slowed down for you?" In the second instance say, "Would it be possible for all of us to meet?"

The Meeting

Once you have an appointment you are ready to prepare for the face-to-face solicitation. This is not as frightening as it seems. First of all, the prospect knows from your letter or your phone call that you will be talking about making a contribution. Since he or she has agreed to see you the answer to your request is not an outright "no." The prospect is considering saying yes. Your job is to move the prospect from consideration to commitment.

The purpose of the meeting is to ask for the gift. As the solicitor, you must appear poised, enthusiastic and confident. If you are well prepared for the interview, this will not be too difficult. Board members and volunteers can go with each other or bring a staff person to such a meeting to provide any information the solicitor doesn't have. If you do go in pairs, be sure you know who is actually going to ask for the gift.

It is important to remember what the solicitor's job is, which is to ask for the gift. It is the prospect's job to either give it, give less, or say no, and it is important that the solicitor does not get personally caught up in the prospect's response. You are not a good fundraiser if someone says yes, nor a poor fundraiser if someone says no. If you are asking enough people, a certain percentage will say no.

Meeting Etiquette

The more the prospect is encouraged to talk, the more likely he or she is to give. After opening pleasantries, keep to the subject of the meeting. Be sure that you have a true discussion with prospect about the organization and the program you are seeking funds for, and that you do not lecture or do all the talking. Ask the prospect open-ended questions, and try to draw out any objections he or she might have.

Toward the end of the half-hour, or when the prospect seems satisfied with what you have said, you are ready to close — that is, to ask for the gift. Repeat the goal of the campaign and the importance of the work of the group in one or two short sentences. Then, looking directly at the prospect, ask for a specific gift: "Will you help with $2,000?" Or, "Could you set the pace with $5,000?" or "I'm hoping you can help with a gift in the range of $500-$1,500." There are no magic words and no statement that is more likely or less likely to elicit a positive response. Find a way of asking the question that suits your personality and ends with the amount or the range of gift that you want.

After you have asked for the gift, be quiet. At this moment, you give up control of the interaction — a control that you have had from the moment you sent your letter. At last, you are asking the prospect to make a decision. Wait for the prospect to speak, even if you have to wait several minutes. Keep looking at the prospect. You can breathe easy now because you have said everything you need to say and you have put your best foot forward. Look relaxed and confident.

The Prospect's Response

At this point the prospect will say one of five things.

1. "No, I can't help you." Although this is an unlikely response at this point, it should be treated with respect. You can ask why the prospect said no, but don't use their answer to talk them out of their decision unless they have clearly misunderstood something. Thank the prospect for his or her time and leave. Send the prospect a thank-you note thanking him or her for agreeing to see you and for his or her candidness. This will ensure no hard feelings on your part or the prospect's, and allows you the option of going back at another point.

2. "I'd like to help, but the figure you name is too high." This is a yes answer, but for a smaller gift. You can say, "Would you like to pledge that amount and contribute it in quarterly installments over a year's period?" Or you can say, "What would you feel comfortable giving?" or "What would you like to give?"

3. "That's a lot of money." This statement is not a decision. This statement says, "Remind me again of my role in this campaign." Your answer: "It is a lot of money. There are not many people we could ask for that amount." Or, "Your gift will be a trendsetter, as such it will be critical in helping us reach our goal." Then be quiet again and let the prospect make a decision.

4. "I need to think about it." Some people truly cannot make up their mind on the spot and if pushed for an answer will say no. Ask the prospect, "What else can I tell you that will help you in your thinking?" and answer any remaining questions. Then say, "May I call you in a few days to see what your decision is?" Set a time when the prospect will be finished thinking and will give you an answer.

5. "Yes, I'll help." Arrange for how the gift will be made (by check, by pledge, by stock transfer; now, later), say "Thank you," and leave.

Immediately after the interview send the donor a thank-you note. Another thank-you note should come from the organization when the gift is received.

Although it is frightening to ask someone for a large gift, it is also thrilling when the prospect says yes. Moreover, it is a good feeling to know that you were able to set aside your own discomfort about asking for money for the greater purpose of meeting the needs of your organization. Most people find that, with practice, asking for money becomes easier and easier.

13.

The Thank-You Note

In 1977, a woman sent $25 to an advocacy group working on women's health issues. The organization was run collectively by two utterly overworked and underpaid staff and 40 volunteers. They had won recognition for their work exposing the dangers of the Dalkon Shield IUD and championing reproductive rights issues. The donor did not receive a thank-you note for her gift. However, she did receive the group's newsletter and she heard about the group from time to time.

A year after her gift she received a letter requesting a renewal. She threw it away. Some time later, she learned that a friend of hers was in the group. "That group sounds good," she told her friend, "but they don't even have it together enough to send thank-you notes for gifts. I can't imagine that they are really fiscally sound or that they use money properly."

Her friend defended the group. "They do really good work. Maybe they should take time to thank people, but saying they don't use money wisely is an unfair conclusion."

The one-time donor replied, "It is fair. It is my only contact with them. They claim to want a broad base of support, yet they show no regard for their supporters. But since you are in the group, I'll give them something." She sent $15.

During the year between this donor's $25 gift and her $15 one, the group had hired me to be their fundraiser. I sent her a scrawled three-line thank-you note: "Thanks for your gift of $15. It's a help financially and also a great morale boost. We'll keep in touch." Two weeks later, this woman sent $1,500.

Valuing All Gifts

Although I had been drilled from childhood about the propriety of sending thank-you notes, I never really believed they were worth much one way or the other until that lesson. After I met this donor, she told me that she often sent relatively small gifts to groups she liked to see what they would do. If she sent $100 or more (a lot of money in 1977) most groups would thank her. But that would not tell her how much regard they had for smaller donors. "Many grassroots groups talk a good line about class and everyone being welcomed," she said, "but the only people they really care about are the program officers of foundations and wealthy donors."

This woman was very wealthy, but she wanted to give money only to groups that had proven that they valued all gifts. I was flabbergasted that a sign of proof could be a sloppy three-line thank-you note, but for her it was better proof than a longer form letter with her name typed in.

Since then I have seen over and over that a simple, handwritten note or typed thank-you letter with a personal note as a postscript can do more to build donor loyalty than almost any other form of recognition. Unfortunately, thank-you notes tend to be one thing that organizations are sloppy or even thoughtless about. They either don't send them, send them weeks late, or, now endowed with computers, send form thank-you notes with the person's name inserted every few lines. These practices are unjustifiable. Sending thank-you notes falls far too low on people's work priority lists. They have to be placed at the top.

People Like Them

It is not clear to me why people like thank-you notes so much, particularly when there is usually very little content in the note. Probably reasons vary. Like our wealthy, testing donor, some see them as a sign that the group knows what it is doing. Others may just like the attention. While psychologists may be able to find out exactly why people like to be appreciated, for fundraisers it is enough to know that it is true. Doing what donors like — as long as we stay inside the mission and goals of the organization — builds donor loyalty. A loyal donor is a giving donor, giving more and more every year.

Don't Do As I Say

What about the donor who claims not to want a thank-you note, or the one who even more strongly states that thank-you notes are a waste of time and money?

The first type of donor, who claims not to want a thank you, but doesn't seem emotional about it, should get one anyway. These are generally people who are genuinely trying to save groups time. You will have greater loyalty if you send a thank-you note anyway. When these donors say, "You shouldn't have done that," or "That's really not necessary," they often mean, "Thank you for taking the time. I can't believe someone would be bothered to notice me."

The second style of donor, who actually resents thank-you notes, probably should get them anyway, too. When you stop sending thank-you notes to those who claim not to like them, you may lose them. If the person is very close to your group, perhaps a volunteer or board member, or someone who used to work for the organization, try calling to thank her or him instead of writing. You can combine your call with another function, such as to remind them of a meeting: "I called to remind you about the meeting Wednesday at 7 p.m. at Marge's. By the way, thanks for your gift — we can really use it."

Overall, experience shows that, all else being equal, when you thank donors you keep them and when you don't you lose them.

Of course, there will be exceptions to this rule, but it is almost impossible to figure out who is really an exception and who is just pretending to be, so thank everyone and save yourself worrying about it.

Do It Now

How can you most efficiently thank your donors, and who should do it? Perhaps the most important rule about thanking donors is that no matter who is doing it — from the board chair to an office volunteer — gifts should be acknowledged within two days of receipt, a week at the outside. If possible, the person who knows the donor should sign the thank-you note.

If you are fundraising properly, you will have dozens of donations coming in from people you don't know. Volunteers and board members can send thank-you notes. It is actually a good way to get board members who are resistant to fundraising to do some, because the thank-you note is part of fundraising.

Buy some nice note cards, or have some made with your logo on the front. There is only a small amount of space to fill on a note card so you can take up the whole space with a few short sentences. That is much better than a three-line thank you on a full sheet of stationary.

People should come to the office to write the notes, and only the most loyal, trustworthy people should ever be allowed to write notes at home. It is just too tempting to put them aside at home. Also, information about a person's gift, while not secret, is also not something you want sitting around someone's living room.

The only equipment for handwritten thank-you notes is legible handwriting. The format is simple:

> Thank you for your gift of $___. We will put it right to work on (name your program or most recent issue). Gifts like yours are critical to our success, and we thank you very much.
>
> Sincerely,
> (Your name)
> Board member

If you know the person, follow the same format, but add something more personal: "Hope your cat, Fluffy, has recovered from her spaying."

It may be that writing thank-you notes by hand or writing all of them by hand is impossible, especially when you get a lot of contributions, such as at year-end, and volunteers aren't as available, or after a successful direct mail appeal when you are swamped for a few days with responses.

Then you go to the next step, which is a word-processed letter. This will go on stationery and needs to be a little longer. Start the thank you several lines down the page, and use wide margins.

> Dear Freda,
>
> Thank you so much for your gift of $100. We have put it right to work at our shelter. As it turned out, your gift came at a particularly crucial moment as our boiler had just given its last gasp. We were able to buy a refitted, good-as-new boiler for cash (saving us $), which we wouldn't have been able to do without your gift.
>
> I am hoping you will be able to come to our art auction next month. We have the works of some well-known local artists and will be featuring paintings and sculptures by some of the residents of the shelter. I enclose two complimentary tickets.
>
> Again, thank you so much! I look forward to staying in touch.

You will notice that the letter refers to some very recent event (the boiler). This gives a sense of immediacy to the gift. If the organization had not used the gift for the boiler, they could have still told the story, as follows:

> Your gift came the same day our boiler broke for the last time. I would have been really discouraged, but your contribution cheered me up. Fortunately, we were able to get a refitted, good-as-new boiler for much less than a new one would have cost.

The letter also invited the donor to an event. You do not need to provide free tickets, nor do you have to be having an event. The point is to refer to things happening in your office every day. Give your donors some sense of your daily work. Even things that seem routine to you can be made to sound interesting. For example:

> Dear Ricardo,
>
> We got a pile of mail today — bills, fliers, newsletters, and then, your gift of $50! Thank you! $50 really goes a long way in this organization, and we are grateful for your support. I just finished talking with a woman who used our educational flier with her son. She said she had expected a miracle, and though of course that didn't happen, maybe something more lasting did. Her son called the HelpLine. It's a start, and that's what we provide for people.
>
> I hope you will feel free to drop by sometime. Though we are usually busy, we can always take a few minutes to say hello and show you around. I'll keep you posted on our progress.

Or:

> Dear Annie Mae,
>
> I just came in from an eviction hearing of one of our clients. I feel really good because we won, and we got some damages to boot! Then, going through the mail, I came to your gift of $25. Thanks! I feel like you are a part of this victory.

Or:

> You wouldn't believe how many people came to our community meeting last night — over 50! People are hopping mad about this incinerator proposal, and I am feeling confident that we may be able to defeat it and finally get the recycling bill passed. Your gift of $50 is going to go a long way in helping with fliers and phone calls. Thanks for thinking of us at this time. You don't know what a great morale boost it is to receive gifts from supporters like you.

If you have a matching campaign or a goal for an annual campaign, then include that:

> Your gift of $100 will be matched dollar for dollar. Your gift brought us to just under $2,000 raised in just two months!

Or:

> Your gift of $75 took us over the $1,000 mark in our goal of $3,000. Thanks!

If you are a volunteer, mention that in your thank you:

> Giving time to this organization is one of the high points of my week. I know we are making a difference, and I want you to know that your gift helps make that difference too.

The Friendly Form Letter

The least effective option for thank-you notes, but one you some-times have to resort to, is the form letter. If you use a form letter, acknowledge that is it impersonal, but give some sense of the excitement that would lead you to use such a method.

Thank you for your recent gift. Please excuse the impersonal nature of this thank you — we are no less enthusiastic about your gift for not being able to write to each of our donors. The response to our call for help with sending medical supplies to El Salvador was both gratifying and overwhelming. We will send you a full report about this effort in a few weeks. Right now, we are packing up boxes of supplies — supplies you helped pay for. Thanks again!

Call Them What You Will, But Thank Them

There are two common questions remaining about thank-you notes. One is, "How do you address people you don't know?" The choices are by first name only, by first and last names (Dear John Smith) or by title (Dear Mr. Smith). There is no clear right or wrong on this point, and no way to avoid possibly offending someone. In general, you will probably offend the least number of people by using titles, "Dear Mr." or "Dear Ms." Certainly, you could write to the person according to how they write to you. A letter signed, "Mrs. Alphonse Primavera" should be answered in kind. If there is ambiguity about whether the donor is a man or woman, write "Dear Friend." If you live in a fairly laid back or not terribly formal place, you can use a first name, "Dear Terry" or "Dear Lynn."

Don't waste a lot of time worrying about this. Having received many thank-you notes that say, "Dear Mr. Klein," I know how off-putting it can be, but it does not cause me to stop giving to the group. Anyone who will stop giving you money just because you (or anyone else) cannot tell from their name whether they are male or female, or whether they prefer to be called by their first name, last name, Mr., Ms. or Mrs. doesn't have much loyalty to your group.

The second question is, "Do all donors get a thank you?" Yes. You have no idea how much a gift of $25 or $5 or $500 means to someone. You need to act as though you would like to get that amount or more again. You also don't know how people use getting a thank-you note to judge whether to continue giving to your organization. Why take a chance?

Do all donors get the same thank you? No, because the notes, if possible, are personalized. But people giving bigger gifts don't get bigger thank yous. If you have thousands of donors, you will not be able to write to them all personally, so sort out the ones you know and write to them. But make sure each donor gets something.

Keep up with thank-you notes as gifts come in. Each thank you is a link to the donor and you should see it as paving the way for the next gift.

SECTION 3
Strategies to Upgrade Donors

INTRODUCTION

The payoff in building a base of donors is in being able to ask people who are giving regularly to consider giving bigger and bigger gifts. The goal of any organization that gains the support of individual donors is to become the favorite organization of their donors. When your donors think about your organization, you want them to think, "That is the group to which I give the most money," or "That is an organization I would do almost anything for." Building on that loyalty, you now help your donors to give your organization the maximum amount of money they can afford. The strategies described in this section are used in that process.

The process of getting people to give more money is called "upgrading" and those donors who respond to these strategies have become the "thoughtful" donors described in Chapter 3, Fundraising Needs and Strategies. It is highly unusual for a person to start their giving to an organization with a thoughtful gift, so almost all thoughtful donors will come out of the donor base that is built using the strategies described in Section Two. The only time someone's first gift might be truly thoughtful is when they or someone close to them has been deeply affected by the issue or the service the organization addresses or provides.

Thoughtful gifts are most often gifts of more than $50; they may be thousands of dollars for annual giving, and will be even higher for capital and endowment gifts. In this section, we will use $50 to describe the minimum thoughtful gift and then discuss much larger gifts. It is important to note, though, that if your organization includes low-income or poor people in your donor base, there will be people giving less than $50 who are nevertheless giving thoughtfully. On the other side are people giving more than $50 who are not giving thoughtfully and could give more. To the extent that you can identify your thoughtful donors who may giving significant gifts for them albeit small amounts of money, you need to treat them with the same respect you treat thoughtful donors who give larger gifts.

In fundraising, we must spend large amounts of time working with people who can give large amounts of money. All donors expect that and would think it odd and not a good use of resources to do otherwise. But we don't overlook other kinds of giving and the significance of gifts to any donor. We do this because it is the right thing to do, but this has a practical angle: someone who gives $5 a quarter through a pledge program may get a better job or a cheaper apartment and change their gift to $5 a month. When he or she gets promoted, the gift may increase to $50 a month. Or, a person may give a small amount for years and years, then die and leave his or her estate to the organization. Through the process of identifying prospects, described in Chapter 12, Personal Solicitation, and through careful and thorough record keeping, we can keep track of all our thoughtful donors, not just the ones who are able to give large amounts of money.

This section, like the last, is organized in order of the amount of personal asking that is required for each gift. The least personal strategies are described first and the most personal — planned gifts — are described last. This also follows the order of their difficulty, from least to most difficult.

14

Major Gifts Programs

Before beginning to solicit major gifts, your organization must define how much money it wishes to raise from large gifts, the minimum amount that will constitute a major gift (in this book it is $50), and how many gifts of what size are needed. You must decide what, if any, tangible benefits donors will receive for their gifts, what materials will be needed, and a core group of volunteers must be trained to ask for the gifts.

Setting a Goal

The first step in seeking major gifts is to decide how much money you want to raise from major donors. This amount will be related to the overall amount you want to raise from all your donors, and can be partly determined based on the following information. (For further information on goal setting, see Chapter 32, Creating a Fundraising Plan.)

Over the years fundraising experts have observed a pattern of how gifts come into organizations. This is the established pattern:

- ◆ 60% of the income comes from 10% of the donors
- ◆ 20% of the income comes from 20% of the donors
- ◆ 20% of the income comes from 70% of the donors.

In other words, the majority of your gifts will be small, but the majority of your income will be from a few large donations. Based on this pattern, it is possible to project for any fundraising goal how many of each size gift you should seek and how many prospects you will need to get each gift.

For example, if your organization must raise $50,000 from grassroots fundraising, plan to raise $30,000 (60%) from major gifts mostly solicited personally, $10,000 (20%) from habitual donors mostly solicited through mail and regular special events, and $10,000 (20%) from people giving for the first or second time, including from all other strategies such as special events, product sales, canvassing, etc. If you have 1500 donors, expect that about 150 of them will be major donors, 300 to 400 of them will be habitual donors, and about 1000 will be first- or second-time donors or donors who give small gifts every year, but for whom your organization is not a high priority.

Most low-budget organizations define a major gift as any gift of more than $50. While not a large gift in the world of large donations, $50 is larger than the average gift to most nonprofits, which tends to be in the $15 to $35 range. It is also a gift that most employed people can afford to give, especially if the group allows people to pledge. Even many low-income people can afford $10 a month or $25 a quarter, which brings being a "major donor" into the realm of possibility for all people close to your group.

Some organizations try to avoid setting goals, saying they will raise "as much as they can from as many people as they can." This doesn't work; the prospects are going to ask how much you need and will not be satisfied with the answer, "As much as we can get." In this situation, the prospect will then give less than he or she can afford or nothing because the organization doesn't seem very well run. Further, without a goal, there is no way to measure how well the organization is doing compared to its plans. You can't build a house saying, "It will be as big as it needs to be" or "It will be as big as we can afford," and you can't build a donor base with vague or meaningless assertions either.

Apportionment of Gifts

It would be great if you could say, "Well, we need $40,000 from 10 percent of our donors, so that will mean 200 people giving $200." But 200 people will not behave the same way — some will give more, most will give less. So fundraising experts have made a second observation: for the money needed annually, you need two gifts to provide 10 percent of the goal, and four to six gifts to provide the next 10 percent of the goal. The remaining gifts needed are determined in decreasing size of gift with increasing numbers of gifts. Using this formula, you can create a "Gift Range Chart" or a "Gift Pyramid."

Let's imagine an organization that needs to raise $100,000 from a wide variety of individual donor strategies. Using the pattern outlined above, $60,000 will be raised from major gifts. Their giving pyramid will look something like this:

Gift Range Chart

Goal: $100,000

Number of Gifts	Size of gifts	Total
2	$5,000	$10,000
4	$2,500	$10,000
5	$1,500	$7,500
10	$1,000	$10,000
15	$500	$7,500
20	$250	$5,000
100	$100	$10,000
156	**$100-5,000**	**$60,000**

The most important and most useful part of the chart is the top part, which plots size and number of major gifts. It should not be seen as a blueprint. If an organization has one donor who can give 10 percent of the goal, then ask for that; you will need fewer gifts at the lower end of the chart. An organization in a rural community may not have the number of gifts needed, so it will have to get fewer gifts of a larger size. The chart serves as a guideline and also a reality check. For example, if your goal is $100,000, but the biggest gift you can imagine getting is $500, then you may have to modify your goal. The chart is helpful for board members and other volunteer solicitors who may have difficulty imagining raising $100,000, but can imagine 100 people giving $100 each.

How Many People Need to Be Asked

Every fundraising strategy, presuming it is done properly, has an expected rate of response. When major gifts are requested by someone who knows the potential donor, knows that he or she believes in the cause, and knows that he or she could give the amount of money being asked, there is about a 50 percent chance the prospect will say yes. If the prospect says yes, there is a further 50 percent chance that he or she will give less than what was requested. So, for every gift you seek through personal solicitation, you will need as many as four prospects (two will say no, one will say yes, and one will give a lesser amount). At the upper reaches of your chart, you should look for four prospects for every gift needed, but because the ones who give less fill in the number of gifts needed in the middle and bottom ranges of the chart, look for two to three prospects for every gift needed in those ranges. Overall look for about three times as many prospects as gifts needed, gambling that, overall, one will say yes, one will say no and one will give less than asked. The chart above, including prospects, would look like this:

Gift Range Chart

Goal: $100,000

Number of Gifts	Size of gifts	Total	# Prospects
2	$5,000	$10,000	(X4) 8
4	$2,500	$10,000	(X4) 16
5	$1,500	$7,500	(X4) 20
10	$1,000	$10,000	(X4) 40
15	$500	$7,500	(X4) 60
20	$250	$5,000	(X3) 60
100	$100	$10,000	(X2) 200
156	**$100-5,000**	**$60,000**	**404**

Overall, an organization needing about 150 gifts will need to ask about 450 people. How you will decide which 450 people to ask is the subject of the Chapter, 12 Personal Solicitation.

Materials Needed for Major Gift Solicitation

In addition to the gift range chart and a list of prospects, there are two more elements that need to be in place. First, you need to decide what, if any, benefits people will receive for giving a major gift. While helping the organization is the main satisfaction for the donor, an added incentive such as a mug or a invitation to a special party or a T-shirt will show that you appreciate the extra effort the donor is making, and will remind the donor of his or her gift to your group. There is no evidence that one kind of benefit works better than another (see also discussion of benefits in Chapter 6, Using Direct Mail).

Certainly, the benefit should not be very expensive. Under IRS law, any benefit that exceeds in value the vague definition of "token" must be subtracted from the gift before the gift can be used as a tax deduction. For example, if someone gives $500 to an organization and receives an etching worth $50, they can only deduct $450 of this gift because $50 is more than "token." If the same group gave a T-shirt or tote bag worth $10, the donor could deduct the whole $500. The IRS is increasingly cracking down on fancy benefits for donors. By and large, this will not affect readers of this book!

The benefit should be easy to mail, which is why many groups use T-shirts or books as benefits. Because of the number of "things" people can get for their gifts to public television, libraries, or major national organizations, a small organization should probably offer something that is unique to its programs. For example, an organization working for stricter controls on the commercial use of pesticides and for alternatives to pesticides sends a short booklet on alternatives to pesticides for home gardens and indoor plants to its major donors. An after-school program for inner-city children aged 8 to 11 asked the teachers to save any drawings the children made that they didn't want to take home. The organization sent the best of those along with the thank-you notes to donors. This benefit is truly of "token" value, but is very popular with donors. Now the organization has one day in which the children are asked to make "Thank-you drawings."

A major donor program can be successfully run without giving any benefits beyond what are offered to all donors, such as the newsletter, if the donors are thanked personally and promptly, and if the organization keeps in touch with them using the ways recommended in the section on renewing major gifts, below.

The second element needed is materials that describe your program. An organization should have a well-designed, easy-to-understand brochure. It does not have to be fancy or printed in several colors, but it should be professionally laid out, well written, and free of grammatical or typographical errors. Return envelopes and return cards are a must, and many organizations have a special brochure that invites people to become major donors. This pamphlet explains the organization, but focuses on ways people can make major gifts. For example, if you have an EFT (electronic fund transfer) program, or a pledge program, or you accept credit cards, or you are seeking stocks and bonds, you can explain all that in the brochure. This also helps volunteer solicitors because they don't need to remember every detail.

Finally, you need to have a core group of people willing to do the soliciting. Some of these people should be from the board of directors, but the board's work can be augmented by a group of volunteers. These people should be trained in the process of asking for money (discussed in Chapter 12, Personal Solicitation). They do not have to have previous experience, nor do they need to know many prospects themselves. But they must be donors, and ideally major donors.

Keeping in Touch with Major Donors

One of the most frequent complaints from donors regardles of the size of their gift is that organizations treat them like water faucets: turn on when the organization wants money; off when they don't. To keep donors interested in your group requires keeping in touch with them, and that is the main purpose of newsletters and other benefits that are discussed in various chapters throughout this book. But people who give thoughtful gifts to an organization require more personal attention than the rest of the donor base. They think about your group and how much they can afford to give and, to greater and lesser degrees depending on their personalities and the size of their gifts, they expect you to treat them thoughtfully in return.

To do this requires some extra work, but it is worth it for the amount of money that will result. An organization should be in contact with its major donors two to three times a year in addition to the time when the donor is asked to renew his or her gift. You will want to be in touch with some donors more often than that depending on the size of their gift and, to a large extent, on their personality. You will be automatically in touch with those major donors who are also board members or volun-teers in the course of your work.

There are several easy ways to keep in touch with major donors that make them feel personally appreciated and do not cost the organization much in time or money. You can choose from the suggestions below or develop your own methods.

1) Send major donors a holiday card during December. The card wishes the donor happy holidays, and is signed by the chair of the board or a board member with a personal relationship to the donor, or by a staffperson. If possible, write a brief note on the card. The card goes by itself — no return envelope, no appeal letter. Unless your organization is religiously identified, make sure the card has no religious overtones including cultural Christian overtones such as Santa Claus, elves or Christmas trees. The same applies to the postage stamp you choose.

2) Send all donors a copy of your annual report and attach a personal note to reports sent to major donors. This note can be on a post-it and does not have to be long. The note says something like, "Thought you'd be interested in seeing this since you have been so criti-cal to our success," or, "I hope you are as proud of our work as we are — your gift helped make it possible." It doesn't matter if you don't know the donor at all — a personal note will make him or her feel appreciated. If you know that something in your report will be of particular interest, note that. "Paul, that program you asked about is featured on pg. 5." or, "Fran, you'll love the photo on the back inside cover!" Staff usually write these notes.

3) Take advantage of things that happen during the year. If you have positive press coverage, if you win a victory in your organizing or litigative efforts, if you are commended by a citizen's group, service club or politician, take the opportunity to send a special letter to major donors telling them of the event. Send a copy of the article or commendation if possible. This letter does not have to be personalized.

4) When you know a donor's birthday, send a card. If you learn that someone graduated from college, or won an award, or had a baby, send a card. Don't spend a lot of time trying to learn all this, but pay attention when the information comes your way.

5) Include personal notes with things major donors will be getting anyway, such as invitations to special events or announcements of meetings.

6) Generally major donors do not get all the multiple appeals that are sent to rest of the donor base, but **when a mail appeal letter is particularly timely** or concerns a particular issue that will be interesting to them, **send the letter to all your donors.**

By keeping in frequent touch with your major donors, you will lay the groundwork necessary to approach them for a renewal of their gift in the second year they give and a request to increase the size of their gift the third year of their giving. You have begun to establish rapport with the donor, even if you have never met the person.

Renewing the Gift

Near the anniversary of the donor's gift, send him or her a letter asking for a renewal. The letter should be personalized and a handwritten note should be added as a postscript. The letter describes the highlights of the year before and attributes some of that success to the donor's gift. One paragraph is devoted to the needs for the coming year and then the letter asks the donor to renew their gift. Be sure to name the amount you want, in case the donor has forgotten how much they gave and also to show that you know how much they gave. Include a stamped, return envelope marked to the attention of the person who signed the letter, and a reply card.

For gifts of $250 and above, consider calling to follow up your letter. For gifts of $1,000 or more, a personal visit is appropriate. For some donors, the visit or phone call will not be necessary, but the offer will still be appreciated. Often, the follow up phone call will go something like this: "May, this is June calling to follow up on my letter." "Yes, June. It's lovely of you to call. I've already sent in my check." June can then ask if May has any questions or can tell her something else that wasn't in the letter (but be brief!). The whole interaction will take five minutes at the most.

A request for a meeting will often have the same result. "Frank, this is Earnest. Did you get my letter?" "Yes, it came yesterday." "Great. I was wondering if we could get together to talk about the possibility or you renewing your gift?" "You don't need to visit me for that. I'll be happy to renew." Earnest still feels pleased that he was given this attention and, again, the whole interaction takes no more than five minutes.

Sometimes people wonder how many times you should ask donors to renew their gift at the same amount before asking for an upgrade. Similarly, once the gift is upgraded, how long is appropriate before asking for another upgrade. The answer is simple: know your donor. The sooner you meet the donor and learn more about him or her, the sooner you will have a sense of whether they like to be visited, whether they are giving to their capacity and cannot upgrade anymore, whether they would rather make up their own minds about when and how to increase their gift, and so on.

Of course, you can't know all your major donors right away, and some you may never meet. When you don't know, follow this formula: get the gift, the following year ask for a renewal, the following year ask for an upgrade. If you receive a larger gift, ask for a renewal, and then the year after the renewal, ask for a gift that is one-third again as much, then a couple of years of renewal and then another upgrade, and so on. If the donor stays at the same level, keep asking for more unless you get information that the level the donor is giving at is what they can afford.

In addition to this formula, use common sense. If someone gives you $5,000, you may need to ask for a renewal for several years before asking for more. If someone gives you $100, ask them to double their gift, but if someone gives you $10,000, think twice before asking them to double. You can always add the phrase "or more" onto any request you make if you really don't know how much more to ask for.

Of course, your organization must be able to justify needing more money in order to ask for more, and that need must be expressed to the donor in a compelling way. Hiring another staff person, for example, is not compelling; serving 20 more children (what the additional staff person is needed for) is compelling.

In planning to have a major gifts component of your fundraising, keep in mind that the first year of recruiting major donors may be the hardest. Do not set your goals too high; you don't want volunteers to be demoralized by failing to reach an unrealistic goal. Major gifts solicitation can be done in the form of a campaign — that is, with a formal beginning and ending time, specific materials, and a committee as described in Chapter 16, Major Gifts Campaigns, or it can be an ongoing program, with different volunteers helping at different times.

The most important step to take in a major gifts program is to start it. Even if you have only one prospect, ask that prospect. If the largest gift you can imagine someone giving is $50, start with $50. A major gifts program builds on itself; simply establishing the groundwork for the program will begin the process of getting major gifts.

15.

Pledge Programs

As found in almost every religious tradition, pledging is the practice of people "tithing" a certain amount of their income, usually ten percent, to their house of worship. Since few can afford to give the entire ten percent at once (if they could, they should be giving more), most donors give the amount promised over some period of time. In an annual giving program, they give it over the course of a year; in a capital campaign, a pledge may stretch over as many as five years. A pledge is a legally binding contract in which a donor commits a certain amount of money and then fulfills the pledge with regular payments. While few organizations would sue a donor who did not fulfill her or his pledge, it is important for donors to understand that this is a serious commitment and that the organization counts pledges as "accounts receivable."

There are two great advantages of a pledge program to an organization: any donor can give more if payments are spread over a time period than they could give all at once, and a well-run pledge program means reliable monthly income.

There are also clear advantages for the donor. People who are committed to an organization can give more than their annual dues by pledging. Most working people could not give $120 all at once but can afford $10 a month. Further, people who give $100, $500 or even $1,000 in one-time gifts may be able to repeat that gift four times a year or even every month. Certainly, they can't make this kind of commitment to every group, but they can and will make it to their favorite organization if the mechanism is in place to ask them.

Pledging is the simplest strategy with which to start the upgrading process. You will have the pleasant surprise of seeing some people increase their giving 400 percent or even 1200 percent as they go from giving $25 a year to that much every quarter or every month.

Introducing a Pledge Program

Once an organization decides to institute a pledge program, it needs to introduce it in all its fundraising materials. First, send a special appeal to your current donors asking them to consider pledging. The appeal letter explains that the reader is a valuable supporter and your organization wants to give him or her an opportunity to give more without undue hardship. For more exposure, use a small amount of space in your newsletter to discuss the pledge program. And include pledging on all your return forms as one of the choices: "I want to give $___ per month/quarter (circle one). My first payment is enclosed." The idea of pledging sometimes takes a while to catch on, but when donors see this option in many different places and grow accustomed to it, more and more of them will take advantage of it.

Organizations sometimes find it helpful to provide incentives for pledging. This can be done by creating a special category for people who pledge, such as a "Gift of the Month Club" or a "Sustainer Council." People who pledge can also be given a benefit not available to other donors, and can be listed in a special category in newsletters or annual reports.

Collecting Pledges

Many pledge programs have failed because the organization did not put time into collecting the pledged amounts or did not have a system in place to keep track of payments. I have pledged to more than a dozen organizations over the years to which I made one or two payments, then forgot about my pledge. Most of the groups have failed to remind me, or reminded me in such a sporadic way that my pledge was paid sporadically. In one case, after being asked to pledge and making payments for a few months, I received a letter asking if I could pay the rest of my pledge in one payment because the group "found the process of depositing so many checks every month too time consuming." Since the main point of a making a pledge is to be able to pay more over time than one can afford at once, I concluded their request reflected a lack of thought, which I feared would be present throughout the group's work, so I stopped giving to the group altogether.

Systems for Keeping Track of Pledges

It is easy to keep track of pledges in your computer or on a paper system. If your database will allow — and if you want to have more than 100 people pledging, you should get a database that can be designed for fundraising — set up fields to record the pledge and the payment due dates. As payments are made, record these.

Send the pledge reminder at the same time every month or quarter, so that it arrives right before the first of the month. If your pledge reminder arrives by then, and if people are billed regularly, you will have the least number of dropouts. Send a form such as the one below and a stamped return envelope. The computer should be able to fill in the necessary blanks and keep track of how much has been paid and how much is still owing.

SAMPLE PLEDGE REMINDER FORM

(sized to fit without being folded into a #7 return envelope)

Organization Name and Address

Date:

Dear Donor Name,

Your monthly (or quarterly) pledge of $_____ is now due. Please use the enclosed envelope to return it. We are very grateful for your ongoing support, and for your commitment to our work.

Director or other staff name

Total amount pledged $_____. Total amount paid to date $_____

Make checks payable to: Your organization, address.

Your gift is tax deductible to the full extent of the law.

If you are using a paper system, record the pledge information for each person on a 5" by 7" card and keep all the pledges in a file box. Each card should contain the donor's name and address, the amount pledged, the date the pledge was made and how often payments will be made. Make a column noting the dates payments are due, and write beside each date when payments are made. A quick glance will tell you whether the donor is behind in payment.

Once a month someone goes through the box, fills out a pledge note, and sends it with a stamped return envelope. Pledge forms like the one above are preprinted and a person fills in the blanks. Pledge collection is an excellent fundraising task for a careful, thorough board member or volunteer.

Most groups find that they collect 85 to 95 percent of their pledges. If a person has been reminded three times without paying, assume that he or she is not going to pay. Some groups have found it helpful to call the donor and see if there is a problem that the organization can rectify. Usually it has nothing to do with the group, but instead that the donor's financial situation has changed for the worse or that the donor didn't realize what a commitment this pledge was. Don't hound people for payment. Simply roll them back into the regular donor program.

At the end of the year send a personal letter with the final pledge note asking the donor to renew his or her pledge. Include a renewal form. The letter is simple and straightforward, such as:

Dear_____,

This is the last payment on your pledge of $250. Your ongoing support has been tremendously important to us this past year. I am writing to thank you for your commitment.

I also hope that you will renew your pledge. We will continue to send you reminders, and you will receive _____, available only to people who pledge. I enclose a form for you to fill out. Thank you again for all your support.

Sincerely,
Director or Board Chair

Other Ways To Collect Pledges

There are two systems for collecting money from donors that require little paperwork on the part of the donor and ensure immediate collection of the pledged amount of money.

1) Electronic Fund Transfer

Electronic Fund Transfer (EFT) allows the transfer of funds from one account to another via a computer network. In use since 1978 when President Carter signed the EFT Act, the process of transferring funds electronically has become increasingly popular and is used in a variety of ways. In fact, electronic banking is increasingly taking the place of check writing, with people paying telephone bills, health club dues, insurance payments and the like using EFT.

The advantages of EFT to an organization are many. Pledge fulfillment is increased to nearly 100 percent because the funds are transferred directly from the donor's bank to the organization's bank. Donors must cancel the EFT in order to indicate that they are not renewing, which gives organizations a much higher renewal rate (in many cases as high as 80 percent, compared to 66 percent normal renewal rate). Organizations with established donor programs find that EFT is one-fifth as expensive as traditional pledge collection systems because there are no mail costs and fewer processing costs.

The main advantage for the donor is that EFT is very convenient — a one-time authorization takes the place of writing and sending a check each month. The donation is listed in the donor's bank statement and an annual statement summarizes all EFT transactions.

The system of electronic fund transfer is run by a network called the National Automated Clearing House Association (NACHA). NACHA is a private processing and delivery network that effects electronic fund transfers nationwide. More than 95 percent of commercial banks and thrifts belong to NACHA. In the rare instances in which a donor's checking institution does not belong to NACHA, the donor can use a pre-authorized check (PAC).

There are no disadvantages to EFT, but an organization must have a solid donor base and excellent bookkeeping and accounting systems in place to deal with authorization forms (see below) quickly and efficiently. Your system must be computerized, and you must have a significant number of donors (in most cases, 100 or more) wishing to take advantage of EFT for it to be worthwhile for you or the bank.

There are dozens of professional firms that will manage the collection process for you, or you can do it yourself, if your bank is cooperative. The advantage of going directly through a bank is that there are no set up fees or fees per individual transaction. The disadvantage is that many banks will not be helpful unless your organization can provide a high volume — out of the range of many small organizations. A professional firm doesn't need quite the volume from your organization because they have it from all their clients combined, plus they have the computer programs, the forms and the knowledge of how to do it.

Organizations are advised to talk with other organizations who are using EFT and with their bank to see what is involved before negotiating with a professional firm.

SAMPLE INCENTIVE OFFER AND AUTHORIZATION FORM
FOR EFT PROGRAM

Join People For Cultural Preservation's Simple Gift Program . . . and receive a cassette of early American hymns.

The Simple Gift Program is convenient. Your gift is paid automatically each month by your bank, and you will never have to write us another check (unless you want to!). A record of your contribution appears on your monthly bank statement. You can cancel at any time by writing or calling us.

The Simple Gift Program increases the value of your gift. The cost of processing your donation is reduced, so more of your money can go right to work in our preservation research and publication efforts.

Here's How to Join

1. Fill in your monthly gift amount, name, address and telephone number on the attached form.

2. Initial the Inflation Guard Box if you would like to increase your gift by 5 percent each year on the anniversary of your enrollment.

3. Sign and date the form.

4. Enclose your check payable to People for Cultural Preservation for this month's gift — transfers will begin in about six weeks.

5. Mail the form and your check in the enclosed return envelope.

Terms of Agreement

My authorization to charge my account at my bank shall be the same as if I had personally signed a check to People for Cultural Preservation (PCP). This authorization shall remain in effect until I notify PCP or my bank in writing that I wish to end this agreement and PCP or my bank has had a reasonable time to act on it; or until PCP or my bank has sent me ten days' written notice that they will end this agreement. A record of my payment will be included in my regular bank statement and will serve as my receipt. My initials in the Inflation Guard Box authorize PCP to increase my monthly charge by 5 percent on each 12-month anniversary of the initial charge.

Monthly pledge $_____

Inflation Guard? ____Yes ____No

Date signed_____

Signed _____

2) Charging Donations with a Credit Card

Paying for goods or services with cash is becoming less and less common in the United States. Checks were the first item to replace cash, although they stand for actual cash. After checks came credit cards, which allow people to defer payments and go into debt more easily. Millions of people have credit cards and many have more than one credit card. The use of fraudulent or stolen credit cards is on the rise, but so are buying on credit and giving on credit.

Many nonprofit organizations including grassroots groups offer donors the option of giving with their credit card. Their reply device includes a space for the donor's credit card number and the amount of the gift. Groups that use credit cards report strong donor acceptance and often report an increase in giving. In the same way that people will spend more with credit cards than with cash, so will they give more.

If you decide to use a credit card option, set it up through your bank. The bank will run a credit check on your organization to see how many checks you have bounced, whether you pay your rent and other bills on time, and what your assets are. If your organization uses credit cards, your credit rating will be a help (or hindrance if you don't pay your bills on time). Someone from the bank will also visit your organization, which is mainly to verify that the organization exists and seems to be what it claims. Sometimes board members, in their capacity as trustee, will be asked to agree that they will supervise the maintenance of this program and that to the best of their knowledge, the organization is sound enough to undertake such a program. (This is part of board liability and is not an extra duty for board members.) The bank may also run a credit check on those individuals. (This is not part of board duty.)

The bank takes a fee of one to five percent of each transaction, depending on your volume, their policy, and whether you have a friend in the bank who can have the percentage lowered or waived altogether. The bank will familiarize you with the procedures it wants you to follow.

Credit cards can be used to solicit one-time donations or to fulfill pledges. The credit card is charged every month with the amount of the pledge.

Three Don'ts of the Pledge Program

Organizations are sometimes tempted to try cost-cutting measures on their pledge programs. They may, for example, send a donor who has pledged $10 a month 12 envelopes at one time, expecting the person to return one envelope containing a payment each month. People cannot be expected to remember to pay their pledges or keep track of the envelopes for the entire year. Even though churches give congregants a box of envelopes for the entire year, they have the advantage of reminding people weekly about their pledges. Further, for people who don't come to church regularly, the church will send a letter reminding the congregant to pay, and the minister or the chair of the finance committee will call.

Other organizations send the envelope to collect each payment, but leave the stamp off it, reasoning that if the donor can afford and is committed enough to pledge, he or she can afford a stamp. The purpose of the stamp is not to save donors money. It is to make it as easy as possible for them to pay their pledge in a timely fashion and to show respect for the commitment they have made. Do not set up a pledge program only to undermine it with these types of penny-pinching measures.

And finally don't set up any pledge program unless you are confident that your record keeping and accounting systems are adequate to handle it. This is particularly important for EFT and credit card collections, which involve banks — institutions that have long and unforgiving memories.

16.

Major Gifts Campaigns

Once an organization has mastered the process of identifying prospects and asking them for money and has a working major gifts program, it is ready to consider moving to a more formal campaign. The two major differences between an ongoing major gifts program and a major gifts campaign is that a campaign is time-limited (it begins and ends on specific dates) and the goal of the campaign is made public. Although a major gifts program has a goal that is part of the overall fundraising plan, the program is in place all year but the goal is not necessarily public. Because a major gifts campaign is time-limited and public, it also provides an opportunity to get publicity about the overall needs of the organization.

During the time of the major gifts campaign, a few volunteers devote themselves intensively to meeting a specific financial goal, giving amounts of time and effort to the campaign that would be difficult to maintain beyond a short commitment.

The Steps of a Major Gifts Campaign

A major gifts campaign requires nine steps, some of which are the same as for any major gifts program. The steps are listed below, then discussed in detail.

1. Set a goal for the amount to be raised and the length of the campaign

2. Identify and train solicitors

3. Identify prospects

4. Prepare supporting materials

5. Assign prospects and solicit gifts

6. Kick off the campaign with a special event (optional, though it can attract media attention and recognize donors)

7. Hold regular reporting meetings to discuss progress and boost morale of campaign volunteers

8. Celebrate the end of a successful campaign with a special event (also optional, though it can attract media and recognize donors)

9. Thank donors, record gifts, and incorporate new donors into ongoing fundraising efforts

1. Set a Goal

The first step in a major gifts campaign is to decide how long the campaign will last and how much money will be raised. For small organizations, a campaign of six to twelve weeks is ideal. To determine a fundraising goal, first calculate how many prospects could be asked in that length of time. Generally a volunteer can ask about five people a month for three months without undue strain. A committee of five volunteers, then, could ask 75 people during three months. Assuming the usual 50 percent rate of success, your group would have about 37 or 38 new donors after such a campaign.

If you have a shortage of volunteers, ask each volunteer to solicit more people per month, but don't expect anyone except full-time volunteers to be able to ask more than ten people in one month unless they are very well connected, comfortable and familiar with asking for money, and can get a number of the gifts with just a phone call.

Knowing how many gifts you can get, now plot how many gifts of specific amounts you will need to reach your goal as follows: Select the lowest amount that will be solicited in face-to-face meetings. Most groups chose $250 as the minimum request for which they will seek a meeting, but many also choose $100. (Rarely would it be worth the time to make face-to-face solicitations for less than $100).

Next determine what your largest gift will be. A rule of thumb is to make the largest gift 10 percent of the total goal. You can also go with the annual major gift formula, which calls for two gifts at 5 percent each of the goal (described in Chapter 14, Major Gifts Programs). With the largest and lowest gifts decided on, you can now chart what size gifts you will need and how many of each to meet the goal. A campaign for $25,000 might look like the chart on the next page.

Assuming a 50 percent rate of rejection, and that half who say yes give less than what was asked for, you would need to ask three to four times as many prospects. To accomplish this $25,000 campaign, then, you would need approximately 20 to 26 people soliciting five people per month for three months.

Goal: $25,000

Gift Size	# of gifts needed	Total
$2,500	1	$2,500
1,000	5	5,000
500	10	5,000
250	30	7,500
100	50	5,000
Total	**96**	**$25,000**

When you make your chart, don't get bogged down. There is no scientific way to do it. Basically, the chart is a triangle with fewer people at the top and more people at the bottom. (In less populated areas, such as rural communities, you might need to have even larger gifts from even fewer people than this chart indicates.) The point of the chart is to recognize that not everyone will give the same amount and to set a limit on the number of people needing to be solicited. Share this chart with prospects and donors; it lets them know that the group has planned the campaign and knows what it is doing.

If you are doing a campaign for the first time, set your goal lower than you think is reasonable so that you are almost bound to make it. This will give an early sense of accomplishment and provide momentum to future campaigns.

2. Identify and Train Solicitors

Invite people to be on the campaign committee as solicitors, assembling the number of people you need to meet your goals. Committee members should fulfill two simple commitments, with a third commitment optional. First, each member should themselves be giving a gift that is significant to them; ideally that gift would be one of those on the gift range chart. Second, each member must agree to solicit a certain number of prospects each month for a certain number of months. Third, and optional, is for members of the committee to provide names of prospects for the master list. If your committee does not provide these names, then you will need another way to get them.

Once enough people have agreed to serve on the committee, set a meeting for them to be briefed about the campaign and taught how to ask for money. The meeting should last about three hours. The agenda includes:

- Overview of the campaign and the organization's need for money (20 minutes)
- Training in how to ask for money including practice solicitation (2 hours), and distributing prospect names (covered below)
- Responding to final questions and setting next meeting time (40 minutes).

The staff or fundraising committee of the board should conduct the meeting, but many groups find it helpful to have an outside trainer lead the training in how to ask for money (see also Chapter 12, Personal Solicitation). It is imperative that every person on the committee be at this training even if they have participated in fundraising solicitations before. The experience of people who know how to do it will be of great benefit to those who are feeling unsure. The committee should have a sense of itself as a team and should develop a strong camaraderie from the very beginning.

In addition to teaching people how to ask for money, distribute the prepared supporting materials as described in Step 4, and assign prospects as described in Step 5.

3. Identify Prospects

Review Chapter 12, Personal Solicitation, for the basics on prospect identification. Ask members of the committee for names of people they know and review your list of current donors to identify people who have given a major gift, people who have the ability to give a major gift, or people who should be asked to give more this year. (For example, anyone on your list who has given the same large donation for two or more years ought to be asked to increase their gift, and this campaign provides an excellent way for this to happen.) Unlike an informal, ongoing program, in a campaign all the prospects must be identified before the campaign can begin.

Now prepare a master list of all the prospects as follows:

Master Tracking Form

Prospect name	Asked for	Solicitor	Outcome	Thank you sent

On separate cards or in a different file on your computer, keep the address, phone number and other prospect information needed for each prospect. Personal information should only be given to the person soliciting the prospect and should not be available to the rest of the committee. Everyone on the committee should receive a copy of the master tracking form. No one should be solicited who is not on the master list to ensure that no one is asked by two people.

All of this information is highly confidential and solicitors must be people who have a clear sense of discretion and can be trusted.

If you have trouble identifying the number of prospects you need, you may wish to lower the goal of your campaign, or to continue your regular major gifts program for a while longer before moving into a campaign.

4. Prepare Supporting Materials

A campaign needs a number of materials for solicitors to use, some of which will already exist in your organization and some of which will need to be created for the campaign. The supporting materials are of two types: a) materials that solicitors will give to donors; and b) materials that are for the solicitors' use only, or that relate to the campaign committee.

For the solicitor to use with donors you will need:

◆ **A campaign brochure:** The brochure, which can be simple and inexpensively produced, spells out the goal of the campaign, the gifts that are needed, and the history of the organization. It invites donors to a celebration at the end of the campaign (if you are having one) and tells them what they get for their money. If you are giving people special benefits for giving to this campaign, list them here. A book, their name on a plaque at the organization, a specially created artwork are all very nice benefits. The benefit should not cost more than $5 per donor. While not imperative, special benefits have an appeal to many donors. Some donors will give more to get the benefit, some will give the same amount regardless of a benefit offer, and a few will tell you that the money could be better spent and will refuse the benefit. Whether to go to the trouble of having a special benefit will depend a lot on your organizational culture, what benefits you have access to, and how the solicitors feel about the need for them.

◆ **A pledge card:** This is a small card on which the solicitor notes the donor's name, what he or she has agreed to give and the method of payment (filled out by the solicitor). Once the solicitation is complete and the card filled out, it is returned to the office and is kept as part of the permanent record on the donor.

◆ **Stationery, envelopes and return envelopes:** Have enough for all the prospects and extras for mistakes. This is used for both initial letters and thank-you notes. It is not necessary or useful to create special stationery or envelopes.

For the solicitors' or committee use only:

◆ A timeline of the campaign steps

◆ A complete description of the campaign and some soliciting tips

◆ A budget of the overall organization

◆ A list of difficult and commonly asked questions about the organization and possible answers

◆ A list of the other solicitors and whom to call for more information

All of these materials should be put together in a "Campaigner's Notebook," which can be as simple as a manila folder, but looks nice, has the name of the campaigner on it, and seems official.

At the training meeting, each person is given a copy of the materials and all the materials are reviewed. In addition each person will be given a copy of the master prospect list and the cards with more personal information about each of their prospects.

5. Assign Prospects and Solicit Gifts

At the meeting, after the solicitors are trained and familiar with the materials and the campaign, they are each given a master prospect list and asked to read through it and choose which prospects they will solicit. Each person should write down the prospects he or she would be willing to solicit, then read his or her list out loud. Everyone else listens for duplication. Should two solicitors have the same person on their lists, they briefly discuss and decide right there which of them will take the prospect (they also have the option of going together to see the prospect). As the names are read aloud and assigned, the group should decide how much each prospect will be asked for. At the end it should be clear that everyone has different prospects and no one prospect will be solicited twice. Having everyone read their lists out loud also helps to ensure that prospects are being asked for the right amount and that the right person is doing the asking. Solicitation can now begin.

6. Kick Off Campaign with a Special Event (optional)

This is not a gala affair, but the press might be invited, as well as all the prospects and all the solicitors. Wine, soft drinks, and hors d'oeuvres should be served. Someone from the committee should give an impassioned, enthusiastic and articulate but brief speech about the campaign, including its goals, the need for the organization, what donors will receive for their gifts (if you have benefits, hold them up for everyone to see). The speech ends with, "We will be contacting all of you individually in the next few weeks to see what questions you have and whether you can help in this important endeavor."

An event can be educational for prospects, informing them of the need, and it also provides a time for people to see who else is involved and who is giving — this peer identification adds an important element to the desire to give.

For campaigns covering large areas (such as whole states or large rural areas) a series of small events would be appropriate.

7. Hold Regular Reporting Meetings

Regular reporting meetings enable solicitors to discuss progress and they boost the morale of campaign volunteers. These meetings should take place at least once every two weeks, and preferably weekly during the campaign. The meetings only last 30 to 45 minutes; many groups hold them over breakfast at 7:30 a.m. so people can attend them before work. The purpose of the meetings is to give everyone a chance to report their progress, which forces everyone to have made some progress between meetings. They can share frustrations, fears and successes. A report on the progress toward the goal should be made (possibly using an illustration, like a thermometer or some other measure). Any additional materials (brochures, return envelopes, extra stationery) can be given out then as well. Again, if a group covers a large area, meetings may not be possible, but phone check-ins become imperative.

8. Celebrate the End of the Campaign with a Special Event (optional)

Though optional, this is an excellent way to recognize and reward the committee as well as the donors. A simple wine and cheese reception from 5 to 7 in the evening, with a speech announcing the successful conclusion of the campaign is fine. Some groups have formal dinners, or ground-breaking ceremonies in the case of capital campaigns, but it is not necessary to be elaborate — simply gracious, warm and rewarding to volunteers.

9. Recognize Donors and Incorporate Them into Ongoing Fundraising Efforts

Aside from raising money, a major donor campaign strengthens donor loyalty, brings in new donors, and upgrades current donors. You need to be in regular touch with all these donors through a newsletter and occasional personal correspondence. Major donors do not get the regular mail appeals that other donors get, so must be kept abreast of the organization in other ways. Major donors, like all donors, must be thanked promptly, and there has to be a method by which the solicitor knows which of her or his prospects has sent in money. All donors to the campaign should receive another thank you at the successful end of the campaign, telling them the organization was able to raise its goal, and stressing again the work you will be able to do with this money.

Major gifts campaigns must be done right to succeed. Don't try to take shortcuts or launch the campaign without proper preparation. A major gift campaign should be both fun and lucrative, and a reward for good planning and good organizing.

17.

Capital Campaigns

A "capital campaign" is a technique for raising money for a one-time need over and above the annual budget. Capital campaigns are usually used to finance buying, building or refurbishing a building; they are being used more and more frequently to begin an endowment. The financial goal of a capital campaign should be at least as large as the organization's annual budget; often it is many times larger. Capital campaigns last from two or three years to five years, and allow donors to pledge a large amount and pay it off over over the course of the campaign or longer (for very large pledges, up to ten years). Donors are asked to give to the capital campaign in addition to their annual gifts, and are explicitly asked not to decrease their annual gift in order to make a capital gift. Capital gifts are extra gifts.

There are no hard and fast rules for how to conduct a capital campaign. In fact, some grassroots groups have conducted "capital campaigns" to buy new computers or send staff to fundraising workshops, which meant their goal was $5,000 or less, their time frame was a few weeks, and people were simply asked to put in a few extra dollars. However, capital campaigns are best used to seek gifts of assets from a wide pool of people and institutions, and not just to seek "something extra" from the annual incomes of current donors (special appeals work as well for that purpose).

They should begin with a goal of no less than $100,000. For needs of less than $100,000, conduct a major gift campaign as described in the last chapter or seek two or three foundation or corporate grants to meet the goal.

Capital campaigns should be aimed at those people among your donor base who may own property or securities and at people who would not help you with a major gift every year, but might give you a big gift once in a while. Generally, the smallest gift one seeks for a capital campaign is $1000. (As in all fundraising, every gift is welcomed and helpful, but people who can afford and are committed to giving to capital campaigns should be able to give at least $1000, particularly if they spread their payments over three to five years.) Capital campaigns can also be used to raise money from corporations, government, foundations, or religious institutions that might not support any of your annual program work.

While your most loyal annual donors will also give to a capital campaign if they can, there are many other kinds of people who give to capital campaigns and are not regular annual donors. For example, a small community organization in Alabama filed a lawsuit against the city they worked in. The attorney who helped with the suit admired the group's feistiness and willingness to take risks. She also admired the sole staff person for working for a low salary and the volunteers for the amount of time they put into the organization on top of their own paid jobs. For these reasons, she handled the lawsuit on a pro bono basis and gave $50 once after that, but because she did not wish to become a regular donor to this group, she did not respond to their annual appeals.

A while later, the group decided to buy a building and asked her to make a lead gift of $20,000. Her pro bono lawsuit had been worth about that much (showing she could probably afford this amount), and they counted on the fact that she still admired them. She did, and she admired their boldness in asking her. She gave $10,000 outright and an additional $10,000 as a challenge to be met by other lawyers. She also told the group not to ask her again.

Universities and private schools often have the experience of an alumnus or alumna who has been a minimal donor prior to a capital campaign making a one-time large gift. Some people like the idea of contributing to something as substantial as a building.

To ask donors to stretch their own giving and to seek donations outside of the "donor family" means having a goal where stretching to meet it is implicit. It must seem to a prospect that the group cannot get this money simply by asking a few people or writing a grant proposal. For grassroots organizations, campaigns of at least $100,000 will give that impression.

Beginning a Capital Campaign

The first step is for the organization to agree that a need exists. The board of directors must fully concur that this is a need and must support the idea of conducting a capital campaign, which is a lot of extra work for everyone and may require an initial outlay of money to hire extra staff and to print materials. Key volunteers who are not on the board and long-time major donors should also be consulted about doing a campaign so that everyone has an opportunity to voice their concerns and to feel part of the decision. There are dozens of buildings in the United States that stand partially finished and seriously underutilized because key people in the organization did not like the idea of building a new building or did not like the proposed use of it and did not have a forum to air their concerns. In other instances, campaigns have had to be called off half-way through because many volunteers and donors had left the organization to protest doing the campaign in the first place. A capital campaign is a very visible activity, and all the people who are important to your organization need to feel good when they see or read about the campaign.

After all the parties have been consulted and there is general agreement on the need, a price tag needs to be set. Similar to the rule of thumb that in a fancy restaurant the total cost of the meal will be double the entree (with appetizer, dessert, drinks and tip), the true cost of a campaign is substantially more than the cost of the project itself. One group recently learned this the hard way. They needed larger office space and decided that buying a building would, in the long run, be less expensive than continually paying rent. They found a building that suited them for $250,000. The owner, happy to sell them the building, offered to remodel it to their specifications as his contribution. The group launched their campaign for the $250,000 cost of the building, forgetting that the price of the building is only part of the cost. When other costs, such as fundraising materials, furniture, insurance, etc. were added in, the true cost of the campaign grew to $310,000 and the organization spent two more years climbing out of a deficit caused by their lack of thinking the whole project through.

The following items need to be added to any actual cost of constructing or buying a building or starting an endowment:

♦ **Fundraising materials.** These can include a case statement, brochures, pledge cards, background information for solicitors, pictures, architect's renderings, special newsletter to capital campaign donors to keep them informed of progress, and a prospectus (see below).

♦ **Cost of staff time.** Someone has to handle pledges, write thank-you notes, report to the board, work with the contractor, decide who will approve paint color or carpet choices, know what to do when someone donates stocks, and handle emergencies. Someone must set up a record keeping system to keep the campaign's income and expenses separate from the annual budget, and to collect pledges (a process that may extend well past the end of the campaign). If you plan to use current staff to do that, then someone will have to do some of their work. In a multi-year campaign, it is unlikely that a group could get by without hiring any extra staff.

♦ **Office extras.** You may need to put in an extra phone, or buy an additional computer. If you hire staff, you may need another desk and chair, filing cabinet, computer, etc.

♦ **For the building project itself.** Someone with expertise in this area will need to help you list costs related to the building. These can include insurance, building permits, design costs, earthquake/hurricane/tornado protection and/or insurance, fire extinguishers, landscaping. In addition, an experienced person can help you estimate how much to budget for cost overruns or unforeseen delays.

♦ **If you are starting an endowment,** you will need to decide how these funds will be invested. You may need to hire a consultant to research the possibilities and make a recommendation to the board.

♦ **Add 15 percent** to cover donors who cannot or decide not to finish paying their pledge. (This will also cover the cost of borrowing money against pledged income that has not come in, which may be required to pay costs that are incurred before pledges are paid. Banks will lend money with pledges as collateral, but you have to pay interest on the loan.)

♦ **Add an additional 10 percent** to the total of everything and you can feel reasonably safe that this will be the cost of the campaign.

Preparing a Case Statement

With the need and cost known and provisionally approved, the organization writes up a case statement for the campaign. This case statement is separate from the organization's overall case statement, although certainly it borrows from it. The capital campaign case focusses on the goal of the campaign alone, and shows how this goal will help the organization meet all its other goals. The case statement implies or overtly states that the work of the group will be significantly slowed down or impaired by the lack of the building, endowment or other project being proposed for the capital campaign. The final page of the case statement is the financial goal displayed as a gift range chart.

The Gift Range Chart

As noted in Chapter 14, Major Gifts Programs, a gift range chart for an annual campaign requires two gifts at 5 percent each of the goal, and a total of 60 percent of the money coming from 10 percent of the donors. A capital campaign gift range chart is much shorter and narrower, with 80 percent of the money coming from about 10 percent of the donors and one gift equal to 10 percent of the total goal.

The chart follows this pattern:

- ◆ 1 gift = 10 percent or more of goal
- ◆ 2 gifts = 5 percent each or more
- ◆ 4 to 5 gifts = 4 percent each or more

After these lead gifts, the number of gifts increases as the gift size decreases in a proportion that makes sense for your group and number of prospects until the goal is reached. However, 40 to 50 percent of the goal should come from about eight gifts. Here is an example:

Goal: $500,000

# Gifts	Gift Size	Cumulative total
1	$50,000	$ 50,000
2	25,000	100,000
5	20,000	250,000
10	10,000	350,000
15	5,000	425,000
20	2,500	475,000
25	1,000	500,000

In this example, 77 gifts will be required. Applying our knowledge of how many prospects will need to be identified, this campaign will need to identify 308 prospects (77 X 4, allowing for half to say no, and half of the half that say yes to give less than is asked for). All of these people will have to be asked in person, and some of them may have to be visited more than once. If any of these gift amounts come from foundations or corporations, proposals will have to be written. Looking for four times as many prospects as donors needed rather than the overall three times that is required for an annual campaign will give the group a little padding to make up for those people who give less than $1000.

Sometimes grassroots organizations are upset with the idea of seeking only gifts of $1000 or more. However, when they do the math of how many people it takes to reach a capital campaign goal and how many people have to be asked, they usually see the logic of aiming the capital campaign largely at people who can give big gifts once in a while.

The final decision the organization must make is about timing of the campaign. You need to look at what other capital or intensive fundraising campaigns are going on during the time you wish to run your campaign, and assess whether any of your prospects will be key prospects for those groups. You need to launch your campaign during years when you expect your annual campaign to be doing well and you need to make sure you do not anticipate any shortfalls in annual income. During the time of the capital campaign, your annual income will not be able to rise, so you must not plan major new programs outside of the capital project.

Once you have prepared the case statement, with costs, gift range chart and timing included, bring the whole package back to the board, key volunteers and staff for final approval. While people may have approved the concept of the campaign, when faced with the realities of the money and time involved, they may wish to change their minds. Without full board and staff ownership, the campaign will fail. Taking the time to make sure that everyone understands the implications of the campaign is imperative because once the campaign is launched publicly, it must be seen through to the end.

Four Stages

A capital campaign is conducted in four stages. The first stage is the "pre-campaign" and starts when the case statement is ready and approved. The second stage is the "launching" stage, which is when the campaign is publicly announced and begins to seek support from beyond the inner circle of donors. The third stage is the longest — it is the "intensive" stage. This is the stage where solicitors are out visiting prospects and gathering commitments. When the campaign has reached anywhere from 75 to 90 percent of its goal, the "wind-up" stage (sometimes called the "topping off" stage) begins.

The Pre-Campaign

You may have noticed that most often people announce capital campaigns by saying, "We are proud to launch our $2 million building campaign today, and are pleased to report that we already have $1.3 million pledged." Do you wonder how could they have raised all that money in just one day? Of course, that money was not raised in a day — in fact, it may have been raised over a period of months or even years during the pre-campaign stage.

The purpose of the pre-campaign is two-fold: first, it is to test the concept of the campaign on people who could actually pay for it. Everyone can feel good about the case and the need for this campaign, but the true test is whether people feel good enough about it to give a big gift. Some campaigns have to be abandoned or seriously re-thought at this phase, but no real harm is done because the campaign has not been made public. The second purpose is to give a feeling of momentum at the public launching of the campaign. The response one wants from the people at the launching is, "Wow, that's great they have so much money already. My gift can move them forward."

The goal of the pre-campaign is to get 30 to 40 percent of the total campaign goal from the top three to five donors. Most fundraisers feel that if you can get the lead (which means the largest first gifts, not just the first gifts that come from board members and volunteers) you will be able to find all the gifts. This sounds like a superstition, but there is much anecdotal evidence to show that this is true. Lead gifts provide a confidence and momentum in the fundraisers and encourage them to work hard getting the other gifts.

Conversely, starting a capital campaign without lead gifts is dangerous because the momentum lags, and if a group doesn't know possible lead donors at the beginning of the campaign it is unlikely to meet them later. It is worth postponing a campaign for months or even years in order to ensure that the first gifts given are also the largest. At the risk of redundancy, let me repeat: an organization does not need to know all of its prospects ahead of time, but it must know the ones capable of making the lead gifts.

The Lead Gifts

The lead donors must not only be able to give big gifts, but must also be people who like to set the pace, to set an example and to take a leadership role. These first large gifts come from people who will take a risk with you that the campaign will succeed and actually pride themselves on being risk-takers. Obviously, they must care very much about your cause and be committed to the capital project. Usually (and ideally), the lead gifts come from a few people who were involved in the planning and approval of the campaign. If those people are not able to give the biggest gifts, they need to know people or institutions who can.

Approaching the Lead Prospects

The process of approaching these people is the same as approaching any major donor, with one slight change. In asking for a major gift to an annual campaign, it is reasonable to assume that most people will give an answer at the meeting or shortly thereafter. With requests for capital gifts, an answer almost never comes at the meeting, and often the prospect wants more information that must be sent or brought to a subsequent meeting. When prospects seem to be stalling or wanting more information, see it as a good sign. A person who says yes to a request for $10,000 in one meeting may be someone who has thought a great deal about the campaign and made their decision, but it also may be someone for whom $10,000 is not a "stretch" gift. Don't be discouraged by prospects wanting to think about it more: making a capital gift is a big decision. Even very wealthy people can't afford to give capital gifts very often and they want to make sure their gift will be well used.

These gifts should be solicited by teams of two people — usually a board member and a staff person, or two board members. The board members must be giving what is a stretch gift for them and should be willing to share information about their gift with the prospect. For example, "I am giving ten times my annual gift to this campaign and paying my pledge over five years." Or, "My husband and I decided this endeavor was as important as our car, so we are giving the same amount as our car payment over the next two years." If the solicitor feels comfortable, he or she may share how much their gift is. The point to make clear to the prospect is that the people asking are giving as much as they can possibly afford and their gift has been made after a lot of thought. They are hoping the prospect will make a similar commitment.

The case statement can be shared with the lead donors and they should also be asked if they are willing to help solicit other gifts. It is flattering and sometimes emotionally moving to be asked for a gift by someone who has given the biggest gift.

Once the very top of the pyramid has been filled in with donors, the group is ready to move to the second stage.

The Launch

The launch of a capital campaign should be marked with a special event. The press, donors, volunteers, foundation and corporate staff should be invited. (The press should be sent or handed a press release that provides all the details.) The invitation to the launch should be very nice because it is the first impression most prospects will have of your capital campaign. The event itself doesn't need to last very long. If you want to make it into a regular special event, you can add a dance or speaker, but this is not necessary.

Large graphics about the campaign should be on display showing how much money has been raised, the gift range chart, and describing the overall goal of the campaign. A board member describes to the gathered crowd how important the campaign is and invites everyone to celebrate how much has been raised so far. Champagne and hors d'oeuvres are served.

The Prospectus

For the launch, you will need to design a document called the "prospectus," which is a brochure or booklet or folder using information from the case statement, but in a shorter and more attractive form. The prospectus will be given to all prospects and it must look good. The prospectus shows the prospect that you know what you are doing and that your group is able to handle these large amounts of money and manage this large capital project. The prospectus includes a statement about the need for the capital project, any drawings or renderings of a proposed building or refurbishing, the gift range chart and summary of money raised to date, a letter from the board restating the importance of the campaign, and a description of the ways a donor can give, such as pledging over a number of years, giving stock, or other methods.

The Intensive Stage

Immediately after the launch the intensive stage begins. Here teams of two people visit prospects with as much speed as that process will allow. Most prospects should be visited at least once during this time. This stage is the longest. As each gift is received, the cumulative total is announced to board, staff and, when possible, donors, so there is a constant sense of movement toward the goal. During this stage, the two most important elements are good record keeping and keeping in touch with volunteer solicitors. Thank-you notes must go out promptly. When people pledge to pay over several years, they must sign a pledge agreement. It can be very simple:

> I, (name), pledge the sum of $____ to be paid in monthly/quarterly installments of $____ for the next ____ years. This is a morally binding pledge, and I know that plans are being made and money is being

spent based on the expectation that I will pay this pledge in the way I have described.

Signed:

The system for collecting pledges, as described in Chapter 15, Pledge Programs, must be in place.

Solicitors must be notified of new gifts and must meet regularly (about every three weeks) to report to staff and each other on their progress. Any problems they encounter must be dealt with promptly. Often prospects will offer to make a gift on certain conditions ("I'll give if three other people match my gift," or "I'll give if the conference room can be named for my mother," or "I'll give if I can have a seat on the board.") Conditional gifts, regardless of how benign the condition is, must go through an approval process at the board level. Solicitors can say to prospects, "That's a very kind offer. Let me see what we can do about it. I don't have the authority to make those promises but I'll get back to you within two weeks." Then the group decides if it wishes to abide by the condition or not. Don't ever take money on conditions that you don't wish to meet. People should not be able to "buy" board seats, for example.

The "Wind-Up" Stage

When more than three-fourths of the money has been pledged, the group goes into a wind-up phase. Here you look for one or two people who can put the goal over the top: "Mr. Jones, we are $10,000 short of our goal — would you finish this campaign with your gift?" To find people who will do that, go back to your original prospects for the lead gifts and see if any of them did not give because they were too cautious or see if any of them said, "Come back to me when you are further along." The wind-up phase is a good time to ask corporations to give, as they will like the publicity of being key to concluding a campaign.

The wind-up phase ends with a large celebratory special event. If you are constructing or renovating a building, this is often a ribbon-cutting or possibly a ground-breaking event (if that hasn't happened already.)

The Post-Campaign

Volunteer solicitors should be given their own party, such as dinner at a fancy restaurant, and should be presented with gifts of appreciation. These are often plaques. The gifts should not be expensive, but should affirm the importance of their work to the campaign. Staff should also be rewarded at this party.

Staff and solicitors should review all records about donors to make sure they are accurate and that all documentation needed is in place.

As you can see, a capital campaign is time consuming and requires keeping track of a lot of detail. Only organizations with a strong working board of directors, a loyal donor base, and a well-designed major gifts program should undertake such a campaign.

18.

Planned Giving

P ossibly the ultimate statement of faith a donor can make in the need for and stability of an organization is to leave that organization money from his or her estate. Gifts from an estate, called "planned gifts," are almost always given by very thoughtful donors who have been part of an organization's life for a long time.

Although planned gifts can be used for annual or capital expenses, the main use of planned giving is to build an endowment. An endowment is an income-generating mechanism that involves setting aside money (principal) to generate interest. The principal, or corpus, is never spent; the interest income can be used as the organization wishes unless the gift has been restricted by the terms of the donor. Interest income is usually used to offset administrative costs since these are the most difficult to raise funds for.

Thinking About Asking

Grassroots organizations rarely get planned gifts and even more rarely seek them. A grassroots group is usually too busy trying to meet the next month's expenses to look that far ahead and often does not think of itself as a permanent institution.

Probably the main reason any organization hesitates to seek planned gifts is a universal one: people feel awkward talking to anyone about their death and especially about their money and their death at the same time. As one board member put it, "It's hard enough to ask for a gift from a living person that they make now; asking for a gift that requires the person giving it to die before we can get it is really in bad taste."

However, as I pointed out in Chapter 1, Philanthropy in America, in the United States bequests (which are the most common form of planned giving) account for five percent of all the money given to charitable causes by the private sector. This is a substantial amount of money. In fact, gifts from bequests are equal to the amount given by foundations and greater than the amount given by corporations. (An old joke in fundraising is that dead people give away more money than corporations. This is used to illustrate how minimal corporate giving is relative to the publicity they receive for it.) Other forms of planned giving, such as charitable remainder trusts, pooled income funds, lead trusts and so on (explained in this chapter), account for hundreds of millions more dollars.

Advantages to Donors

There are many advantages of planned giving for donors. These advantages should be accentuated and should give you courage to talk with your donors about planned giving. A bequest, for example, costs the donor nothing. It is deducted from the estate of the donor, lowering the amount of estate tax that will be owed.

Estates are currently taxed at the rate of 55 percent of their worth, which is higher than income tax or capital gains tax rates. Estates of less than $600,000 are not taxed. However, many people who have never considered themselves well-to-do will leave estates with greater than $600,000 value, once the value of appreciated property (real estate, stocks, IRAs, etc.) is taken into account.

Many forms of planned giving go into effect during the donor's lifetime and, in addition to lowering estate taxes or, in the case of irrevocable trusts, avoiding probate altogether, can pay the donor or save the donor money. (Probate is the judicial administration of estates, including the verification of a will, if one exists.)

What is most important about planned giving is that it allows a donor to help ensure that what he or she stands for and believes in and contributes to will continue into the future. People who have supported an organization for years and years have a chance, at little or no cost to themselves, to see that the organization continues to be supported after they have died.

The Importance of a Will

Almost all planned gifts, from the simplest bequest to the most complicated generation-skipping lead trust are made with terms laid out in a will.

Everyone should have a will because anything you own during your lifetime you also own after your death and you have the authority to direct what happens to your property after you have died. But seven out of ten people don't have a will, and of the 30 percent who do have a will, half leave their entire estate to their spouse. To get a sense of just how much money is distributed from estates without wills, in 1989 $100,000,000 a week went through probate courts in the United States from estates without wills!

Introducing your donors to planned giving is a service to them because it causes them to think about getting their wills made or updated. This may mean that your nonprofit group gets some money, but it also protects the donor's family and other interests.

If you die without a will (called "dying intestate"), the law specifies who will receive your estate:

♦ If you are survived by a spouse and not survived by a child or parent, your spouse receives all your property.

♦ If you are survived by a spouse and a parent (and not a child), your spouse and your parent share your property.

♦ If you are survived by a spouse, child and a parent, your spouse and your child share your property, and your parent receives nothing.

♦ If you are not survived by a spouse or a child or a parent, your brothers and sisters and the children of your deceased brothers and sisters share your property.

Motivating Donors to Make a Will

The first step in planned giving is to convince your donors that they need a will. The second step is to encourage them to leave something to your organization in their will. A few case studies about what happens to people who don't have wills motivates most donors to create one.

Names have been changed in the two examples that follow, but they are true stories.

A 40-year-old woman we'll call Mary Springhill died of breast cancer. She had no children and her parents were deceased. She was separated but not divorced from her husband. Legally, he is the surviving spouse. Mary was a successful artist and her estate, including a house, a new car, and some savings, is worth a little over $400,000. Mary had never gotten around to writing a will. Then, during the time she had cancer, she was too sick to think about preparing one. Mary had left her husband three years prior to her death after enduring his physical and emotional abuse for more than 15 years. Now he is the beneficiary of her entire estate.

Pro-choice activist Alice Williams, age 33, was recently killed in a car accident. She and her parents had clashed about her pro-choice views as well as her generally progressive attitude toward many issues. Her parents were active in their fundamentalist Baptist church and had told their daughter on a number of occasions that she was "going to hell." Although they were on speaking terms and Alice spent some holidays with them, their relationship was very strained. Alice believed she was too young to need a will and that her estate did not warrant the cost of going to an attorney to draw one up. (Like many people, Alice erroneously believed that only attorneys can make legally binding wills.) At 21, Alice had inherited $100,000 from an aunt. She had never spent the money, although she occasionally augmented her meager salary with the interest it generated. Through her work, she had a life insurance policy worth $25,000. Without a spouse or children, Alice's estate of $125,000 went to her parents. Alice may not have objected; however, in the belief that the money could, as they put it, "nullify some of the evil work poor Alice had done," her parents gave it all to a variety of anti-abortion organizations.

Especially early on in the AIDS epidemic, a high number of AIDS patients left no wills, causing estates to return to parents who may not have spoken to them in years. Other classic cases involve a daughter caring for an aging parent until the parent's death, then finding that the estate is to be shared equally with a brother or sister who had had no part in the parent's care or the expenses for it.

Most people underestimate the worth of their estate and overestimate the time or cost involved in setting up a will. They do not realize that when there is no will, dealing wth someone's estate is a tremendous amount of work. Finally, besides the distribution of property, a will can carry wishes about how the person wants to be buried, whom they want looking after children or pets, and any other legal or moral obligations heirs need to be aware of.

A Warning Before Proceeding Further

As a nonprofit, you cannot be involved at all in the creation of someone's will. You can encourage people to create a will, you can offer workshops on wills featuring attorneys or estate planners as the workshop leaders, you can discuss what you know about wills with donors, but you must not get involved in giving legal advice or in helping people write their wills. No one in your organization should ever give advice to a current or potential donor about the best planned giving instrument, or provide help to draw up wills or trust agreements, or negotiate any agreement with a donor that has legal ramifications for the donor's estate.

The reason for all these cautions is that people who work for non-profits are subject to being accused of "exerting undue influence," thus opening the way to legal challenge of a will. The way to avoid that accusation is to know only enough about planned giving instruments to give general information. Each donor must confer with his or her lawyer and financial planner, as well as other family members, before making any decision as final as many of these estate decisions are. As a representative of your organization, you can attend some of these meetings, and you will want to confer with your own lawyer concerning planned gifts that require your organization to be a trustee. Your organization's board of directors should also be fully informed before any commitments to donors are made.

The Bequest

The simplest form of planned giving is the bequest — that is, something left to a charity in a will. Most organizations start with bequests; many seek only bequests and do not set up any of the more complicated forms of planned giving.

One of the most famous and oldest bequests was given by Ben Franklin in 1790. He left the equivalent of $4000, to be divided between the people of the state of Pennsylvania (76%) and the city of Philadelphia (24%) on the condition it not be touched for 200 years. In 1990 the 200 years was up; Franklin's bequest was worth $2.3 million. A group of Franklin scholars given authority to recommend the best use of the money decided that the city's money be kept in a permanent endowment at the Philadelphia Foundation and the state's money be shared between the Franklin Institute and a consortium of community foundations around the state.

Making a Bequest

Anyone can make a bequest. All that is required is that you are alive and of sound mind when you make your will, and that you own something that you can't take with you. Many grassroots groups think that bequests are only for wealthy people. In fact, however, if all you own is a 1976 Chevy Nova, you can leave that car to a nonprofit organization and they can sell it for $200 and have the money.

In 1987, an 84-year-old woman in east Tennessee left her church a bequest that equalled $50,000. She had never earned more than $3,000 a year and lived on her Social Security income and from the vegetables she grew in her garden. Her husband and son had been killed in a mining accident and she had no other relatives. Being very poor, many of her needs were taken care of by the members of her church. The value of her bequest came from the value of the land she lived on and two antique quilts she owned. Her story is dramatic but not unusual, as most people have more "hard" assets than liquid assets.

All bequests are revocable during the life of the donor — a will can be changed any number of times. Your organization may be included in one will and left out of a later version. Thus unrealized bequests (bequests promised to you but not yet available) cannot ethically be counted toward a fundraising goal.

Wording of Bequests

The General Bequest

This is the simplest bequest, where a donor gives a stated amount to the nonprofit group without attaching any conditions. This bequest reads as follows:

> "I give and bequeath to (exact name of your organization) the sum of $___ (or a specific piece of property) to be used as the board of directors directs."

To be absolutely certain there is no confusion about which nonprofit organization the donor meant, it is a good idea to include the address of the group.

Income Only to be Used

> "I give and bequeath to (name of the organization) the sum of $___ to be invested or reinvested so that the income only may be used as the board of directors directs."

Request of a Percentage

> "I give and bequeath ___ percent (name a specific percentage) of the total value of my estate to (name of organization)."

Bequest of Residue

This is a provision in a will leaving the remainder of one's estate to an organization after all other bequests are fulfilled.

"The rest, residue and remainder of my estate, both real and personal, wherever situated, I give and bequeath to (name of organization) to be used as the board of directors directs."

Contingent Bequest

This leaves a bequest to the nonprofit if any of the other beneficiaries are unable to receive their bequests because of death or other circumstances. Everyone should have a contingent bequest in their will in case the will is quite dated and circumstances have changed since it was drawn up.

"Should (name of person) predecease me, the portion of my estate going to (person) I give and bequeath to (name of organization)."

Designated Bequest

This provides a sum of money for a specific or designated project or program.

"I give and bequeath to (name of organization) the sum of $___(or the property or percentage) to be used for (specific description of program, scholarship, building, etc.)" Ideally, a designated bequest has some kind of contingency, such as, "Should this program no longer be needed, the bequest may be used as the board of directors directs."

The most flexible bequests (and those best for the nonprofit) are percentage bequests and contingency bequests.

Other Kinds of Planned Gifts

About 60 percent of planned gifts are made as bequests. However, there are several other giving instruments that your organization should know about.

To understand the following planned giving strategies, it is necessary to understand two principles concerning taxes and value. A tax is a fee assessed on the transfer of something of material value from one person or entity to another. When you sell something for a profit, there is a "gains" tax. When your estate is valued at $600,000 or more after your death, an "estate tax" is levied on those who inherit it. One of the few things of value that can be moved from one place to another without tax are gifts to charity. A large function of planned giving, then, in addition to expressing a donor's commitment to a charity, is to lower their capital gains and estate taxes.

The second principle is that everything you own (your assets) has two kinds of value: present value and future value. For example, if I have $1,000 in a savings account earning 10 percent simple interest, I own $1,000 now, but I will own $1,100 in one year, $2,000 in ten years, and so on. From the point of view of a charity, I can give the entire asset now (the $1,000), or I can give the entire asset later (that is, in my lifetime or as a bequest). Or I can split the value, giving some and keeping some — for example, giving the $1,000 principal to a charity, but getting the interest on that principal as long as I live. By giving away one value (the principal) what I keep (the interest) may have more value to me, in part because I have saved myself paying taxes on the larger value, the principal.

With these two principles in mind, you are ready to understand the most common planned giving instruments.

Charitable Gift Annuity

A charitable gift annuity is a contract between a donor and your organization in which your organization agrees to pay the donor a fixed amount of income annually (called the "annuity") during the life of the donor in exchange for money or assets transferred to your organization. The amount of the annuity, which you set, is determined by the value of the gift and the age or life expectancy of the person(s) who will receive the annual income. For large gifts you might want to offer a larger annuity. A person closer to death receives more because of the shorter number of years the annuity will be paid.

Once the amount of the annuity, or annual payment, is fixed, it does not alter regardless of the value of the asset. This benefits the organization when the corpus is able to grow and generate more income than the nonprofit is paying out; however, it can be hard on a group if the value falls. Your organization is legally obligated to continue paying the amount you contracted for regardless of the subsequent value of the asset.

Here's an example: a husband and wife, both age 68, wish to increase their retirement income and make a gift to their favorite cause, which happens to be a church. They give $30,000 to the church, which promises to pay them $2,000 in annual income for as long as either of them lives (which is a return of 6.7 percent per year on the $30,000). The couple is allowed an income-tax deduction on the $30,000 gift and, of the annuity income they receive, the portion generated by the church investing in tax-exempt securities is exempt from income tax.

The church is able to invest the $30,000 in an account that bears 8 percent interest, which generates more than enough money to make the annuity payment and pay the administrative costs. When both donors have died, the church will have the $30,000 plus any interest they have saved beyond their annuity payments to the donors. The donors could probably have gotten more money from a commercial annuity, but they would not have had the tax deduction and they would not have helped their church.

Deferred Payment Gift Annuity

This annuity is like the charitable gift annuity, except the payments are deferred until the donor reaches a certain age. This can be an attractive option for younger donors.

For example, a donor, age 35, wants to make a significant gift and guarantee some retirement income. She has a high income now, so the tax deduction is attractive, but she does not need annuity income. In fact, she wants to defer the income from the annuity until after retirement, when her lower income will mean lower taxes. The calculations for this type of annuity should be done by a professional, as they depend on actuarial tables of the age at which the donor desires payments to begin and the age of the donor at the time of the gift.

Trusts

There are a wide variety of trusts that may or may not include charitable provisions, but there are four that are most commonly used.

Pooled Income Fund

A pooled income fund is similar to a mutual fund. The "pool" is made up of contributions from many donors (although it can start out with just one). The contributions are commingled to minimize investment risk and maximize income. Your organization, or an investment firm you designate and oversee, manages the funds. The donors are each paid an annual amount based on the number of shares they own and the amount of money the fund has earned. This can vary from year to year. All of the income from this type of fund is taxable because a pooled income fund cannot invest in tax-exempt securities. When any particular donor dies, the amount of his or her original investment is removed from the pool and belongs to the charity.

For both charities and donors, the pooled income fund is best for smaller gifts. Where any of the other instruments requires at least $2,000 and often more to be worth setting up, a contribution to a pooled income fund could be as little as $500 and still be worthwhile for the charity, while giving the donor earning potential from a much greater amount of money. (Because larger amounts of money are able to generate more interest, one person's share of the interest from their $500 contribution will be greater if that $500 is part of a $1,000,000 investment than if it is earning interest on its own.) Also, the cost of managing the investment is spread over all the shares in the pool, so only small administrative costs need to be passed on to each donor.

Charitable Remainder Annuity Trust

Like an annuity, the annuity trust pays a fixed amount of income for the life of the donor or beneficiary or for a specific period of time, which cannot exceed 20 years. By law, the annuity cannot be less than 5 percent of the initial fair-market value of the donated asset. The donor can choose how frequently he or she is paid, but it must be at least once a year.

The goal of an annuity trust is maximum income. If the asset makes more than the amount you are paying the donor, you have realized some extra income for your organization. However, if the asset makes less than your required payment, you have to fund the payments out of income accumulated by the trust previously or out of the principal of the trust. From the point of view of the organization, an annuity trust is preferable to an annuity because once you have exhausted the trust principal to maintain your agreed upon payments, the trust collapses and your payment obligations to the donor cease. Of course, you also no longer have the ability to earn money from that donation.

In an annuity, on the other hand, you always owe the donor the amount you contracted for, even if the amount they gave has long since been used up.

Charitable Remainder Unitrust

A unitrust is similar to an annuity trust, except the payout rate (minimum 5 percent) is based on a fixed percentage of the total value of the trust, determined annually. Growth of the corpus, rather than maximum income, is the investment goal here. This type of trust works well for people holding highly appreciated stocks which may not be paying much income. To sell the stocks would incur a huge capital gains liability, but to transfer them to a unitrust will avoid capital gains and will often give the donor a higher return than before. Income to the donor can go up in this arrangement because it is based on the changing value of the fund.

Lead Trusts

The other type of trust you may have read about or heard of is the lead trust. The amounts of money involved in setting up a lead trust are beyond the scope of most institutions. If someone wants to set up a lead trust with your organization, call a lawyer and estate planner for details.

The main difference between the remainder trusts described above and a lead trust is understood again in the split interest theory. In a remainder trust of any kind, the donor gives the "tree" (remainder interest, or what remains after income interest contracts have been satisfied) and keeps the "fruit" (income interest). In a lead trust, the donor keeps the tree and gives the fruit by giving the income from the trust.

What Does All This Mean for Your Organization?

If you have read this far, you have probably thought, as I often have, "I can't understand this, and even if I could, I don't know anyone to whom this could apply, and even if I did, I wouldn't know how to bring it up, and even if I did, they couldn't understand it, or if they did, someone else probably asked them and I am too late."

These feelings and all others of inadequacy are totally normal. However, once you put your mind to learning what you need to know, allowing yourself to not understand all of it, and finding a lawyer or estate planner who does understand more of it, you will realize that planned giving is not that difficult! All along, the obfuscation of planned giving terms and ideas has been part of the structure that keeps small groups small and impermanent.

I have known donors who had a favorite grassroots organization to which they made significant donations and for which they volunteered, only to make planned gifts to their university or another much larger institution. They made this decision because they could not be sure the grassroots group could handle a trust or annuity or other planned gift vehicle. This is a vicious circle, and those of us in fundraising roles in small organizations need to break it by learning as much as we can and convincing some of our bolder older donors to take the leap with us into planned giving. Once a few do it, others will follow.

Introducing Your Planned Giving Program

There are many ways to begin a planned giving program, but for grassroots organizations the best way is also the easiest and most low-key: add a planned giving component to your current mailings. Then add two mailings a year to donors who have identified themselves as interested in learning more about planned giving. Once you and your donors become more familiar and comfortable with planned giving strategies, you can launch a campaign, develop an overall brochure, recruit volunteers to solicit planned gifts, and so on.

Start with your newsletter. Once or twice a year, describe some aspect of planned giving. These articles focus on two things: the need for your organization to exist for a long time, and therefore to have an endowment, and the need for the donor to have a will that expresses his or her commitments. The donor's commitments and your needs join at the moment the donor provides for your organization. Use some real life stories, and give people examples of language they can use to create a codicil (amendment) for their will. Indicate that you are happy to meet with anyone who would like to discuss their estate in more detail.

Many people are happy to answer questionnaires, so one way to introduce planned giving in your newsletter is to include a questionnaire such as the following:

Reviewing Your Plans

Do you have a will? __Yes __No (If the answer is no, stop here and find out how to create one immediately.)

Have your reviewed your will in the last three years?

Have you experienced significant changes since you last reviewed your will (moved to another state, had a child, children got married, bought a house, etc.)?

Have you included a common disaster clause in your will?

Have you included the organization you care about in your will?

Follow this questionnaire with the article.

In every newsletter except the ones with the article, include a notice (like a classified ad) that your organization is receiving bequests and is able to work with other planned giving instruments. The following are two examples of ads:

> If you have provided for (name of your group) in your estate plans, please let us know. If not, let us show you how you can. Call or write: (group's name and address).

> If you had a Gift Annuity with us, you would have received a payment this month. Find out how a gift annuity can benefit you, while you maintain your commitment to us. Call or write (group's name and address).

This is a low-key approach, but begins to make the donors think about the long-term existence of your organization and will generate some inquiries. Best of all, it costs you very little to start your planned giving program this way.

Special Mailings

Between newsletters, start a mailing program with materials specifically geared to planned giving. Many experts recommend mailing to donors four times a year; however, you will have to weigh planned giving mailings with other mailings. A method that works well is to mail a brochure specifically about some aspect of planned giving to all your donors twice a year, including a return coupon for those wanting more information. Donors who respond are then put on a list to receive further mailings.

The first mailing you send to your whole list can be a small booklet called a "Personal Record Book" or "My Records" or something like that to get donors thinking about their wills and therefore about their bequests (see sample pages). This booklet can help people begin to record their assets — the first step in creating a will.

Your organization can order personal record-keeping books in bulk from planned giving consulting firms with the name of your organization on the front, or you can make one up for your donors. Keep them small and thin, not too lengthy. The record book is a nice gift to donors from you at little cost. It causes the donor to think about his or her will, even if the donor simply sets the record book aside to fill out later. Include a return coupon such as the following and an envelope so that people can write for more information. Make sure the return coupon fits in a #7 return envelope.

Return Coupon #1

Please put me on your mailing list to receive information about planned giving strategies.

Please send me specific information about

__ Forms of bequests

__ Charitable remainder trusts

__ Making gifts of property

(List the kinds of planned gifts your group is able to receive)

Name _____

Address _____

_____ Phone _____

☐ I have included (name of your group) in my will.

Those responding with the return coupon now become the base of donors to receive further mailings. Be sure to respond quickly to any requests for information, and if anyone has checked that you are in their will, note that in their donor records and send a thank you.

The second mailing that goes to all donors is either a pamphlet or a special letter that discusses all the possible forms of bequests. It is usually called something simple such as "Giving Through Your Will," and it provides language specific to your organization for any type of bequest a person may make. You can also order these pamphlets in bulk with your name on the front or you can use the language provided in this chapter about bequests.

Again, this mailing goes with a return coupon and return envelope. People who may have meant to write to you before, or who didn't read your previous mailing may respond now. It is not necessary to use a postage-paid envelope. Let the donor provide the stamp.

Space these two mailings six months apart and do them every year. In between, send mail only to those who have asked to be on your planned giving mailing list.

Planned Giving Mailing List

This list is made up of people who have identified themselves as wanting mail about planned giving. This list contains really hot prospects. It also contains names of fundraisers from other organizations who want to see your material, people who love to get mail and write away for everything, and people who thought planned giving meant you were planning to give them something. One job is to sort out the truly hot prospects from the others and focus any personal attention you want to give to planned giving prospects on the true prospects.

To do so, in your first mailing to this list describe your organization's planned giving options in more detail, using examples and possibly providing more worksheets. Topics for these special mailings would include charitable remainder trusts, pooled income funds, gifts of real estate, and any of the more complicated strategies that you are set up to handle. Again, you may order generic descriptions of these strategies with your organization's name on the front, or make up your own. If you choose to write your own, ask an attorney familiar with estate planning to verify the information. Whether you print your own or order from a company, don't order too many. Tax laws change with great frequency and changing interpretations of tax laws can render brochures obsolete very quickly.

A detailed return coupon goes with these mailings and allows you to separate prospects. It is action-oriented and might look something like this:

Return Coupon #2

Please send me more information on:
__ Making a gift of appreciated securities
__ Generating income from my gift
__ Converting real estate to new income
__ Generating a current tax deduction from my
   personal residence or farm
__ Transferring income to (name of your group) and
   principal to my heirs

Date of birth _____

Type of asset I am considering _____

Value (if known) _____

Name _____

Address _____ Phone _____

Best time to call _____

People who fill these out in detail want to be called; call them. Of course, there are still hot prospects who don't fill out these forms, and there are other strategies to identify them.

Hold A Seminar

A good community service that can also generate some planned gifts is a seminar on estate planning. Invite people who have indicated an interest in planned giving. Have an estate planner there and plenty of materials both about your group and about estate planning strategies. If you can, get someone who has made up their estate plan and included your organization to discuss how they did it.

The purpose of the seminar is to help people think through what they are going to do with their estates, so you don't want to spend a lot of time talking about your organization. However, you will need to mention yourselves a few times to drive the point home that if a person includes a charity in their will, it should be your charity.

A seminar lets you meet people, making follow up easier. One follow-up technique is to form groups of people who want to discuss estate planning or planned giving options with the help of an expert. The group meets about once a month to discuss one topic in depth. The group can also discuss more difficult personal questions, such as when children should have access to their inheritance, the kindest thing to do with pets at the death of an owner, living wills and so on.

19.

Using Donor Analysis

To build an effective donor base an organization should periodically analyze the makeup of its current donor population. Try to assess what attracted these people to your organization and how you can attract more of them. Conversely, see what kinds of people you have not attracted but would expect to be represented among your donors.

There are six steps to be followed in doing this analysis. They depend on conducting two surveys of your donors: one that describes them by sex, age, race, income, occupation and other such concrete information (demographics); the other that describes their lifestyles, values and attitudes (psychographics). The six steps are:

1. Determine who your donors are through demographic and psychographic surveys, described in this chapter.

2. Use information from the psychographic survey about why donors give to keep them giving and to provide them with opportunities to give more often.

3. Based on who your donors are, identify who your prospects are. Based on why your donors give, get those prospects to give.

4. Use public education, media, house parties, conferences, and so forth to turn different segments of the population into prospects.

5. Use fundraising strategies to turn those prospects into donors.

6. Go back to step one.

Know Your Donors

The first step is to know who your donors are. There are three tasks to completing this step:

♦ Know exactly why your organization exists, what your goals are, and how you intend to accomplish them.

◆ Survey your donors demographically. Then, compare the demographic characteristics of your donors with what you had expected based on the nature of your organization.

◆ Determine the values and commitments of your donors through a psychographic survey. This survey tests donor loyalty and helps you think about how to make donors more loyal.

For the first task, review Chapter 4, Making a Case for Your Organization. When you feel that your organization is clear about its mission, goals and objectives, then you are ready to consider whom you would expect to support the organization and to conduct a demographic survey of donors to see who actually does support it.

A small committee should develop the demographic survey based on the example here. The sample includes questions that may only be relevant to certain types of organizations. Choose the items most relevant to your donor population. (A demographic survey only asks about and analyzes actual facts about people — it does not generally address issues of values and beliefs. The psychographic survey will do that.)

Before conducting the survey, the committee predicts who they think should be donors. The answers to a series of questions they ask themselves provide a baseline from which to note significant differences between the group's self-perception and the perceptions of its donors. These are the questions the survey committee answers for itself:

◆ What beliefs and values would we expect our donors to have? How would they get those values, and how are those values and beliefs reinforced or challenged in the culture?

◆ What types of people have these values and beliefs?

◆ How does our group convey our beliefs in our work?

◆ How do we think we have recruited donors up to now? (Mail appeals, special events, canvassing, etc.)

Then the board and staff should complete the survey, not to describe themselves but to develop a composite profile of who they think would be the group's average donor.

Once the leadership of the organization has answered these questions, the committee then administers the demographic survey to the organization's donors. The survey should be accompanied by a letter explaining the reasons for seeking the information and that answers are to be given anonymously.

As a point of comparison, the committee should also learn what it can about the demographics of your town or city. To find local or regional demographic information, consult the Census Bureau, Chamber of Commerce, and other groups that have done similar surveys. A national group would need to get comparable demographic information. A reference librarian can help with this. Comparing the profile you get from your demographic survey with that of your city or town lets you see whether and how the make-up of your group differs from that of your population base.

Eliminate from the actual demographic survey board members, volunteers, staff, and anyone very close to the organization who is also a donor. Survey those people who give mostly by mail and who are for the most part personally unknown to the majority of the leadership.

Some specialists believe that you need a certain percentage of response to have an accurate perception of your donors. What percentage, however, depends on how many donors you have to begin with. If you have 200 donors, you will need at least a 20 percent response to have a significant body of information to go on. On the other hand, a group with 200,000 donors would have enough information from a one or two percent sample.

Your response tells you what the demographics are of those donors who respond to the mail survey. To round out the picture, you will need to phone some of your donors. You can simply ask them if they have seen the survey and if they have responded. If they have not, ask if you can take the information now. Reassure the donor that you are a surveyor and will not be recording their name or any identifying data.

Compare the results of your survey with your predictions. Note gaps, surprises, populations that are under-represented, or types of people you didn't expect would be included among your donors. Here is an example to show what this part of the process can teach an organization.

An Example: Midwestern Hospice

A hospice program in a midwestern town of 150,000 people conducted a demographic survey such as the one in the example.

Their internal survey compiled by a board committee first, came out as follows.

Beliefs and values our donors tend to have:

 ◆ A person should be able to die at home if he or she chooses.

 ◆ Every family should be able to have access to the support services needed to have a terminally ill family member at home, regardless of their ability to pay.

 ◆ People can die with dignity, and they can live until they die.

How they would get these values:

 ◆ Reading Elizabeth Kubler Ross, Cicely Saunders (the founder of the hospice movement) and the like.

 ◆ Personal experience with the terminal illness of a friend or family member.

 ◆ Their religious beliefs.

How these values would be supported or challenged by the culture:

These attitudes would mostly not be supported by the culture. They would be challenged by:

 ◆ Many in the medical establishment, who promote hospitalization and do not generally favor keeping a terminally ill person at home.

 ◆ The general fear, anxiety and avoidance of death.

What types of people have values and beliefs that would cause them to give to the hospice?

 ◆ Quakers and people of other particular religious orientation (for example, some liberal Protestants).

 ◆ Psychologists, social workers, clergy of certain denominations.

 ◆ People who believe in the integrity and importance of the family.

 ◆ People over 65 and middle-aged people with older parents to whom they are close.

 ◆ Teachers of elementary and junior high schools.

 ◆ Others using our services.

How does our group convey our beliefs and our work?

 ◆ Through direct mail, brochures, and press releases, coverage in local newspapers, and appearances on some radio talk shows. Also a quarterly newsletter keeps people up to date.

How have we recruited donors up to now?

 ◆ Mostly by mail (more than 75 percent), through services provided to client families who remained donors after the death of the client, through word of mouth, and through board member efforts (at most 4 percent).

What will the demographics of our donor population be?

♦ Most donors will be white, professionals, in the $30,000-50,000 income bracket, married with children, as many men as women. Our donors will be college educated and a significant percentage will have graduate degrees. More than half will be active in a church or other religious institution. (This profile also conformed to the profile of the town's population.)

The Results

Of 1,000 donors surveyed, 200 completed the demographic survey, and an additional 50 responses were collected by phone.

Most of the donors were women (75 percent), and the most common profession was "homemaker" (25 percent). No other profession was commonly mentioned. Occupations included self-employed plumbers, teachers, janitors, administrative assistants, middle managers, small business owners and retired people. All the respondents had completed high school, but only 20 percent had attended college; very few had graduate degrees.

Furthermore, at variance with both the organization's prediction and the town itself, only 50 percent of the donors said they were religious, and only 50 percent of those people reported church attendance.

The average income was lower than predicted, with most donors in the $20,000-30,000 range.

The group was correct in predicting strong family commitments. Most were married (75 percent) and more than 90 percent had children or grandchildren.

Most of the donors had heard of hospice through the newspaper or radio, and 50 percent had heard and joined because of other volunteer work. Only 23 percent had joined from a mail appeal. Most had written to hospice first, then received information and a request to join. About 15 percent had become regular donors after giving a memorial contribution.

A major conclusion that can be drawn from the differences between the predicted and actual responses for fundraising purposes is that this hospice was well known and respected among other nonprofit organizations, but was not reaching professional people who did not volunteer in the nonprofit world. Whereas the hospice had among its supporters many people who did not fit the profile of the town in their religious commitments, it probably also had great potential to develop donors from the large religious majority.

Education was also not a major factor in the current donors' backgrounds, and only a minority had indicated personal experience with the hospice or religious beliefs that would lead to their support of hospice care. These factors pointed to a strong need for a psychographic survey to learn where current donors got their values and beliefs.

The Psychographic Survey

Describing people based on their lifestyles, values and attitudes is called "psychographics." Together, demographic and psychographic data give an overall profile of donors and prospects, allowing you to focus your fundraising and education efforts on the needs, wants and desires of your donor population and to find prospects who share the commitments and ideals of your organization.

Once the group has completed and analyzed the demographic survey, it is ready to conduct a psychographic survey. This is a more in-depth personal survey and is generally given to fewer people.

The psychographic survey helps you know why people give to your organization, why they are loyal to it, and what makes them more — or less — loyal. With this information, you can maintain and strengthen existing commitment and gain new donors with strong loyalty. This process may seem lengthy, but by completing it you will gain important information that will ultimately save you time and money in recruiting new donors.

The first step in conducting a psychographic study is to divide your donors into categories according to how they give. First, identify people among your donors who qualify in one or more of the following ways:

1. People who give or pledge large gifts ($100 or more) at least once a year.

2. People who give any size of gift three or more times a year (assuming that your group asks your donors for money at least three times a year).

3. People who have given for three years or more.

People who pledge fall into category 1, unless they give in addition to their pledge payments, which would put them in categories 1 and 2.

Now, sort these donors into further categories as follows:

A. People who belong to categories 1, 2 and 3 above.

B. People who belong to categories 2 and 3 above.

C. People who belong to categories 1 and 3 above.

You will probably not have more than a few dozen people (if that) in category A. If you do, however, then take a random sample of 50 or so for this survey.

You are now ready to conduct the survey. Here's how:

1. Interview in person as many people in category A as possible.

2. Interview by telephone as many people in category B as possible.

3. Send written surveys to people in category C, with phone interviews of a random small number of these people.

Each group should be asked the same set of questions. The personal interviews, which can be done one at a time or in informal settings of several donors and an interviewer, will yield the most wide-ranging opinions. The telephone and written surveys will be easier to analyze because the answers will be more fixed, but will not yield the kinds of additional comments you can expect from personal interviews. All questions should be tested on a small group of people to make sure they are sensitive, necessary and not ambiguous. (See box, "On Asking Questions.")

Keep in mind that surveys of donors have serious limitations. For example, you probably will not be able to determine the value of listing donors' names in your newsletter, or giving them plaques, membership cards and so on through a donor survey, because so few donors will admit the importance of those benefits to their giving. Also, most people aspire to be more idealistic and high minded than they really are, so they will check options that reflect their ideal of themselves rather than their true behavior. However, it is important to know what ideals you do strike in people so you can aim your fundraising efforts at those.

Number of People to Survey

It may not be possible for small organizations to get what statisticians would consider "scientifically significant" numbers. Obviously, the more people you survey, the more accurate your response, if all other variables are the same. Small organizations, however, do not have a huge donor base to survey and do not have the money to conduct extensive research. Generally speaking, a well-worded survey administered to 100 or more people will be fairly accurate. Smaller numbers, particularly small numbers of in-person interviews (in-depth interviews of key donors) will nevertheless yield information that is useful and can be tested on new prospects.

What Have You Learned?

When you have completed your survey, compile all your data. You now have a profile of your donor base by sex, age, race, income, occupation, and other demographic data from the demographic survey, and by commitments, priorities, self-image, and commitment to your group from the psychographic survey.

Sit down with your committee and discuss what you have learned. What are the surprises? How do your donors' broad perceptions of your organization differ from those of board members and volunteers, or from your mission statement? What are the most important programs to your donors compared with the priorities of board and staff?

If you discover serious differences in priorities or perceptions between your donors and your leadership, you do not have to change your organization to fit your donors, nor do you have to alienate them. You must, however, spend the time to do some consciousness-raising and education. On the other hand, you may discover your donors are more bold than your board, or that board, volunteers and donors are basically compatible in their thinking about the organization.

A diversity of values and opinions among your donors shows you have broad appeal. By careful approaches to different populations, you have the potential to expand your donor base among many types of people.

Putting the Information to Work

To use the results of your demographic and psychographic surveys to find new donors, first list all the strategies that you currently use for getting donors. (If you are doing this in a group, write all the strategies on a piece of butcher paper or on a blackboard where everyone can see it.) Your list will probably include direct mail, phone-a-thons, special events, products for sale, fees for service, foundation and corporate grant proposals, and major gift solicitation.

Now, list your survey results and note what fundraising strategy would be best for finding donors similar to the ones you already have. To illustrate, let's look at the surveys point by point and how you can use their information.

The results of the demographic surveys have given you the age, income bracket, occupation, education, religious and political identifications, and other information about your donors. Ask yourself: Where are more people like that? What do they like to do? How can we find them?

For example, a group discovered that 25 percent of their donors live in a particular neighborhood of the city. Those same donors generally have incomes between $30,000 and $70,000: they are upwardly mobile career-oriented individuals, mostly without children. They are a market with a good deal of disposable income. Also, according to the survey, most of them are Democrats, and for the most part, they have no religious affiliation.

Using this data, the organization identified from all its possible fund-raising strategies one that would allow it to focus on that neighborhood. They decided to ask donors who had given $100 or more for two or more years to host a house party for the group and to invite their neighbors. At each party, the guests were educated about the work of the group and asked to participate by donating to the group, holding a house party of their own, and voting on certain issues at an upcoming election.

From their data, the group knew that most of the people would be voting the way they recommended anyway, so the only new behaviors they were asking for are were donation and a house party. They set a goal of five house parties hosted by current donors, and ten more hosted by people recruited by donors. This turned out to be a very effective strategy to reach an upper-income group in a relaxed setting and bring them in as major donors.

The same group also decided that because so many of their donors were in an upper-income range, the group could provide information that would be useful to others with similar income. In conjunction with several other nonprofits, they hosted a seminar on socially responsible investing. They advertised widely in the neighborhoods where they already had many donors and attracted many new people to their seminar. The focus of the seminar was not on the organization but, during the seminar, the organization was able to give a pitch for itself.

Another organization compiled the names of all the magazines mentioned in their survey responses. The one mentioned most often was *The Nation* followed by *Utne Reader* and *Off Our Backs*. They decided to rent mailing lists from those publications for the geographic area they served (where available) and use direct mail to reach those people. Because those publications are primarily received by subscription, rather than bought at a newsstand, and are generally ordered through the mail, they reasoned that the readers of those magazines, in addition to their political beliefs, also have in common that they buy by mail.

To back up their mail appeals, the group placed classified ads in these magazines during the two months that they were sending mail appeals. The ads offered a publication for sale that the group had produced, but the real purpose of the ads was to increase their name recognition in order to increase response to the mail appeals. Although it is impossible to tell exactly what results this dual strategy produced, it seemed to work. The organization expected a 1 percent response to its mail appeal; it received just over 2.5 percent. In addition, they received some orders for the publication advertised.

Another group observed that more than half of their donors indicated in the psychographic survey that they talked about the organization to their friends and co-workers. Some respondents even wrote in that they always shared the organization's newsletters with friends or brought them to work. Using that information, this organization launched an "each one reach one" campaign. They sent a special appeal to current donors asking that each donor ask one person to join the organization. They included a copy of their newsletter, a fact sheet on the organization's latest work, a return card and envelope and a card on which they could request more return cards and newsletters, in case they wanted to ask more than one person. The current donor was asked to sign his or her name on the return card before giving it to the prospective donor. Everyone who brought in a new donor was sent a small gift. Some people recruited ten donors, some only one, and one person recruited 25 donors!

Many organizations discover from a psychographic survey that their donors do not have any set formula for determining how much to give to nonprofits and that they either don't know what their annual charitable giving is or that it is less than two percent of their disposable income, which is the national giving average.

Some of these groups are launching educational efforts to teach people to be better donors. Their newsletters contain stories from thoughtful donors, their appeals compare the cost of a meal or clothing with the cost of a donation. These strategies help make the point that social change needs to be a priority — not something done after all other needs and wants are taken care of. One anti-nuclear organization did an appeal on this theme: "Most people spend several hundred dollars a year to insure their homes and cars against theft, fire, flood or other destruction. Our world needs this insurance. Please calculate how much you spend on insurance, and then send us a check, keeping in mind that peace is our only insurance against nuclear destruction."

The answers to each aspect of your survey should be used as a brainstorming point to determine the implications of the information. How can we take advantage of this information in recruiting new donors? What strategy will be most effective in reaching similar people?

Groups that thrive will be those that think carefully about their donors: who they are, what they respond to, and where there are more of them. Knowing the donors will be the key to success.

On Asking Questions

Only seek information necessary to your group. A group working on housing issues or pollution control might find it useful to know what percentage of their donors use mass transit and how often. However, a group working on women's health does not need this information, unless it's related to access to care.

Don't ask questions that assume a behavior. For example, asking the question, "Our last newsletter discussed workfare. Did you agree with our position?" assumes that the person read the newsletter and remembers what position your group took.

Remember that you may be asking questions that some donors find embarrassing or sensitive. Be sure you give people multiple choices in your written surveys and that you do not ask socially unacceptable questions directly in your telephone or personal interviews.

Use simple, sixth-grade vocabulary. This ensures that donors will understand the questions easily, increasing their incentive to answer.

Don't bias your questions. For example do not ask a question such as, "Our board of directors feels that more prison construction does not reduce crime. How do you feel? Would you support the board in their effort to defeat building more prisons?" Instead ask, "What is your opinion of more prison construction? If our organization were to work against it, would you support us financially in that particular endeavor?"

People generally prefer to mark a category than give a specific answer, so as much as possible include categories (such as income ranges) rather than asking for a specific answer (what is your income).

Always give people the option to answer "Don't know," or "Not applicable."

SAMPLE DEMOGRAPHIC SURVEY

Please answer the following questions. If you do not know something, write DK; if the question is not applicable, write NA.

1. Zip code or neighborhood where you live: _____
2. How long have you lived there? _____
3. How many people share your house/apt/duplex (circle one) with you?
4. Your age: under 18   19-25   26-35   36-45   46-60   over 60 (circle one).
5. Your sex: ☐ M   ☐ F
6. Your race _____
7. Your ethnic identity _____
8. Do you have children? ☐ No ☐ Yes If yes, how many? _____
    What are their ages? _____ Do they live with you all the time/part of the time (what part?_____)/none of the time? (circle one).
9. Are you:
    ☐ Married/Partnered   ☐ Single   ☐ Divorced/Widowed
10. Your income level:
    ☐ under $10,000   ·   ☐ $31,000-40,000   ☐ over $100,000
    ☐ $10,000-20,000   ☐ $41,000-50,000   ☐ over $250,000
    ☐ $21,000-30,000   ☐ $51,000-99,000
11. Your education:
    ☐ High school graduate   ☐ Graduate school
    ☐ College graduate   ☐ Postgraduate training
    What academic degrees do you have? _____
12. Your occupation: _____
13. Do you attend a church, synagogue or other religious institution? (circle one)
14. Are you registered with a political party?
    ☐ No ☐ Yes: Which one? _____ Active? _____
15. How long have you belonged to our group? _____
16. How did you join?
    ☐ Mail appeal   ☐ Friend   ☐ Phone appeal
    ☐ Special event   ☐ Other

SAMPLE PSYCHOGRAPHIC SURVEY

Your group will need to make up a survey that gives you appropriate information. It should ask the following kinds of questions (the specifcs here are meant as examples only).

1. How long have you belonged to our organization?
   ☐ 1 year ☐ 2 years ☐ 3 years ☐ 5 years
   ☐ Longer (specify) _____

2. Why did you join? _____

3. What other nonprofit organizations do you give to? _____

4. What is the largest gift you make to any group?
   ☐ $15-25 ☐ $151-250 ☐ $1,001-2,500
   ☐ $26-50 ☐ $251-500 ☐ More than $2,500
   ☐ $51-150 ☐ $501-1,000

5. What is your total annual giving to charity?
   ☐ $100 ☐ $1,000 ☐ Don't know
   ☐ $500 ☐ Other $_____ ☐ _____ % of income, if known

6. How do you determine your giving to charity?
   ☐ As a percentage of income ☐ As a set amount each year
   ☐ No set formula ☐ Other _____

7. Which, if any, of the following words describe you, and to what extent?

	Yes	Sort of	Not really	Not at all	Don't understand
Feminist					
Environmentalist					
Christian					
Democrat					
Civic-minded					
Family-oriented					
Activist					
Radical					
Liberal					

8. If you had to cut back on your giving, when would you eliminate our group?
   ☐ Immediately ☐ Not until I had to
   ☐ Soon ☐ Never

9. If your income were to increase dramatically, would you:
   (a) Give more money to charity?
   ☐ Yes ☐ No ☐ Maybe
   (b) Give more money to our group?
   ☐ Yes ☐ No ☐ Maybe

10. What is the most important issue we address? (list your issues): _____

11. In describing our group to a friend who had never heard of us, what would you say? _____

12. Do you talk about our group to:
   ☐ Your friends   ☐ Sometimes
   ☐ Your colleagues at work   ☐ Rarely
   ☐ Your family   ☐ Never
   ☐ Other (specify) _____

13. If you talk about our group to anyone, do you think most people you talk to have heard of our work?
   ☐ Most   ☐ Almost none
   ☐ Some   ☐ None
   ☐ Very few

14. If our organization keeps doing work of the current quality, do you foresee continuing to support us?
   ☐ Yes   ☐ Maybe   ☐ Probably not
   ☐ No   ☐ If possible

15. If probably not, or no, please say why: _____

16. Where do you get news about world affairs or current events?
   ☐ Television   ☐ Newspaper   ☐ Don't keep up
   ☐ Radio   ☐ Friends

17. What magazines do you subscribe to? _____

SECTION 4
Other Methods of Fundraising

INTRODUCTION

The more appropriate title for this section would be "Some Other Methods for Fundraising" because an entire book could be devoted to ways of raising money that are not mentioned in this book. However, the following five chapters outline the most common methods that grassroots organizations use. These methods incorporate the most important aspects of any fundraising solicitation: researching the prospects, creating a clear plan to approach prospects, and asking for the money.

In all the other sections of this book, readers are given enough information to begin the strategy without needing to read further (although you are always encouraged to read further and talk to more people). In this section, readers are given basic definitions and some preliminary how-to's, but more in-depth reading and research would be required before adding these methods to your fundraising plan.

20.

Fees for Service

In a small industrial city in Michigan, the director of a program serving seniors described his experience in starting a fee-for-service income stream. His organization provides a wide range of services to people 65 and older, including Meals on Wheels; transportation to medical appointments; helping people do their taxes or deal with Social Security, Medicare, and private insurance; leisure activities in a community center as well as field trips; and help with aging parents. All of these services were free. For most of its history, the agency's $300,000 budget was provided by funds from United Way, the city, and a few other government sources. The program was run inexpensively because 75 active volunteers did much of the work.

Then, without notice, the city cut their contribution to the program's funding entirely. With the city itself in a state of decline and unemployment high, senior services were no longer a priority. The United Way also cut their contributions — by 50 percent — with further cuts expected. Reluctantly, this director created a free-will donation system to encourage users of the service to contribute toward its cost. Above a box for donations in the community center he posted a big sign that read:

The cost of providing services is as follows:

One delivery of a meal (Meals on Wheels)	$ 5.00
One trip to and from a medical appointment	$ 3.00
Support group counsellor (per person)	$ 7.00
Private counselling (per hour)	$ 20.00
Lunch at the community center	$ 2.00
Field trips per person per day	$ 10.00
Magazine subscriptions (average)	$ 25.00
Books for the library (average)	$ 17.00

Any amount you can pay toward these services is gratefully accepted and will be put right to work.

Thank you.

This same announcement appeared in the program's newsletter and on a sign in their van. This approach is low key and not threatening. No one actually asks for money. To donate, one has to be able to read the sign, then put money in a box or hand it to the person in charge.

In the year following posting this information, the director reported a 300 percent increase in the number of people using the various services the center provided. Puzzled, he investigated. Were there 300 percent more seniors in town? No. Were 300 percent more seniors falling into need for these services? No. Finally, he surveyed center users about what brought them to the center, how they found out about it, and what they liked about it. Among other things, he learned that people liked being able to pay for the service. Several people made comments to that effect: "I never used this place before because I don't like taking things for free. I am not so poor to need free service. I can pay my own way." "I can take care of myself pretty good and I don't need handouts. I've worked hard all my life." "I like coming to the center and seeing people, and the prices are affordable. Sometimes I put in a little extra for someone who isn't as well off."

This experience has been repeated over and over again as organizations have been forced to start suggesting donations to their clients. Most people prefer to pay something than to get a service for free and, to some extent, giving services away to people in need robs them of their dignity.

Fees for service, whether voluntary or mandatory, can bring in more clients and strengthen your program. Fees can also provide the income stream that keeps an organization afloat.

Many nonprofit organization have mandatory fees. They charge well below the "market rate" for their service, but in order to get the service, you have to pay a fixed price or a fee made by some determination such as income or reimbursement from insurance.

This chapter discusses how to determine fees and how to collect them for organizations that have traditionally provided free services to clients and now wish to charge voluntary fees.

What is a Voluntary Fee?

You can charge voluntary fees in one of two ways: You can still provide service for free but request money to help cover the cost; or you can ask that people pay something for the service, but whatever they pay is acceptable.

Which system you use depends on the nature of your clients. Organizations serving the homeless will probably not require a contribution. Cultural organizations, organizations serving the working poor, mental health providers, and so on may opt to require some payment.

Or you can mix the two methods. For example, one homeless shelter provides shelter, showers, and clothing for free and does not attempt to charge. But they have a suggested voluntary donation of $.50 for meals, and a mandatory processing fee of $10 for job placement (collected after the person has received their first paycheck). This agency now receives donations for almost 70 percent of their meals served, with many people giving $1.00 and a collection rate of 80 percent on their job fee. Another shelter provides free meals, but charges $.50 for seconds, and $.10 for coffee or tea. Water and juice are free.

Staying Legal

Charging fees is not illegal, but if you are asking for donations rather than fees, they must be perceived as voluntary by the client for you to stay within your nonprofit status. No coercive measures can be used to collect voluntary fees. A coercive action would be one that makes a person feel the service was not really free or that he or she was the only one asking for free service, or some other method of seeming to manipulate a person into paying or paying more than they want to. What is coercive is a matter of perception, but some actions are more obviously coercive and need to be avoided.

For example, one free meal program separated those who had given from those who had not. Those who gave were placed at tables with tablecloths and given dessert. In another instance, admission to a class on how to prepare for job interviews was free, but the person registering people loudly announced each donation so that someone sitting across from her could record it. Although thoughtless and probably unintentional, this practice caused some who had intended to take the course for free or even for a low price to pay more than they had wanted to; others simply left before reaching the registration table.

People tend to be embarrassed by any practice that makes them feel as though they don't have enough money. Any system that can embarrass someone may cause them to feel pressured to pay more than they want to or can afford, and the voluntary fee is no longer truly voluntary.

(Ironically, this same embarrassment can arise from an agency insisting on providing service for free, which can also keep people from seeking services they need.)

The second legal obligation is that your fee, whether voluntary or mandatory, be well below what a for-profit would charge for the service.

Setting the Fees

There are several ways to set your fees. The least effective (judged by amount of money raised) but least intrusive is to post a sign near a collection box that simply reads, "Donations," or "Donations welcome," or "Your gift ensures that we can continue to provide this service to others. Thank you." You will tend to get only people's spare change; however, you will never be accused of forcing someone to give, and this can be a good way to introduce the idea of giving to your clients.

If all your services cost about the same amount, you may want to suggest a range for the voluntary contribution. You would post a sign that said, "The cost of providing our services ranges from $10-25. Any amount you can pay will ensure that we can continue to provide these services. Thank you." If you want, you can add an explanation, "The budget for the services you are receiving was previously provided by the government/United Way/foundations, but these funds have been cut back. To make sure that we can continue to help people, we are asking all our clients to give what they can. Thank you."

The most effective system is one similar to that used by the senior center discussed earlier. A wide range of costs was established, and people could donate toward only the service they had used. Just as when fundraising from individuals, asking for a specific amount will result in more people giving something than leaving the amount up to the prospect, so suggesting specific amounts for services rendered will bring more donations overall, and will show that you are serious about raising money and you know what you are doing.

Most service providers have someone who staffs a desk by the front door. This person should be trained to ask for money, particularly if any of your clients cannot read a posted sign. The front-desk person adds to whatever they would normally tell people, "The service is free, but we ask you to give a donation if you can. The donation box is over there." Many clients will ask if there is a charge, which makes it easier to explain. For clients accustomed to getting the service for free, explain that you are still providing it for free, but that you are asking people who can help to do so. If you hand out literature to your clients, include a card explaining your need and a return envelope. They can drop the envelope in the box or send it later.

Introducing the Process of Collecting Fees

At first, volunteers and staff will probably be uncomfortable with the process of asking clients for money, regardless of what process you use. First, validate everybody's feelings: Yes, it is difficult to ask for money, and it may be more difficult to ask people for money who have very little. And, it would be a much better world if people did not have to pay for things to which they are entitled: housing, health care, education or food, and did not have to feel embarrassed about that. However, the U.S. government has a different understanding of entitlements which has resulted in significant cutbacks, and cities and states no longer have enough money for these programs. While all of that is being solved, your organization has to keep on providing services. Your clients would much rather you exist than watch you go out of business. They will help if they can and will feel good about helping. Once you have a few experiences of asking for money and seeing people feel good about giving, this initial discomfort will go away.

When Service is Not Given in Person

What if your way of providing service is over the telephone or by information that is mailed? Your organization has a harder task collecting fees for service. Certainly, you cannot ask someone calling a crisis hotline for a donation once they have calmed down. Voluntary contribution for service will not be possible in those cases. However, if you are providing non-crisis information, after you are finished, ask if you can send more information about your organization and how it is supported. If they give you their name and address, immediately send them a fundraising letter.

If your service includes mailing information to people, include a card and return envelope. The card should tell how your group is supported and ask the person to return the envelope with a donation as soon as possible. A card is more effective than a letter because the letter may get put aside while the person is looking at the other information you sent. However, he or she will be inclined to put the card with the envelope, and respond once they have determined that your information is useful. You may also wish to use a "wallet flap" envelope where the outside flap serves as the "card."

Setting up a voluntary system for collecting money from clients will create a steady income for you, and it may be larger than you think. Further, the system may inspire people who are not clients to give. Many times volunteers are just as uninformed about how your organization is supported as are clients. Once educated, volunteers often give regularly. Finally you may get more clients, which serves your broader mission, and may bring in more fees.

21.

Payroll Deduction Programs

U sing payroll deduction programs has proven to be one of the most efficient and effective methods of raising money for some organizations. Payroll deduction has been in use since Henry Ford introduced the concept to his employees in 1940. Today, more than $3.5 billion is pledged through payroll deductions every year. The pioneer agency for this type of fundraising is, of course, the United Way, with affiliates in almost every town of more than 25,000 people in the United States. Ninety percent of the money raised through payroll deduction giving goes to the United Way, with the rest going to a wide and growing variety of alternative federations of groups focussed on arts, service, health, environment, women's, and other issues.

A payroll deduction plan is a cross between a pledge program and an electronic funds transfer program. Employees specify how much money they want to donate each pay period and that amount is deducted from their wages. On a quarterly basis the employer sends the collected money to the federation, which keeps a percentage to cover its own costs and distributes the rest to its members.

There are several ways to benefit from payroll deduction programs, including becoming a beneficiary of the United Way or of one of the other federated funds in your area. Even if a group isn't affiliated with a federation, it may be able to receive money from any of the funds through a Donor Option Plan.

Because the United Way is the oldest, largest, and most powerful federated fund, health and human service groups should start by applying to it for funding before pursuing any alternative workplace solicitation program. If you are turned down by the United Way you have a strong case with the other federated funds or a case for starting your own fund. If you are accepted you need go no further.

United Way

The United Way of America is actually a federation of United Ways around the country. While United Ways have many things in common, each has a great deal of autonomy. Direct service nonprofits will have to approach the United Way in their community. A service agency may be accepted by a United Way in its community while an agency providing the same service in a another community may be rejected by its United Way. United Way does not support arts or environmental groups unless the work of the group involves health issues or provides health education.

Application forms and details of the application process can be obtained from your local United Way. The process is usually long and tedious, involving an extensive written application, site visits, and reviews by various United Ways committees. The bulk of United Way funding has customarily gone to a variety of "mainstream" direct service organizations, such as Boy Scouts, Red Cross, Salvation Army, YMCA, and YWCA. Traditionally the United Way has not funded women's or minority organizations, groups with advocacy programs, or groups working for social change.

In many communities (and nationally) the United Way has been severely criticized for its lack of responsiveness to social change and social justice concerns, and it has responded by making significant changes in funding policies. In some cities a progressive United Way leadership has funded shelters for battered women, groups working with the disabled, gay/lesbian health clinics, AIDS organizations, and some advocacy programs.

To find out what types of organizations the United Way funds in your community, talk to groups that receive United Way funding and to those that have been turned down by them. If possible, meet some United Way officials and discuss your organization's needs with them. If it seems from this research that your group falls within United Way guidelines, then proceed to apply.

Pros and Cons

There are obvious advantages to getting United Way funding. First, a group usually receives a sizable amount of money that can be counted on from year to year. Even though groups must reapply each year and allocations do change, once an agency is accepted by United Way it will usually continue to receive grants for many years.

For organizations truly interested in self-sufficiency and in diversifying their funding sources, there are many disadvantages to United Way funding. First, organizations receiving United Way funding are not allowed to do their own fundraising from September to November. This so-called "black-out" period is when the United Way conducts its payroll solicitation campaign. To lose three of the best months of the fundraising year is a serious drawback. Unless the allocation from the United Way is significantly larger than what your organization could raise in that time, it is not worth submitting to this structure.

Second, because many people think that agencies supported by United Way need no other funds, many donors will not give to organizations receiving money from the United Way.

Third, many Americans simply do not like the United Way. They do not like being pressured to give at their workplace and they see the United Way as wasteful of funds and bureaucratic in structure. While this perception is false for many United Ways, the reputation of your local United Way will affect your organization's own reputation for better or worse.

Because most organizations, especially those doing work related to health or human service, will be asked by individual donors, foundations and corporations whether they have applied for funds from the United Way and if not why not, groups need to explore the possibility of becoming a member even if such exploration leads them to the conclusion that such a move would be impossible (you don't qualify) or unwise (your grant from the United Way is not enough to put up with the rules). Then the group can present its reasons for not being involved. This will help donors realize that your organization is responsible and knowledgeable.

The Donor Option Plan

Even if your organization does not qualify to be a United Way-funded agency, you can still receive donations through the Donor Option Plan. This plan is not available in every community, but when it is available it allows employees to designate the agency they wish to receive their contribution.

Generally, local United Ways do not promote the Donor Option Plan and sometimes try to discourage employees from using it. The United Way sometimes maintains that the Donor Option program is expensive for them and complicated to manage. They will ask local groups not to advertise it and not to solicit gifts through Donor Option.

Nevertheless, there is nothing the United Way can do if you do advertise Donor Option plans to your donors. Ask your donors to notify you if they have given to you through Donor Option, so that you can check up on the pledge if the United Way fails to notify you. Find out from someone in the United Way or from a workplace that gives to United Way how someone can designate your group (this process varies widely) and let your donors know exactly what they should do to designate their payroll deduction for your group.

Alternative Funds

If your organization cannot or does not wish to receive United Way funding but still wishes to pursue a payroll deduction plan, you will want to explore alternative funds. First, find out if there are any in your community and what their grant-making capabilities are. Most alternative funds belong to an organization called the Alliance for Choice in Giving, headquartered in Washington D.C. (as is the national United Way). You can write to them for more information about what federations your organization might be qualified to join, as well as information about starting your own fund. Their address and phone number are: 2001 "O" St, NW, Washington, DC 20036, (202) 296-8470.

The alternative fund movement has grown dramatically; as of 1993, there were 162 local alternative funds in 39 states. Some of the newer funds may not yet be able to make large grants but have excellent technical assistance programs. Others are giving away money but may not yet have gained access to many employers and must raise money in ways other than payroll deduction.

There are also ten alternative federations that raise money for national organizations. Samples of these are Earth Share, which raises money for national and international environmental organizations; Children's Charities of America, which funds teaching, feeding, and protection programs for children nationally and abroad; and the National Black United Federation of Charities, which promotes organizations working towards the betterment and advancement of the African-American community.

Starting an Alternative Fund

If there is no alternative fund in your community you can start one. This is a major undertaking and, like a small business, takes several years before it will pay off. However, it can eventually be lucrative if you have the time and the skills required. Setting up an alternative payroll deduction plan is simple in theory. Your organization calls together organizations similar to yours in either size or issues addressed or with a broad agenda in common to form a federation. This entails the same work as forming any not-for-profit. The federation acts an as umbrella for the member groups and other groups that may apply. The federation seeks employers' permission to solicit donations from employees and distributes the money to member groups, first taking their own operating expenses from the collected funds. The overall fundraising costs are much lower than if each group were to try to do this type of fundraising on its own.

There are many decisions to be made in forming a federation. Who will be a member? How does the federation choose new members? What will the application process be? How will the money be distributed? Will it be divided evenly among all the members or given out according to each agency's need, or given out in accordance with the wishes of the donor, or a combination of these three approaches?

Once the federation has made these decisions (which can take many meetings and many months of negotiation and discussion), it must gain access to the workplace to solicit the funds. Since the United Way has had a virtual monopoly on employee contributions for some time, it is understandably reluctant to share the stage with alternative funds. And employers may find it easier to limit access to the United Way only. Interestingly enough, however, studies show that when employees have several choices of funds to give to, and when they have Donor Option programs, total giving goes up. Some United Ways have discovered to their surprise that they did better when other funds were also allowed to solicit.

Finally, because a great deal of money can be involved and because the politics of the organizations forming an alternative federation are often in clear conflict with those of the United Way and individual employers, groups may find themselves embroiled in legal battles to protect their right to free speech in soliciting employees.

22.

Canvassing

Canvassing is a fundraising technique that involves a team of people from your organization going door to door requesting contributions for your group's work. The canvassing technique is used primarily by local groups and by local chapters of state or national organizations. It can be an excellent acquisition strategy and, by returning to neighborhoods, it can also be used for retaining donors.

While part-time or temporary canvasses can be run with volunteers, most canvassing is a full-time operation involving salaried or commissioned employees who work 40 hours a week and solicit in neighborhoods on a regular, revolving basis. Well-run canvasses can bring in from $50,000 to $500,000 or more in gross income. Because they are labor-intensive, however, the high overhead of most canvasses absorbs at least 60 percent of their gross earnings.

Advantages and Disadvantages

There are three main advantages to canvassing as a fundraising strategy. First, an established, well-run canvass can provide a reliable source of income to your organization, and this income can be quite substantial. Second, the face-to-face contact with dozens of people each evening can bring in more new members than almost any other strategy; this volume of personal interaction is not duplicated in any other fundraising strategy. Third, canvassers bring back to the organization the public's opinions and perceptions of what your organization is doing.

There are also disadvantages to a canvass. If it is done on a full-time basis it requires separate office space to accommodate its large number of staff as well as extensive bookkeeping and supervision. As with a small business, canvass income can be unreliable if the top canvass staff is not good or if too many canvasses are operating in an area. The canvassers themselves can give the organization a bad reputation if they are unkempt, rude, or unpleasant to the people being canvassed. More and more, people are frightened by a stranger coming to their door and may not even open it. A final disadvantage is that many donors do not like the concept of canvassing because of the high overhead involved. While the amount of gross income can be impressive, much of that is lost to overhead costs.

Elements Needed to Run a Canvass

Four elements must be present for an organization to operate an effective canvass. First, and most important, the organization must work on local issues. People give at the door when they perceive that an issue affects them and their neighborhood. The work of your organization can have national impact and your organization might be a branch of a national group, but in door-to-door canvassing, you must explain how this issue affects the resident directly.

Second, people must feel that even a small donation will make a difference. Most people make a cash donation to a canvass, and even a check will rarely be for more than $25. People must feel that their small donation is needed and will be well used.

Third, people must feel confident about your organization. Their confidence will be inspired by your organization's accomplishments, which must be clear and easy to discuss. Newspaper articles about your work are a major boon to canvassing. A specific plan of action that can be explained simply and quickly and that sounds effective is essential. The work of some organizations lends itself particularly well to canvassing. Work on issues of general importance and interest to the majority of people, such as health care for all, lower utility rates, or crime prevention is easy to explain and of universal concern. Litigation can work if the suit is easy to understand, with a clear "good guy" (your group) and "bad guy." Complex regulatory reform, issues requiring historical background, legal knowledge, or patience in listening to a long explanation do not lend themselves to canvassing.

Finally, you must be able to distinguish your organization from any other organization doing similar work without implying any disrespect for the other organization. In some communities where there are not only two or more groups working on similar issues but also several groups canvassing, potential donors get confused and then angry that they are being solicited so often for issues that seem interrelated. People will explain to your canvassers that they just gave to your group last week, that someone from your organization was just there. No amount of protest from you will change their minds. The only thing that will help is to clearly distinguish your group from any other.

All these requirements for a successful canvass, except the focus on local work, are also necessary for many other fundraising strategies, particularly mail appeals and phone-a- thons, where the object is to get the donor's attention quickly and hold it long enough to get the gift.

Setting Up a Canvass

First, check state and local laws and ordinances concerning canvassing. If canvassing is heavily regulated in your community, it may not be worth the time involved to comply with the regulations. Some communities have tried to stop canvassing operations altogether by means of ordinances governing what you can say when soliciting door to door and establishing strict qualifications for canvassers, including expensive licensing. If your canvass violates even a minor regulation it could be forced by the city or state to cease operation and may bring bad press for your organization. Many of these ordinances have been challenged in court and found unconstitutional, but most organizations have too much work to do to also take on costly and lengthy legal battles in this area.

State laws governing canvassing can be learned by contacting the state attorney general's office, which generally monitors all rules related to charitable solicitation. Many states publish handbooks on canvassing regulations.

Local ordinances are sometimes more difficult to discover, since several city departments may have jurisdiction over different parts of the canvassing operation. Contact the police department and ask for notification and application procedures for a canvass. Be sure to write down whatever the person tells you, and get his or her name so that if you get a different story from another police official you can refer to this phone call.

Contact the city attorney's office for information regarding solicitation of money for charity. Sometimes the mayor's office has some jurisdiction over these matters. In general, informing as many people as possible about your canvassing operation will ensure the least amount of interference later.

Study the Demographics

After making sure that you can comply with the law you must determine if your community's geography and population density and the income range of the people being canvassed are favorable to a canvass. Gather demographic data on your area: for various neighborhoods, find out the population density, the property values, how many of the people are homeowners, what type of work most people do, what the income levels are, and so forth. This information is available from various sources, including driving around and getting a sense of the neighborhoods, asking local people, reading the newspaper, talking with volunteers and board members who have lived in the area and consulting with the Chamber of Commerce.

Remember one important caveat in assessing demographic data: A canvass rarely does well in an affluent neighborhood. Affluent people generally do not make contributions at the door. Their charitable giving is usually done through major gift solicitation, personal mail appeals or special events. Canvassing operations do best in middle- and lower-income neighborhoods, where giving at the door is more commonplace. Another demographic item you need to evaluate is whether the population is dense enough per square mile to make it worthwhile to canvass. Canvassers need to be able to reach 80 to 100 homes per night. This means that there must be enough people in the area and that the terrain must be flat enough to allow canvassers to walk quickly from house to house. It is much harder to run a successful canvass in a rural area simply because of the distance between houses and the small number of people.

Finally, you need to evaluate whether the area is safe for canvassers. A good canvasser may be carrying $100 or more by the end of the evening, much of that in cash. Canvasses in high crime areas (which still can be successful) sometimes send their canvassers in pairs, but this doubles the labor cost. Others have a roving car to check in on canvassers and to pick up cash.

Staff

Once you have determined that your area can support a canvass, you are ready to hire canvass staff and prepare materials.

The staff of a canvass varies from place to place but generally includes several individuals with the following roles:

◆ **Canvass Director:** Supervises the entire canvass operation, including hiring and firing canvassers, researching areas to be canvassed and mapping out the revolving sequence for the areas to be canvassed in a year, keeping the organization in compliance with the law, keeping up to date on new laws and planning and updating materials.

◆ **Field Manager(s):** Transports and supervises a team of five to seven canvassers. Assigns the team to various parts of the neighborhood, collects the money at the end of the evening. This person also trains new canvassers on the team and participates as a canvasser at the site.

◆ **Secretary/receptionist/bookkeeper/office manager:** Manages the office, including keeping records of money earned by each canvasser, replacing canvass materials as needed, scheduling interviews with prospective canvassers for the canvass director, answering the phone, and generally acting as back-up person to the canvass operation. This person does not canvass.

◆ **Canvassers:** The people actually carrying out the canvass. Canvassers work from 2-10 p.m. five days a week. They usually have a quota - an amount of money they must raise every day or every week. Their pay is either a percentage of what they raise (commission), a straight salary, or a base salary plus commission.

Canvassers must represent the organization accurately and be respectable ambassadors for the organization. The individual canvasser is often the only person from the organization whom donors will see and may well be the only face they will ever associate with your group.

Because the pay is low and the hours long and arduous there is a high turnover in canvass staff. In the summer, college students help expand canvassing staff. Recruiting canvassers is more difficult in the winter months.

Canvassers must be equipped with various materials. These include any identification badges or licenses required by the city or state, clipboards to carry materials to be given away, brochures about the organization, return envelopes, newspaper clippings about the work of the group, and a receipt book.

Many canvassers use a petition to get the attention of the person being canvassed. The canvasser will ask, "Would you sign a petition for . . ." and briefly explain the cause. While the person is signing, the canvasser will ask for a donation as well.

Canvassers should try to get the gift right at the door. However, for people who need to think about it or discuss it with a partner or spouse, the canvasser should leave a brochure and a return envelope. A brochure should also be given to people making a donation, because on reading it some of them will send an additional donation. Do not assume when people say they need to think about your request they mean they are not going to give. This is a common mistake. Leave the materials and act as if you believe the person. Many people do not make any decision on the spur of the moment, and people who need to think about what their gift will be to your group may well become major donors.

All of the information should be carried on a clipboard, which makes it easy to display and lends a degree of authority to the canvasser. People are more likely to open their doors to someone who looks as though he or she has a good reason to be there.

When canvassers begin their work day they are appraised of the neighborhood they will be canvassing and told of any new information or special emphasis on issues that they should present to this neighborhood. Then they have a late lunch/early dinner and are driven by their field manager to the canvass site. They begin canvassing around 4 p.m. and end at 9 p.m., when they are picked up by their field manager and taken back to the office. They turn in their money, make their reports, and finish around 10 p.m.

Because canvassing is hard work, essentially involving face-to-face solicitation with a "cold" list, it is critical that the rest of the organization's staff and the board members see the canvass staff as colleagues and as integral to the total operation of the organization. To help build this support, many organizations require non-canvass staff to canvass for an evening every couple of months.

Second only to quality of canvass staff in ensuring the success of a canvass is an efficient record-keeping system. After each neighborhood is canvassed an evaluation of the neighborhood should be filed along with the demographic data on that neighborhood that led to its being chosen as a canvass site. These data can then be reevaluated in the light of the canvassers' experience. Any special considerations, such as "no street lights," can also be noted in the evaluation.

Many people worry that theft by the canvassers will be a problem. Theft occurs no more often by canvass workers than by any others. Careless bookkeeping, however, can cost money and can give the impression that money has disappeared. At the end of the evening, both the canvasser and the field manager should count the money brought in. The amounts are entered under each canvasser's name on a "Daily Summary Sheet." The money and the summary sheet are then placed in a locked safe, and the secretary/bookkeeper should count the total again in the morning and make a daily deposit to the bank. At the end of the week the bookkeeper should tally the total receipt of each canvasser and prepare the payroll sheet.

Canvassers who fail to bring in their quota for more than a week must be retrained or fired. Strict discipline is important in a successful canvass, and keeping performance records will help to maintain a good canvass team.

Canvassing is an excellent strategy for some groups, and if done properly it can be lucrative. However, there are many pitfalls, and it is neither a simple nor a low-cost strategy. Canvassing changes the nature of the organization. It doubles or triples staff size and requires office space and additional equipment. Only groups that have thoroughly researched the pros and cons of this strategy should consider beginning a canvass.

23.

Setting Up a Small Business

The idea of a nonprofit starting a small business seems sound at first: sell something people want to buy and use the profits to finance your organization. For many years, nonprofit organizations have run small businesses — thrift stores, gift shops, ticket sales for performances, concessions, and so on. Some nonprofit organizations have well-known multimillion-dollar businesses, such as the Girl Scouts' cookies, the Salvation Army's second-hand stores, and UNICEF's gift shops.

Despite these glowing examples of success, the unfortunate fact is that most nonprofits that have started small businesses have failed in this endeavor. Their failures were caused by the same factors that cause 9 out of 10 small businesses to fail: Undercapitalization, poor management, inability to respond to market conditions, and underpricing of goods.

Nonprofits have additional problems. First, staff and board members are often not business people themselves. In fact, they may have a distaste for business and capitalist ventures and feel uncertain about the politics of starting a small business. Further, staff and board members are already putting in a great deal of time and may feel unable to work harder. Almost any staff person knows the feeling of being constantly behind in his or her work, always barely catching up, always conscious of tasks that never get done. Board members, squeezing in time for the organization between jobs, families, and other commitments, know this feeling also. To establish and supervise a business on top of these time commitments is often unrealistic.

To start a small business an organization must be financially sound. A successful small business takes three to five years to show a profit and should not be seen as a "quick fix" to financial difficulties. Even after three to five years of development a small business can provide, at the most, 10 percent of an organization's budget.

In his study of small business ventures, *Business Ventures of Citizen Groups,* Charles Cagnon explains, "Many non-profits have an annual budget of over $100,000. It would require a remarkable business to make an impact on a budget of that size. For example, a typical business would have to receive gross revenues of nearly $1 million in order to earn $50,000 in net profits which could safely be removed from the business and applied to the non-profit. (Even though some industries are more profitable than others, a 5% net profit is a conservative rule of thumb.) A business that would produce $1 million in gross revenues could easily require 20 employees, particularly in the retail and service industries which citizen groups are likely to consider. . . . To put it another way, for a business to contribute a modest $5,000 to the non-profit's budget, the business would probably have to generate $100,000 in gross revenues."

In estimating the projected profit margin from a business, groups must keep in mind that not all the profit can be given to the organization's work; some money must be reserved for business slumps and to reinvest in the business to ensure its long-term growth.

Types of Small Businesses for Nonprofits

There are two broad categories of business that a nonprofit may engage in under existing tax law: "related" and "unrelated" business.

In a related business the profits from the business are exempt from income tax. To qualify as a related business the business activities must " contribute importantly" to the accomplishment of the organization's mission.

The key element the Internal Revenue Service uses to evaluate the continuation of the organization's tax-exempt status is the determination of whether the nonprofit organization has an unfair advantage over a profit-making business and is thus engaging in "unfair competition." Because a nonprofit organization's related business does not pay income tax, it can reinvest that money to expand the business faster than a for-profit concern. Under pressure from the Small Business Administration, small business owners, and sometimes the general public, the IRS is being more and more strict about what types of businesses nonprofits can run and what kind of taxes they can avoid. Because so many small businesses are imperilled by large chains, by an ongoing recession in many parts of the country, and by increasing labor costs, they watch closely the benefits that nonprofits get in starting and running businesses and insist that the business that a nonprofit runs be closely related to its work.

To avoid the accusation of unfair competition and to avoid losing your tax-exempt status, your group can opt to incorporate the business as an entirely separate entity and pay income tax. The business then donates its profit to your organization. Remember: The laws governing businesses are complicated, somewhat vague, and occasionally changing. Groups should always consult an attorney and business advisor about their situation before proceeding with a business.

With an "unrelated" business, the product or services offered for sale do not advance the mission of the group. In that case the organization must pay tax on the business's income at a regular corporate rate. A serious problem with an unrelated business is that if the business activity is "substantial" compared to the activity of the nonprofit organization, the nonprofit may lose its tax-exempt status. This happens in cases in which the business becomes so consuming that the purpose of the organization seems to be to run the business rather than to run the organization. To constitute a business, work must be carried on regularly. Therefore, an organization can sponsor completely unrelated special events on an infrequent basis and it will not be considered taxable business.

There are a few circumstances under which income tax is not collected from unrelated businesses, including:

◆ The bulk of the work is done by unpaid volunteers

◆ The products sold have been donated to the nonprofit

◆ The revenue comes from the rental of property for which little or no property management services are provided

◆ Revenue comes from interest, dividends, investments, or royalties.

Are You Ready for a Small Business?

Several elements must be present before an organization is ready to start a small business. First, the organization should have a strong donor base, regular special events, and an ongoing program of recruiting new donors. The organization should not need the money from the small business, especially in the immediate future. A small business is a diversification strategy for a group that has already diversified to the more traditional fundraising strategies and is looking ahead five years or more to other strategies.

An organization must also have people who are very committed to the idea of a small business and who themselves own or have owned successful small businesses. These people can constitute a planning group to do the research necessary to decide if and what kind of a small business is appropriate. An organization with all of these requisites in place can then consider starting a business.

The organization must have or borrow start-up capital to open the business. This almost always takes more money than is planned and longer to recoup than is anticipated. Undercapitalization — lack of sufficient start-up capital and enough money to put into the business after it starts and before it begins to show a profit — is a major reason for small businesses failing. Nonprofit organizations, which often live from month to month, are highly unlikely to have the financial reserves to risk on starting a business. Even for groups that are financially sound and have some financial reserves, deciding to risk them on the gamble of a business is a difficult decision. Borrowing the money does not solve your problem because the money must be paid back. The board of directors, some of whom will sign for a loan and may even put up collateral for it, are then personally liable for the loan. So a small business may mean not only risking all the assets of the organization but some of the personal assets of volunteers as well.

The Risks

An organization must reflect on several major risks in undertaking a business venture. The most obvious risk is that the business will fail. If the business goes bankrupt, the nonprofit corporation and its board of directors may be liable for any debts the business has incurred. If the product is faulty, the staff unfriendly, the price too high, the place dirty, and so forth, there is the danger that the business will tarnish the organization's reputation. A bad business reputation attached to your organization will not only affect the success of your business, it will also hamper your fundraising and organizing endeavors.

A second risk is that the business will not fail outright but will become a financial and emotional drain to the organization. All of its profits will have to be reinvested into the business or, if it operates at a loss, the organization will have to decide whether to invest more borrowed money in it. This is a drain in many ways, not the least of which is the stress involved in deciding whether to persevere, hoping that over time the business will become successful, or to cut your losses and bail out. If you decide to persevere, how long do you keep the business going? What will progress look like? All the fancy business plans in the world cannot ease the anxiety involved in running a business on the edge.

A further risk, as discussed above, is that the organization will lose its tax-exempt status.

The Gains

The advantages of a successful business are tremendous. First, of course, the organization can count on a reasonable amount of income from the business on a regular basis. Second, the skills acquired in learning how to run the business are useful in all aspects of fundraising and financial management for the entire organization. Many organizations that have small business ventures have discovered that the management of the overall organization is greatly strengthened. When an organization is strong and well managed it is more attractive to donors and more money can be raised.

Third, just as an excellent annual fundraising event increases visibility for a group, a business does so on a daily basis. A good business draws people in who may never have heard of your organization. Some of these people may become more involved with your group as donors and volunteers; others will simply patronize your business because they like what you sell even if they don't care about the goals of your group.

For direct-service organizations a business can sometimes provide valuable training and job experience for clients.

Starting a Small Business

The planning phase prior to starting a small business can be years long. The shortest time frame will probably be a year if you do a proper job of getting board and volunteer ownership, thoroughly investigating the law, and developing a formal business plan. The beginning of your process should be an investigation of other nonprofits that have businesses in your community. Interview the director or manager of the business. Is it successful? How long did it take to show a profit? How did they decide on their product or service? Patronize their business. What does it feel like to be a customer? Read a few books about starting small businesses. The Small Business Administration has a wide variety of free periodicals and your local library will probably have a shelf full of "how to" books about various businesses.

Think about what else you want from a business besides money. There are many faster ways for an organization to raise money than starting and running a business, so other goals must be paramount in pursuing this idea.

You may want to test the idea by offering products for sale through your group, such as T-shirts or totebags. Note the ease or difficulty with which you distribute these items and the kind of profit you are able to make. If your organization is good at selling products and you seem to have a natural constituency of buyers and/or entrepreneurs among board and staff, then proceed. You will always learn valuable skills from the process of planning a small business venture, so even if you don't open the business, your time will not be wasted.

24.

Religious Institutions, Service Clubs and Small Businesses

eligious groups, service clubs and small businesses often provide some funding to community groups, neighborhood projects, and projects with low budgets. With rare exceptions, national organizations will not get money from these sources, as they tend to concentrate their giving on local projects. Also, the more your organization's work challenges the status quo, particularly on issues of distribution of wealth, the less likely you will be to get money from businesses and service clubs.

Religious institutions, service clubs and small businesses can be asked to support specific projects or to give specific items such as office supplies, raffle prizes, or the use of space. These groups should also be approached as audiences for speaking engagements to broaden your visibility. Once you have received money or services from any of these sources you have a good chance of having the gift repeated. Few groups, however, will find any of these to be major sources of funding.

Religious Institutions

In Chapter 1, we noted that religious institutions receive about half of the money given away by the private sector in America. Religious institutions use most of the money they raise to pay for their own programs: maintaining buildings, paying staff, providing dues to their national offices, offering scholarships for seminary students and supporting various mission programs in America and abroad.

Organized religion is a also a major source of funds for other secular nonprofit organizations. It is hard to know exactly how much is given away by churches, synagogues, and mosques because IRS reporting requirements for religious institutions are slightly different and looser than those for corporations or foundations. However, reliable studies show that organized religion's philanthropic giving to nonreligious activities exceeds that of foundations and corporations combined, putting religion right behind individuals as the largest source of charitable giving.

Most grants from religious sources are in the range of $500 to $10,000. Some large sources, such as the Campaign for Human Development (Catholic) or the United Thank Offering (Episcopalian) give $30,000 to $50,000 to some of their grantees. Within local churches, the Women's Guild or the Altar Society may give some $50 and $100 donations to a few local groups.

Each religious body has its lines of accountability (some more, some less) flowing from the local house of worship through regional structures to national offices. Not all religious institutions have national offices, but most that give money do. In churches, the regional structures are called "judicatories" and you will need to be familiar with how they are organized in each denomination to understand the giving process of most churches. If you want to understand the structure of any Christian denomination, the Yearbook of American and Canadian Churches (check your library) is an excellent resource for getting the whole picture.

All local churches and synagogues can give contributions if they choose. The best guide to which local religious institutions are in your area is the Yellow Pages. See if people in your group are affiliated with any of the religious institutions listed. In most cases, in order to seek a gift from a religious institution, your group will need to have a relationship with the minister, rabbi, or a leading layperson. Then, there are several avenues for obtaining local funding:

◆ A minister or rabbi can give a group money (generally up to $500) from a **discretionary fund** over which he or she has authority.

◆ In churches that take up a collection, the minister or laypeople can call for a **"second collection"**: After the collection for the church has been taken at Sunday service, the minister or representative from your group will describe your work to the congregation and the collection plate will be passed again. The proceeds from this second collection go to your group.

◆ Within most churches and synagogues there are **various guilds and clubs**, each of which does its own fundraising and many of which distribute the money as they wish. Generally, any house of worship will have at least one women's guild, several mission programs (the money from which can be used for "domestic" missions), and youth projects.

◆ Churches and synagogues may **make their facilities available free of charge**. These can include meeting rooms, office space, use of a photocopy machine, limited use of a telephone or fax, and so forth. For groups just getting started, these services can be invaluable, as the church or synagogue can also act as your mailing address and may agree to receive phone messages for you until you are established.

In some religious bodies, there are also regional or national programs that make contributions, or there may be ecumenical efforts in one community focussed on one population or set of issues. The best known of these are the Catholic Campaign for Human Development, the United Church of Christ's Board of Homeland Ministries, the United Methodist Voluntary Service, the Jewish Fund for Justice, the American Friends Service Committee (Quaker), the Unitarian Universalist Veatch Program, and the ecumenical Commission on Religion in Appalachia (CORA). Many orders of nuns and priests provide funding to local groups as well. Much of this information is available at your local Foundation Center Collection (see list at the end of the book).

Remember that certain denominations take stands on specific issues. One obvious example is the Catholic Church's stand against freedom of choice in abortion and birth control. Many churches have reaffirmed their position that homosexuality is incompatible with Christian life. Almost all religious institutions place a strong emphasis on the integrity of the family, the importance of marriage, and other traditional values.

Service Clubs

Every city, town, and village in America has service clubs whose members are active in civic and community affairs and often raise funds for various community causes. The most common service clubs are Rotary, Kiwanis, Lions, Oddfellows, Shriners, Moose, Elk, Ruritan, Soroptomist, Zonta, and the Junior League. Some of these clubs restrict membership to one sex, but increasingly these clubs welcome both men and women.

Sometimes service clubs simply adopt an organization or a program for which they then sponsor an annual fundraising event. Organizations adopted for such support are usually Boys' and Girls' Clubs, camps, scholarship funds, school programs, or vocation-specific programs such as a trip to Washington, D.C. for young people wanting to go into politics, specially equipped vans for disabled people needing to get to college classes, and so forth. Service clubs will also give funds to buy equipment and will occasionally give to capital campaigns.

A group can approach a service club in one of two ways. If you have a contact with someone in the club who knows the club's fundraising program ask if that person will advocate with the club for a donation to your group. If you have no appropriate contact, offer a speaker from your group for one of their monthly meetings. If you don't know anyone in a service club, write or call the club for the name of the volunteer in charge of the program for monthly meetings, and then write or call him or her and volunteer a speaker from your group. Most groups will gratefully accept your offer.

Clubs' politics, commitment, and size and level of activity vary greatly from community to community. Therefore, research the clubs in your town to find out what, if anything, they can do for you.

Small Businesses

Groups seeking money from corporations and large businesses are often surprised by the generosity of owners of small stores and sole-proprietors of businesses compared with the frequent lack of response from bigger operations with more money.

Small businesses are best approached for in-kind rather than cash donations. Businesses can give raffle prizes, buy ads in an adbook, give your group items at wholesale cost (or at greater discounts for volume purchasing), underwrite special events, and buy tables at your luncheons or dinners. The key element in securing a business donation is to show the business person that his or her business will materially benefit from supporting your group. For example, in soliciting a raffle prize, stress how many people will see the raffle ticket with the business's name on it and how many will read the listing of supporting businesses in your newsletter. One raffle prize is a small investment for all that advertising.

Businesses that sell supplies that your group uses, such as office supplies or paper products, sometimes find that they need to discontinue a product line that isn't selling or to reduce inventory. Be sure you let them know that you will be glad to receive donations of such products.

Businesses can also extend credit to your group, enabling you to buy needed items and to pay when your cash flow is better. As long as you are trustworthy and keep in touch with them, businesses may be willing to carry a debt for quite some time.

Most business people belong to one or more business associations (which are sometimes service clubs whose members are all business people) that meet regularly and need speakers. By being invited to one of these meetings you can meet many business people at once. Use the same procedures as for getting a speaking engagement with a service club.

The economic conditions of your community and the health of small businesses generally will affect your ability to raise funds or services from them. If you show, however, that it is in their self-interest to help you, you will be able to expand your fundraising to these areas.

SECTION 5
Fundraising
Management

INTRODUCTION

F undraising for low-budget organizations generally falls apart over one of the following three things:

1. Strategies are not used properly and thus are rendered ineffective

2. The organization doesn't have a clear case, or loses sight of its mission and goals in its search for funding

3. Fundraising is not managed properly — there are bad record keeping systems, the fundraising staff have their own jobs and several other peoples, and the organization cannot keep to its plans.

It is to forestall #3 that this section exists. Starting with the office and basic working conditions, and moving all the way to finding staff, consultants and volunteers for fundraising, this section explains what has to be in place for effective fundraising to happen.

25.

The Fundraising Office

ew offices of low-budget organizations are adequate in size, equipment or support staff. Though buying state-of-the-art computer equipment and hiring more and more administrators and secretaries is not an option, there are some basic requirements for equipment and support that fundraising staff need to carry out an effective program. The same requirements hold true whether your fundraising program is run by volunteers or by paid staff. Those that cost money will all pay for themselves, and these costs should be seen as front money. Other elements cost time, which also must be seen as a front cost. If these requirements are not met, fundraising staff cannot be expected to work to their optimal capacity.

Space and Materials

There must be a separate space in the office for fundraising staff, files and materials. This would preferably be a room or at least a partitioned off area. This space must be quiet and include a desk of adequate size with drawers, a chair, a three-drawer (at least) filing cabinet and a telephone. (Some of this equipment can be obtained for free from corporations.) A bookshelf and other storage space, such as a closet, is also important. The space must have proper lighting and ventilation. This space should not be used by people other than fundraising staff and volunteers. Too much of the information here is confidential; files, mailing lists, reports, letters, and other papers need to be kept in order and should not be touched by anyone who is not dealing with them.

Fundraising staff should also have access to a good computer with a word processing program and a data base for donor records. Preferably, one computer should be dedicated to fundraising.

The organization must take the fundraising process seriously. Both paid and volunteer fundraising staff should be seen as professionals needing certain tools to carry out their job. A computer, desk, filing cabinet, phone and separate space are the tools of a fundraiser in the same way, and with the same importance, that hammers, saws, levels and the like are the tools of a carpenter. Just as you can't build a building without construction equipment, you can't build a donor base without fundraising equipment.

In addition to an adequate office set-up, a fundraiser should have a basic library of fundraising books (see Bibliography for a recommended list), as well as a dictionary, thesaurus and style manual to aid in writing and planning.

Obviously fundraising staff should not have nicer office space or fancier equipment than everyone else in the office. The whole organization should examine its working conditions from time to time and make it a priority to improve them if needed. It is ironic that many social change or social service groups will work in conditions that include too much noise, dim light, inadequate equipment, and so on when they would be outraged to read about such conditions for other workers. Good working conditions cost time and money, but poor working conditions cost more: in lower productivity, stress, burn-out, loss of creativity, loss of information, and the like.

26.

Managing Information

A major part of fundraising involves dealing with information — about people, sources of money, timing, strategies. But fundraising does not just involve knowing things; the creativity to make fundraising successful comes from knowing how to put things together: asking the right person at the right time for the right amount; scheduling the right event and inviting the people most likely to be interested to attend; using volunteers to the best of their abilities.

In order to use all the information available in the most effective ways, a fundraiser must know how to manage the information in his or her office. Often when you visit the office of a fundraising staff person, you notice piles of papers on the floor, table and windowsill, unlabelled computer disks, a desk strewn with notes, post-its stuck to every surface, and a telephone perched precariously atop the overflowing in-basket.

Too often we mistake the inability to handle paper with overcommitment on the part of the staff person. Since overcommitment is also a major element of many fundraisers' work styles, one compounds the other. A fundraiser confided recently to me that she was secretly relieved when her office flooded and many of her papers were destroyed. She now had an excuse for not getting work done she wouldn't have gotten to anyway.

This era is being called the "information age." Certainly, it is an age of words on paper and disk — books, magazines, papers, ads, computer programs — and the vague and unpleasant sensation that there is much more that you should know about every subject than you can possibly digest. Within the scope of the fundraiser's job, this chapter will provide help in dealing with the overload of information.

Information You Need for Fundraising

In order to know what to keep, what to throw out, what to delete, what to order, and what to file, you must make a list of priorities about your job. What information do you need to be on top of, and what doesn't matter? While the answer to this question will vary from person to person, most fundraisers must keep track of the following information, which is the most important information to their work:

1) Information pertaining to current donors

2) Information pertaining to prospects

3) Information about the organization that will be used to get more donors and prospects

4) Reference material about past fundraising activities

To keep track of this information, set up four filing cabinet drawers and four main directories on your computer to reflect these priorities: current donors, prospects, information that will attract donors, and reference material about your fundraising activities. Papers that you now have pertaining to anything else should go into the recycling box. Among other items that will get tossed are all newsletters from other groups unrelated to your group, all advertisements for seminars and classes, all catalogues, all annual reports of foundations your group will not be applying to and all old annual reports of prospective foundations, all old to-do lists and all reports on all causes unrelated to your group. Into the fourth file drawer, for reference material, put one copy of your group's past newsletters, one copy of proposals funded, evaluations of direct mail appeals and reports on special events, board minutes and reports, and financial statements.

Every piece of paper should be held up to this test: Can this help you get money from someone? If yes, who? how? Put it in the prospect's file, or in the reference drawer if it might be needed for reference (such as board finance reports). If no, throw it out or give it to another staff person.

Simple Rules

Once you learn a few simple rules about what to keep and what to save, keeping track of information will not actually be that difficult.

First, review the basics. What is your job? What do you have to know? What would people reasonably expect you to be able to lay your hands on quickly? Even if you are the only paid staff person, you still have a limit to your job.

◆ You must have records of official meetings of the organization and reports offered to the board, the public or the IRS about the organization. Keep one (at most two) copies of minutes, audits, 990's, newsletters, direct mail appeals, annual reports, etc.

♦ You must have records on the donors: their names addresses and gift history, as well as information that would help you or someone else ask them for more money or for some other type of involvement.

There are other items you probably should have if you are a one-person shop — you decide. But do you really need copies of newsletters from organizations you are not interested in? Dozens of samples of invitations? (Pick the best 10 and throw the rest away.) The latest reports from the most prolific think tanks on every subject from the ozone layer to police brutality, campaign reform to the role of women in rural Hindu communities? No. What is your group? Read only what pertains to you.

Having set priorities on what kind of information you need, sort all your papers into those categories and throw away anything that doesn't fall into them. Especially throw away the volumes of information you now keep that you feel you "should" read. The stuff that you bring home but never quite get to, and take on business trips but get distracted from by other reading. If you feel like you "should" read it, you probably won't. Get off your own case and lighten up. It's all right not to read everything, or even not to read most things.

The final rule of thumb about what to throw out is that if you haven't looked at it in six months, and it is not needed for the IRS or as an archive copy, throw it out.

A to Z

Next, think through your filing system. Many people simply put their files into alphabetical order and call it a day. I was once in an office in which the personnel policies were filed right behind a donor named "Alice Pershing." This mixes donor files with administrative files and makes everything hard to find.

Create broad categories, then file inside those categories. Categories might include: board, donors, prospects, foundations, finances, programs, personnel, publications. Inside some of those categories, you may want sub-categories. For example, the board section might have the following sub-categories: board members — current, past, potential; board reimbursements; board minutes; staff reports to the board, etc. Some of these categories will then contain alphabetical files, but some will be easier to find if you file them chronologically. For example, board minutes and reports to the board should be filed chronologically.

To test your filing system, ask a friend or another staff person to come into your office and start naming things for you to find. You should be able to lay your hands on any piece of paper you are in charge of in 30 seconds. If you can't do that, reassess your system. Once your system passes this test, see how well it works for someone else. Suppose you were hit by a train — how understandable is your office? If it takes someone else more than five minutes to figure out where something is, your system is too mysterious.

Handling What You Keep

The next challenge is to deal with the stuff you keep. Make it a rule not to handle any piece of paper more than once, and try not to break this rule more than a few times a day. Make a small mark on every piece of paper you are handling and note how many marks it has before it is finally laid to rest. More than three is a bad sign.

The Intangible Files

Finally, there is the subject of files in your computer. This is more insidious because you don't often notice how much room these are taking up — the "clutter" is invisible, so it is easy to let hard disks get overloaded and chaotic. I have watched people scroll their directories and sub-directories with the same intensity and frustration with which they previously tried to sort through their papers, unable to find what they were looking for.

The same standards apply to computer files as to paper files: Will you need it again? What category and sub-category should it be listed under?

When you save something on your computer, think about what you name it. There are people who name their files after their lover of the moment, or the day of the week, or even some obscure abbreviation of something in the file, but all of this makes the files obscure even to the one who named them. Again, apply the standard, "If I were hit by a train, could someone else find this?" Give it a name that makes some sense.

To help you stay on top of your papers and computer files once you get organized, post a 3" by 5" card with the one, two or three things that will most help you keep clear on what to keep. One person has this on his card:

"Is it a donor?

Is it a prospect?

Could it lead to a donor or a prospect?"

Another has this:

"When in doubt, throw it out.

After all, what is the worst thing that can happen?"

Another's says:

"If this were my last day at work and I was sorting through my stuff, would I give it to the person succeeding me?"

In our business information is like food. It is only useful for what it does for us, and trying to keep it only causes it to spoil. Seeing information in that light will let you be in control of it, so that you can use it to do your work.

27.

Managing Time

Effective time management often marks the difference between a good fundraiser and someone who is never going to make it in this field. The most important thing to remember is that the fundraising job is never done and you are never caught up. In this case Murphy's Law says that expenses rise to meet income. The more successful the fundraising plans are, the more plans the organization will make to spend that money. Consequently no amount of money raised is ever enough. Fundraising staff (paid or unpaid) must set their own limits, because no matter how supportive the organization may be of the fundraising staff's work, it is still relentless in its need for more money.

Here are some guidelines for using your time to best advantage.

Every Day:

♦ Reserve one to three hours during which you cannot be interrupted by phone calls. Either get someone else to answer the phone or use an answering machine. Use that time for research and writing.

♦ Spend fifteen to thirty minutes at the end of the day writing up a to-do list for the next day. At the beginning of the day review your to-do list. Unless something that can't wait comes up, do only those tasks already on your to-do list. Put new things on tomorrow's list.

♦ Write, or have a volunteer write, thank-you notes. Don't get behind on these.

Every Week:

♦ Update your donor records.

♦ Go over your fundraising plan for the month and make sure you are on target. Don't put off tasks such as getting a letter to the printer, calling a foundation, setting up meetings of the major gifts committee or special events committee. Do these tasks on time.

Every Month:

♦ Call all board members, even if just to say hello. Make sure they feel needed and wanted by the organization. Those board members working on particular fundraising tasks need encouragement, gratitude, and sometimes help. (During campaigns you will need to call these people more frequently.)

Beyond these rules of thumb, understanding information as time-related is also integral to running an efficient office. Once you have organized your office, files, and desk in a way that allows you nearly instant access to the information you need and provides a sensible system that someone else can follow, as described in the last chapter, you need to assign a time by which you will have used or acted on the information you are so effectively keeping track of. There are two principle methods: calendars and action plans.

Calendars

Buy or make three calendars:

1) A "year-at-a-glance" calendar. This calendar needs to be big enough to hang on the wall, showing all twelve months at once, with each month divided into 1" by 1" boxes for the days.

2) A "month-at-a-glance" calendar. Some people get these calendars as desk-top blotters. You can also buy a desk-top calendar from a worthy group so you have uplifting stories or fabulous nature photos to look at. Just be sure that the space for each day has enough room to write a few lines.

3) An appointment calendar to carry with you in your purse or briefcase. This is a simple daily calendar, with all the days of the year laid out two or so to a page.

While you can certainly invest lots of money in fancy calendar systems that have places to record expenses, birthdays, car mileage, meeting notes, priority to-do's, meeting agenda items, tax information and the like, I have yet to meet anyone who actually used all those systems. Further, in my experience the fancier the calendar, the less reliable the person. I always know when someone pulls out the ten-pound, multi-colored and tabbed calendar, and turns to the special section for "commitments made" to write something they just said they would do, it will probably never happen. On the other hand, when someone takes the free calendar they got from their insurance agent or an inexpensive one bought at an office supply store and writes what they have committed to on the day they made the commitment, I am reasonably certain it will get done. In terms of calendars, then, the simpler the system, the more workable it is likely to be.

Now, take your "Year-at-a-Glance" calendar and put X's through the following:

- ◆ Major holidays, and one or two days before and after those holidays
- ◆ Your vacation
- ◆ Your birthday (don't work on your birthday)
- ◆ The day (or two, if you wish) after any work meeting or conference that you know will be grueling or that you have to travel a long distance to attend.

What you have left is close to the true number of days you could get work done.

Now put a large dot on the dates of board meetings, annual meeting, special events, proposal deadlines, newsletter deadlines and any other meetings or deadlines that you can anticipate. Take a fine-line marker and draw a line from each deadline back as many days as you think it will take you to prepare for it, and if there is work generated by the event, then extend your line for one or two days after the event. Whatever work days don't have lines, dots or X's are days you can do the rest of your work.

You now have a clear visual picture that allows you to assess quickly, "Can I take on this commitment?" "Does it make sense for me to attend this conference when I will be exhausted from our annual retreat?" "Should we conduct our major donor campaign during our audit?"

Remember also that some of the days of the year will be used up by illness (yours, your children's, etc.), by goofing off or not working efficiently, and by emergencies that take precedence.

Now take your "Month-at-a-Glance" calendar and in the day boxes write the major task areas that have to be taken care of each day in order to keep on schedule. This calendar does not take the place of a "to-do" list. However, most people do not keep the relationship of their "to-do" list and their calendar clear enough. For example: someone calls you and asks for an appointment. You look at your appointment calendar and, seeing a clear day, make the appointment, only to realize later that the day was kept clear because of the approaching deadlines covered by the to-do list. Whenever possible, set your meetings, appointments, lunch dates, and so on by referring to your yearly or monthly calendar. A day does not stand alone. Do you really want to have a 7 a.m. breakfast meeting with a major donor the morning after a board meeting that will run until 10 p.m.?

Your daily calendar that you carry with you is used for appointments, addresses, phone numbers, making future meetings and appointments when you are not in your office, notes from meetings, etc. However, every two or three days (some people do this at the end of every day), move all relevant information from your daily calendar onto the monthly one or onto a to-do list. Note in your daily calendar deadlines and days that are filled with writing or preparation.

Make appointments with yourself also. One man who had a hard time saying no to anything would make up names of people and then assign meeting times to them in his calendar. He does this because of the obnoxious habit some people have of looking at other people's calendars to find open space. Often at meetings, he says, someone will say, "How's Wednesday at 2?" Leaning over to peer at someone else's calendar, the person will say, "Bill, looks like you have an open afternoon." So when Bill knows he has a hard day of work, even though it involves no appointments, he writes in fake appointments and puts the letter "hh" beside these, which stands for "ha-ha." He knows they are fake, but they jar him into not saying yes. He can say, "I have a meeting" which for him, like most people, is easier than saying, "I have to write the campaign brochure." It also spares him the agony of someone saying, "This will only take 20 minutes — it will be good for you to have a break from your writing."

Avoid having a home calendar and a work calendar. People who do that almost always miss their Monday morning appointments and are constantly trying to recall whether they can make an evening meeting on Thursday, because they think it is Jill's soccer match, or is it Wednesday? Your daily calendar shows your whole day, from home to work and back home. Put your important home-life appointments and activities in your single daily calendar.

Things to Avoid

1) Avoid saying to yourself or others, "I am so busy," or "I don't know how I'll get everything done." Both these statements could be true, but they don't accomplish anything except to use up time and make you feel overwhelmed. Most people are busy and few people get everything done. Tell yourself instead, "I can get this done. I have enough time."

2) Skip meetings or conferences that you do not need to attend. Conferences, training workshops, seminars and classes are very popular now, feeding on the feeling that we never know enough. They are both expensive and time consuming and rarely worth it. Choose those events where you will really learn something or see people you truly want to see. Then go, and be there. Too often we decide to attend a conference half-heartedly and spend most of the plenaries and workshops making notes or to-do lists for when we get back. A sign that a conference is not worth it for you is when you have to phone your office more than once a day while you're gone.

3) Avoid too many meetings. While we have work to do in meetings and, admittedly, a certain amount of the work we do at meetings is socializing and building camaraderie, many meetings are not essential and almost every meeting lasts too long. Question every meeting. Is it necessary? If it is, do I need to be there? Can I be there for part of it and not all of it? If you can, make sure there is an agenda with times beside each item. People tend to talk for the amount of time that is listed. You can negotiate the need for extra time as it comes up.

4) Avoid time drains. If you often have the feeling that you worked hard all day and that you are using your calendars properly but you still got little done, it is important to look for time drains. For most people, they take two forms: the telephone and people coming by your office to chat. Here are two ways to shorten time drains:

♦ *Shorten your phone calls.* Move the phone off your desk so that you have to stand up to answer it. If you stand up to answer the phone and remain standing while talking on the phone, your phone calls will be much shorter and you will not be tempted to make phone calls that are not part of your work plan.

♦ *Discourage people from dropping by.* Either take all chairs out of your office so there is nowhere for someone to sit, or put papers on them so that the papers have to be moved in order for someone to sit down. If someone comes by whom you don't need to talk with and you don't have time to talk to, you can tell them that you will call them later or set a lunch date right then, or you can stand up and remain standing while talking to them (they will not sit down if you are standing). If need be, while *you* are talking to them, look at your watch or your calendar. This will remind your visitor of time without you being rude. You never need to act hurried or rushed with spontaneous visitors as long as you don't get panicked about how your are going to get rid of them.

Action Plans

One of the hard things about working with individual donors is that this work has no externally determined deadlines, so you have to create your own. Once you have your calendars set up, you are ready for the next step in organizing your fundraising office.

Whenever you work with a donor or a prospect, make a note in their file of what you intend to do next. This is called your "action plan." It can be recorded in a separate field in your computer data base or a separate entry on a donor information card. An "action plan" is brief, such as, "Invite to house party," or "Call with outcome of organizing effort in Roane County," or "Send report on toxic waste dumping as soon as available." Then add a date to the action you plan to take. Now take this date and put it in your "month-at-a-glance" calendar. Note the donor's last name or some identifying phrase that will remind you to check their file for what you were going to do on that date.

If you are systematic about your donors, each donor or prospect will have a date on which you are going to work with them and move the process of cultivating them along. By spreading these dates out over the year, you can give more personal attention to donors and not get jammed with donor meetings during a campaign or at the end of the year. If you have thousands of donors, obviously you will have to decide which ones you want to work with personally, but the action plan concept can be used for group activity also, such as "Oct. 1: all $50-100 donors receive news alert mail appeal."

A fundraiser's job is often compared to the circus performer who balances plates on sticks by keeping the plates twirling, and runs from stick to stick to keep the spin going. If she misses, the plate falls and may break. The calendar is the stick, and the action plans are the plates. This is how you keep your plates spinning and not falling. The overall idea is to have as little to remember as possible. You shouldn't have things in your memory that you could write down or enter in your computer. This frees you to use your mind to be creative or to learn new details about people, and write those down later.

The wide variety of tasks involved in fundraising are both exciting and one of the many difficulties of the job. You can minimize the difficulties by relatively simple procedures to keep your office running efficiently. A calendar and action plan system allows you to use the information you accumulate and raise maximum dollars for your work.

28.

Record Keeping

Accurate, up-to-date and thorough records are a necessity for an ongoing fundraising program. Without such records, you have little capability to ask donors for more money, to target projects to specific donor interests, to track response to appeals, or to carry out any of the other requirements for fundraising from a stable group of individual donors.

By now, most organizations are using computers for word processing, doing mail merge, maintaining mailing lists and so on. If you are on a paper system, you still need to keep good records. Most of the information in this chapter will be the same for those doing record keeping on paper as for those using computers.

The name, address and other information about each donor needs to be maintained in some kind of data base — this can be a box of 5" by 7" cards, an off-the-shelf software program that you customize for your organization or a data base program designed for fundraising. What is best depends on the size of your list. If you intend to work with more than 250 donors, you should aim to have a computerized data base rather than a paper system. If you have more than 1,000 donors, you will probably want to buy a software program designed for fundraising unless you are a computer whiz yourself or have a volunteer who is. Although fundraising software programs tend to cost at least $1,000, several of them have extended low- or no-interest payment plans, and several have versions you can "grow into"—that is, you buy a data base that holds fewer names and possibly has fewer functions; as you grow, you apply the cost of your previous data base to an upgrade that holds more names and has more capabilities.

Look for a data base with these five capabilities:

1) It stores a lot of names (preferably an infinite number).

2) It stores a lot of information about each name, using as many fields as you need.

3) It can sort those fields quickly and easily.

4) It can produce reports by sorting and compiling information, such as total number of gifts from the summer appeal, amounts pledged vs. amounts received, difference between this year's direct mail and last year's, and so on.

5) It can merge with a word processing program to create individualized letters, and can format labels of different sizes for mailings.

If you are thinking of buying a fundraising program, ask for a "demo disk." The disk will show you what the program can do and give you a sense of how "user friendly" it is. Before buying anything, be sure all your questions have been answered and that you understand the answers. Don't be afraid to ask elementary questions and don't let sales people make you feel stupid or old fashioned for not being up on the latest technology or the latest vocabulary. Finally, find out what kind of support the company provides once you purchase their program: Is there an 800- telephone number for questions? Can you call as often as you need to? How are charges for this support figured? What kinds of training programs does the company have and how expensive are they?

Many organizations have bought either a fundraising or a data base program they then had to customize without fully understanding it, and then could not afford the additional cost of the support package and so did not use the program. There is a marked difference between the number of nonprofits that have computers and the number that use them to their fullest capacity for fundraising.

Whether you are on a paper system or a data base, think through what information you will want to gather and maintain. You don't need to know as much about someone who gives $25 as about someone who gives $2,500. You will want to know more about someone who gives money several times a year for ten years than someone who gives one gift and then doesn't give again.

What to Record

For all donors you need to know the following information:

♦ **Name and address.** Get this off of the photocopy of their check, if they give using a check. Information written on people's checks is generally accurate, particularly the spelling of their names. People are offended when their name is misspelled, regardless of whether their handwriting is legible or not.

• **Phone number.** Record this if it appears on the check, or if the donor wrote it on their reply device.

• **Form of salutation** to use in writing this donor. Note whether to use Dear Mr./Ms., Dear Joe, Dear Anna and Mary, Dear Rev. Lloyd, etc. If you don't know, use a formal but non-sexist salutation: Dear Ms. Smith is preferable to Dear Mrs. Smith. For couples, try "Dear Friends."

• **Gift history.** Note date of gift, size of gift, and what the gift was in response to (such as board member request, direct mail, canvass, etc.).

• **Renewal date.** In many cases this will be in the "Gift History."

• **Correspondence record.** Note "thank you sent" and the date, and any other correspondence you have. Actual copies of the letters will probably be in a paper file or in another file in your computer.

• **Other information.** This category, or "field" as it will be called on your data base, may remain empty if you have no other information, but it can be used to note anything you know about this person that is pertinent to their being a donor or a prospect for a bigger gift. For example, "Sister of board president" would go here. Or, suppose a gift of $30 comes in from Joe Cumberland, but the check says "Joe Cumberland; Janice Ruark, MD." First, you can check to see if Janice Ruark is also a donor. If she is not, just make a note "check in his name and Janice Ruark, MD." This may be useful, or it may never lead anywhere. Sometimes a reply card will carry the name of a person, "Lydia S. Turner," but the check says, "Sampson Family Foundation." Make a note of that. Probably the "S" in Lydia's name is for Sampson. Under your "action plan" (see previous chapter), make a note to look up the Sampson Family Foundation at the Foundation Center Library.

If you trade lists with other groups, you may want to have a box on your reply device that says, "Do not trade my name." This information would go in another field, and would be indicated by a letter or other code. If you were going to trade your mailing list, you would ask the computer to produce a list of everyone except people with that code.

This is all the information you keep on people who have given only once so far, or who give less than $50 and have done so for less than three years, or for people you know are not going to give more.

For people who give more than $50, or have given any amount for more than three years, start keeping the information outlined in Chapter 12, Personal Solicitation. If you have a fundraising data base, it will have suggested categories that can help you think through what you need to know. If you have a data base that you program yourself, you will have to determine all the categories.

There are two useful categories that can be easily added to either a data base or a paper system. They are "Missing Information" and "Next Step." It often happens that you know some details about a donor but not enough to include the donor in the upper ranges of your gift range chart, for example, or to ask them to give an extra gift for a capital improvement. In this case it is helpful to focus on what you would need to know to feel comfortable asking them for more money or an extra gift. Perhaps you need to know more about their friendship with a board member. Are they very close, or simply acquaintances? Perhaps you need to know what other charitable commitments the donor has made. Maybe you need to know more about what the donor thinks about a particular issue that your group is working on. Or maybe it is something simpler, such as their phone number. Make a note of whatever it is under "Missing Information." Once every month or so, ask the computer for a printout of the fields "Name, address," and "Missing Information." Then you will have complete list of what you need to do to get your donor records in better order.

The other useful category is "Next Step." Obviously, a logical next step may be to find the "missing information," but this category can be used more proactively. Often the next step is not to ask for more money, but to be sure to send some article of interest that you promised the donor. Maybe Sally, your board member who lives down the road from this donor, needs to invite the donor to a house party or a meeting. Maybe this donor has a lot of contacts and you want to ask her to give you a list of them right before the spring major donor drive. Note what the next step is and a date by which it should be done. Then, by asking the computer for "Name, address and Next Step," you have a complete to-do list for working with donors.

The Importance of These Records

People sometimes feel that gathering this information so systematically and writing it all down is an invasion of the donor's privacy and makes the organization nosy and somehow manipulative, viewing people only in terms of money. It is very important to remember three things about donor records:

1) If you don't record this information you will forget it, and you will not be able to raise money effectively. Many people have "birthday books" where they write down all their friends' and relatives' birthdays. No one thinks this is an invasion of privacy — in fact, they are pleased to be remembered on their birthday. You are trying to use donor resources to the best advantage, which is what donors want and deserve. There is no point is asking someone for more money who only gives once a year, but it is a waste not to ask someone who likes your organization and would gladly give more often if asked. Further, how will the organization know that your long-time loyal donor, Tania Lopez, hates to be called at work if someone doesn't record it? Or that Steve who owns the Deli said he would cater your Annual Meeting for free if you get back to him by March? Finally, you are obligated by law to keep a record of gifts received so that if a donor is audited by the IRS, and the IRS needs to verify the amount the donor gave to your group, you can provide that verification.

2) You don't record anything that you don't need to know. Your goal is for every donor to be as loyal to your group as possible and to give you as much money as they can afford because of that loyalty. Everything you record about a donor should be information that helps you toward that goal. So, no matter how interesting it might be that Max was once lovers with Fred, don't record it. If a donor who is also a friend confides to you that she spent time in prison and is having trouble with the parole board, don't write it down. Think of this: if a donor asked to see his or her record, would you be embarrassed to show it? Why? What's in there that shouldn't be? You are recording information that is easily obtainable or that people would not object to your knowing, such as how many children they have, or where they work.

3) This information is highly confidential. Only a few people, such as the executive director, the development director, and the treasurer of the board (and sometimes the bookkeeper or administrator) should have access to all the information. (Most data bases will include some kind of password system. One password allows access to Name, address and phone; a second password accesses Gift History; a third password allows one to see all the information. Only a few people should have all three passwords.) Donor records such as paper files, back-up disks, correspondence, and so on should be kept in a locked file cabinet with limited access. People who can see this information must understand its delicate nature and use the same discretion in revealing it as is used in recording it.

Keeping Your List in Shape

Update your donor records on a regular basis. Don't pile up more than 10 names that need to be recorded or you will get careless with numbers and spelling when you do record them. Many small, understaffed groups put off updating their records until the night before they need the mailing list for the newsletter; then a staff member and a volunteer frantically try to get everything in order. That list is inevitably full of errors.

Watch for duplicate entries, particularly when you are going to use the list for a mailing. Donors dislike getting more than one copy of your newsletter or other mailing. A data base will not know that J.P. Miller and John Miller are the same person, or that Sally Jones at 22 Pine St. South is the same as Sally Jones at 22 S. Pine.

Safety First

Whatever system you use, be sure to have a back-up system that you use often. If you are using a paper system, make a copy of your donor records once every six months and keep it in a safe deposit box or at a board member's house. Keep copies of legal documents and any records that would be difficult to replace in a location away from your office. When using a computer, be sure to back up your work every day that you use the computer; every month, make a back-up disk of your donor records that is not kept in the office. You need to think through what would happen if your hard disk crashed, or if your building burned, or if there was a flood, vandalism, earthquake, hurricane or any number of other disasters that could ruin your record keeping system.

For many fundraisers, record keeping is the bane of their existence. But keeping records takes far less time if you do it regularly and without getting far behind than if you wait until the last minute, do it badly, and then have to spend time cleaning up your mess. Record keeping needs to be seen as being as necessary and habitual as brushing your teeth.

29.

Hiring a Development Director

As small organizations grow, they grapple with the ongoing need to raise more and more money. Inevitably, they must consider hiring someone to take charge of the fundraising function. This is a difficult decision. A group is gambling that the investment of salary — money they often barely have — is going to generate much more money than they are currently raising. And it will, if the person is effective, the board already accepts its role in fundraising, and the organization has its basic infrastructure in place (up-to-date records, clear goals and objectives). However, there is little margin for error. What if the person isn't skilled enough, or isn't a good worker?

What if everything is in place, but the program takes longer than planned? How will the organization support itself in the meantime?

Three issues must be clarified before any decision to hire fundraising staff can be made.

1. There must be clarity as to the role of a fundraiser or development director. It is most important to understand that the person whose primary responsibility is overseeing fundraising does not actually raise money. With the input of the board or fundraising committee, she or he plans for fundraising (developing year-long plans that spell out each strategy and set goals).

This person maintains fundraising records and the mailing list; sends out thank-you notes, or oversees that task, if there is clerical staff; reports to foundations or large donors on specific projects; does prospect research; writes and sends mail appeals, renewals and other fundraising letters; and goes on major donor visits as needed. She or he works closely with the board, helping them make and then fulfill their fundraising commitments. This person may also write grants and research foundations and corporations, if that is a part of the organization's plan, and there may be other fundraising strategies that he or she must oversee or implement. The development director primarily works behind the scenes, establishing a structure for effective fundraising by volunteers.

Many board members and paid staff imagine that hiring a development director will save them from further fundraising tasks. "Let's pay someone to do this so we can do the real work" is a common and potentially fatal suggestion. While the paid fundraising staff obviously relieves the load of other staff and may relieve the board of some tasks, everyone's involvement in and consciousness of fundraising must stay the same or increase for the expanded fundraising program to be successful.

2. There must be clarity about what you want this person to do for your organization. Many people wonder why the task of fundraising has so many different job titles attached to it, such as "fundraiser," "fundraising coordinator," "development director," or "resource developer." In many social change organizations, the fundraising coordinator is called just that, in a straightforward way. In other, usually larger organizations, this position is called the director of development. Sometimes small groups think this title is a sign of elitism or an attempt to disguise the crassness of raising money, similar to saying "your support" rather than "your money" in fundraising appeals and letters. However, there are actually important differences between fundraising and development.

Fundraising is the process of bringing in the amount of money an organization needs to carry out its programs from year to year. Besides raising an operating budget, development also includes most of the following activities:

- Creating a long-range plan and updating it on a yearly basis (augmenting the case statement)
- Instituting a planned public relations program
- Maintaining a planned and frequently evaluated process for bringing on new board members
- Providing fundraising training for board, staff and volunteers
- Carrying out ongoing planning and evaluation of the financial needs and fundraising plans for the future of the organization
- Developing the group's capability to conduct capital campaigns and start planned giving programs.

One development director characterized it this way, "In fundraising, you make do with what you have. You keep the organization going and out of debt. In development, you start with what you have and you help it grow."

3. It must be clear that hiring a development director will actually solve the problems you have. Analysis of your situation will show whether your problems lie in fundraising or need other solutions. To begin this analysis, answer the following questions:

a) Is your board active in fundraising? Does every board member participate in fundraising in some way, whether organizing special events, getting mail appeals out, or asking for money face to face?

b) Does it sometimes seem that board and perhaps staff spend more time planning for fundraising than actually raising money?

c) Do board members and other volunteers involved in fundraising seem to suffer from a lack of knowledge of what to do rather than a lack of enthusiasm?

d) Is the executive director or other staff constantly pulled away from program development and organizing to do fundraising? Does she or he feel torn about setting priorities for use of time?

e) Is your budget over $200,000, or do you need to raise more than $100,000 from non-government, non-foundation sources?

If the answer is yes to three or more of these questions, you should seriously consider hiring a development director. This person would direct and kindle the fundraising energies of the board, plan for fundraising, train others in fundraising tasks, and enable program staff to get on with program work.

If, however, you need help with data entry, writing the annual report, compiling financial reports, answering the phone, dealing with the mail, handling checks, sending thank-you notes, etc., you should consider hiring support staff, such as a secretary or office manager.

If your list of needs includes a better and more involved board, you need to strengthen your board and provide some motivational training for them before you hire a development director.

If you want someone to help you plan and carry out a time-limited project, such as a direct mail or major gifts campaign, consider hiring a consultant.

Paying Development Directors

Imagine this scenario: An organization is debating whether to hire a development director. They have little front money so they worry about finding the right person and meeting a salary. As if in answer to a prayer, a handsome stranger shows up and offers to raise $150,000 (their budget) for a 20 percent commission. If he doesn't succeed, he explains, they are not out anything; however, they pay him 20 percent of any money he raises. He says he can do it in six months.

There are several reasons that this is an absolute no-no. First, no one else in the organization is paid on commission. People are paid a salary in recognition that their work is a process and that they may be very good at their job without showing a lot of immediate progress in ending racism or stopping pollution, or whatever the group is working on.

Second, a commission tends to distort salaries. In this case, this fundraiser would be paid the equivalent of $60,000 a year, nearly twice as much as the director, who makes $35,000.

Third, this person will not bring his own list of contacts. He will be working with the organization's donors. He says he has some contacts from previous jobs, but are they appropriate for your work? And do you want him taking your donor information to his next job? Further, his whole livelihood depends on donors saying yes to his requests. Even a totally honest fundraiser working under these conditions would be tempted to distort information, seeing his rent check in the eyes of each prospect. Also, many big gifts take cultivation and several visits. He may be willing to settle for a small gift in order to get it quickly rather than take the time it would require for proper cultivation.

Fourth, what will the donors think if and when they find out that 20 percent of their gift went to this temporary staff person? Few things make donors angrier than learning that a significant part of their designated gift was used for expenses.

Fifth, as was stressed earlier, one person should not be in charge of actually raising money for an entire campaign. Suppose he is both honest and successful. When he leaves, the group is $150,000 richer, to be sure, but no wiser in regard to fundraising.

Finally, the person coordinating the fundraising should absolutely believe in the cause and be a part of the team of people putting the campaign together.

For these reasons, paying on commission is highly frowned on in fundraising and all the trade associations for fundraisers, including the

National Society of Fundraising Executives, the National Association of Hospital Developers, and the Council for the Advancement and Support of Education, have issued statements decrying the practice of commission-based fundraising.

Some people in small organizations will say, "That's fine for them to say, but we don't have the cash to hire someone and it is risky to hire a person when you can't afford it, both for the person and for us if they are not successful." But for all the reasons above, a small organization especially cannot afford the risk involved in hiring someone on commission.

The development director's salary should be based on other staff salaries. If you have a collective salary structure, then it is the same as everyone else's. If there are pay differentials, then it is less than the director's, but more than the office manager. In a hierarchical structure, the development director is a management staff person, usually reporting directly to the executive director.

Many times you hear that you have to pay "a lot" to get a capable person. This is not true. A good person for your group is someone who first and foremost believes in your group and wants to be part of it. This person will express his or her belief through fundraising, just as someone else is expressing their belief by doing direct service, organizing, or policy development. If someone who meets the criteria of believing strongly in your work has fundraising skills but can't afford to work at the salary level you are offering, you may need to reevaluate everyone's salary.

How to Find a Capable Development Director

Once you have decided that you need a development director, you need to create a fair and accurate job description and begin the hiring process. Many job descriptions fail to attract candidates because they contain too many responsibilities. Avoid the temptation to add components to the job that are not related to fundraising or public relations. It is fair to ask the development director to edit and oversee the publication of the newsletter; it is unwise to ask that person to also be the accountant.

You should be able to describe the job in one page (see example). Think about what skills are essential as opposed to those that are desirable but not imperative. When interviewing, ask for writing samples, since writing will be a large part of almost any fundraiser's job.

Advertise in publications geared to nonprofits. Unless you are in a small town, avoid advertising in the newspaper. (You will receive a lot of resumes of unqualified people.) Post your job description at the Foundation Center Collection nearest to you (see list at end of book) and in places where social change activists hang out or shop, such as coffeehouses, alternative or women's bookstores, health food stores, progressive churches and synagogues. Send the announcement to other nonprofits and call directors and development directors that you know and tell them the job is available.

Don't be stuck on hiring someone with all the "right" qualifications and experience. If you find such a person, hire them immediately. But if you don't find such a person, look for other sorts of qualifications that are evidence of skills related to fundraising such as running a small business, teaching, or personnel management. Any job that requires that a person be a self-starter and have experience planning, working with diverse groups of people, and good organizational skills is a good background for fundraising.

Look closely at volunteer experience, and encourage applicants to describe their work as volunteers. Many people know more than they realize about fundraising from having volunteered. People with little or no volunteer experience are not good candidates because they will have little idea of how to work with volunteers.

In addition to broadening your criteria in hiring someone, be willing to hire a consultant for a few days to help your new staff person get a running start on their job, or send the new development director to one or two of the many classes and courses that are offered on fundraising. The theories and how-tos of fundraising are not particularly difficult to understand, even though they take a lot of work to implement. Getting someone who is underqualified but bright, committed and eager to do a good job is almost as good as getting an experienced person with the same attributes.

SAMPLE JOB DESCRIPTION

Development Director — Position Available

Starting Date: June 1
Deadline for Resumes: April 1

Harry and Jane's House serves the homeless population of the four counties of eastern Rhode Island. Formed in 1983 after itinerant day laborers Harry and Jane Smith were found frozen to death on the steps

of the Methodist Church, Harry and Jane's has sheltered 400 ,
every year. In addition to shelter, we provide job counselling, access .
medical care and a school program for children. The total budget of the
shelter is $400,000, with $200,000 provided by city and state funding.

Harry and Jane's House seeks its first development director to help
ensure stable funding and to expand the range of services it provides.

Major Responsibilities: The Development Director will be responsible for expanding the shelter's development program which currently
includes income raised through major gifts, direct mail, special events
and foundation grants in addition to the government funding named
above. Under the supervision of the Executive Director and in partner-
ship with the rest of the staff, the Development Director will expand the
shelter's fundraising program in the following areas:

1. Seeking major gift donations in the $100-5,000 range
2. Expanding the direct mail program
3. Expanding the board of directors' role in fundraising, particularly in soliciting new and upgraded gifts.

The chosen candidate will also take primary responsibility for written materials, special events, and foundation proposals.

Prospect research and identification will be a shared responsibility
with the Executive Director and fundraising committee of the board.

Qualifications: The successful applicant should have at least three
years of direct service experience as a volunteer or paid staff, preferably
in the areas of housing and homelessness, as well as at least three years
of fundraising experience, including major gift planning and solicitation,
good writing and communication skills, and experience working with
boards of directors.

The successful applicant will have demonstrated ability to work
well with a diverse constituency, will be self-motivated, work well
under pressure and be able to handle several projects at one time.

It is highly desirable for candidates to be computer literate and to
be familiar with Rhode Island.

Ideally, the candidate will have previous experience working in a
shelter for the homeless.

Salary and benefits are commensurate with experience and existing
pay and benefits at the shelter.

To Apply: Please send cover letter summarizing what you would bring
to this position and why you want to work in a shelter, along with your
resume, two writing samples and three references.

Send to: Search Committee, Harry and Jane's House, Address.

Phone inquiries: Call Executive Director Sharon Helper at _____.

Women and people of color encouraged to apply. The shelter is an
equal opportunity employer.

30.

Hiring a Consultant

There are times in the life of almost every group when a fundraising consultant can be helpful. These times are characterized by one or more of the following situations:

1. You need someone with skill and knowledge who cares about the issues your organization is concerned with, but is far enough removed to have perspective on how your organization can improve its overall fundraising or some particular aspect of it.

2. You need help deciding on a course of action: Can you really launch a capital campaign now? Would direct mail be a good strategy to explore?

3. You need someone to carry out a time-limited task: run a special event, train the board in fundraising, plan a major gifts campaign, design a direct mail program, write a grant proposal.

4. You need someone one day each week or month to help design a work plan, provide guidance and be available to answer questions for your bright, energetic but inexperienced fundraising staff.

5. You are between staff and need someone temporarily to run the development function of your organization.

Consulting is characterized by being time-limited. You can hire a consultant for a few hours a week, a few days a month, or contract for a number of months. A consultant does not usually get involved in carrying out day-to-day fundraising operations. She or he is generally employed to give advice and guidance.

It is partially because of the latter that the idea of hiring a consultant carries a negative meaning for many people. The jokes, "A consultant borrows your watch to tell you the time," or "free advice for a price," are said only half in jest.

The problem is compounded by the sheer number of consultants working in the United States. There are sleazy and unreliable consultants in the fundraising profession, but a more common problem with consultants is that many have little knowledge of their professed subject. Sometimes people call me to ask how they should go about becoming consultants. When I ask what experience they have had, they respond with a list of the books they have read and the trainings they have attended. They think consulting would be exciting because one travels a great deal and gets to know a wide variety of nonprofits. Further, consultants do not carry the ultimate responsibility of the fundraising success or failure of any organization.

What my inquirers fail to see, however, is that consultants carry a different level of responsibility: the advice we give must be correct. If implemented, it must work. Further, by being hands-off, consultants must trust others to carry out plans that the consultant designed. This means the plan must be communicated very clearly, and must be designed at the level of skills and resources the people carrying it out have, or have access to.

Consultants must know what can be learned by teaching, guiding and giving advice, and what can only be learned from experience. They must know what they can do for an organization, and what an organization can only do for itself. Here is a list of the kinds of activities fundraising consultants can and cannot do:

Consultants can:

♦ Train and motivate people in all aspects of fundraising

♦ Create fundraising plans and help implement and evaluate those plans

♦ Research prospective donors (individuals, corporations, foundations, religious institutions), and write proposals if needed

♦ Set up a data base for keeping track of donor information

♦ Conduct feasibility studies

♦ Conduct direct mail campaigns, including acquiring lists, designing the package, tracking results, and sometimes producing thank-you notes

♦ Help board members understand their responsibilities, and help organizations recruit and train good board members

♦ Study and recommend structural changes in an organization to improve functioning and fundraising efficiency

♦ Help hire fundraising staff, including writing job descriptions, advertising, and interviewing candidates

♦ Organize special events

♦ Set up any other fundraising strategy that an organization has decided to use

◆ Manage mailing lists and donor information. This can include sending out pledge reminders, thank-you notes, and renewal letters. (Generally, it is not cost effective for small organizations to pay a consultant to do these tasks).

Fundraising consultants cannot:

◆ Actually solicit money from individuals, unless they go as part of a team with someone from the organization

◆ Use their personal contacts to raise money. Consultants often know a great deal about wealthy givers in the community and, with discretion, can share that knowledge in prospect research. However, consultants do not go from job to job with their own list of prospects. Most of the time consultants do not actually raise money. If a consultant offers to do all your fundraising for you, run the other way. This is not an effective solution because, at best, it postpones the necessity of getting the board, staff and volunteers involved in fundraising

◆ Guarantee their work. There are no absolutes in fundraising. There is a body of fundraising knowledge (largely based on common sense) and there are many applications of this knowledge. No strategy will work every time for every group.

How to Choose a Consultant

Once you have decided that your particular situation may be helped by a consultant, what do you look for in that person?

1. Track Record. Ask how much fundraising he or she has done, and with what success. Has the person worked with organizations similar to yours both in purpose and strategy, and in similar locales? A successful consultant for social change groups in Manhattan may be less useful for rural advocacy groups in North Dakota. Superb consultants for large institutions may not be as good with all-volunteer operations with budgets of less than $25,000. If questions of gender, sexual orientation, race, class, or disability are very important in your organization, ask the consultant what experience they have working on these issues as well, or with diverse groups of people.

2. References. If you don't know the person by reputation, ask for the last three groups she or he has worked with. Then call those groups and ask about the consultant. Was the person helpful? Did the consultant listen well and really understand the situation? Would this group hire this consultant again? You can also check references, but you may get a more candid evaluation from non-reference groups.

3. Compatibility. If you envision a relationship with the consultant involving more than a one- or two-day training, you may wish to meet the person. This meeting, which should take about half an hour, should be free. You then get to see if you like the person and would feel good taking his or her advice. It sometimes happens that an excellent fundraising consultant is not the right person for your group because the personalities will not mesh. If the organization dislikes the consultant, both their advice and your money are wasted.

4. Confidence. Ask what the consultant will do for you, or what they recommend. Avoid asking for long written plans. Elaborate "work plans" or proposals are often standardized; each one is essentially the same as the next, with the name of your organization substituted for the name of the previous organization. You can ask for a resume, if you find that helpful. By the time of this meeting, you are not looking so much for proof of fundraising knowledge as for ability to put that knowledge across. Ask yourself, "Is this person believable?" "Does she or he convey confidence, enthusiasm and good will?" "Will the people who have to work with this person like him or her?"

5. Belief. Finally, the consultant must be able to articulate the mission of your organization and believe that your group should exist. The consultant does not have to be a donor to your group, and does not have to think that your group is the greatest idea since sliced bread, but he or she needs to care about what you stand for and want to help you out of conviction as well as needing a job. This is particularly important if your group is controversial or has a "troublemaker" image. Avoid consultants who advise you to "tone down" your message or broaden your goals "to make everyone feel included." A fundraising consultant's job is to help your group raise money — not to water down the group then help this newer, lightweight group raise money.

Paying Consultants

There are no standards or guidelines for how much to pay a consultant. A high price does not mean better performance or more accountability, but a price that is too good to be true probably is. By hiring a consultant, you are investing in the present so you will have more money in the future.

Most consultants charge by the day or by the hour, but some charge by the job. The daily rate is less per hour than the hourly rate, and several days is less per day than one day. Consultants also charge for all their expenses: hotels, meals, telephone, photocopy, and travel are the most common. You can cut some of these costs by offering to house the consultant in someone's home and providing their meals.

Establish clearly just what you are paying for. For example, you pay for the consultant's time. But when does that time start? In some cases, the time starts when the consultant reaches the office of the client or the training site. Even if it takes a day to get there, they do not charge until they are there. Other consultants start charging the minute they leave their house or office. Find out if the consultant charges for phone calls, and at what rate.

If you are hiring a person for several days or months of work, build in evaluation points. For example, you might say, "At the end of one month, we will evaluate progress and decide whether or not to continue, or whether the plan needs to be modified." This is best for the consultant also, who may need to re-estimate the time involved, or may have run into some unforeseen obstacles. It is important to have a written statement spelling out your understanding of the consultant's role, fees and expenses, which you both sign. For the same reasons listed in the last chapter on hiring a development director, do not pay the consultant on a contingency or commission basis.

SECTION 6
Budgetting and Planning

Lily Tomlin once said, "I always wanted to be somebody. I guess I should have been more specific." I think of this quote whenever I think of planning. Organizations want to run well, have enough money, and do good work. But the work of defining exactly what those things would mean often doesn't get done. Consequently the group does not make very much progress and cannot even rejoice in its accomplishments because they were unplanned and probably not fully appreciated. Planning and budgeting (in fact, a budget is a plan for how money is to be raised and spent) are easier to explain than to do, but it is much more difficult to operate without a budget or an overall fundraising plan than with one.

Because time is our most precious non-renewable resource, all efforts that use time respectfully, efficiently, enjoyably and with maximum benefit for time invested ought to be our top life priorities. Grassroots organizations use thousands of hours of volunteer and staff time and will gain the most from that time by taking the time to plan.

31.

Developing A Budget

When asked about their budget, many small organizations will reply that they simply spend what they can raise. This budget process will do for a while, but its cost in frayed nerves, sleepless nights, and inability to expand programs makes almost any other system preferable.

The people responsible for raising money often feel too busy to make a comprehensive fundraising plan. However, a simple planning mechanism can enable them to develop a plan quickly so that they can spend most of their time implementing and, where necessary, modifying the plan.

The first step in developing a fundraising plan is to develop a working budget. A budget is simply a list of items on which you will spend money (expenses) and a list of sources from which you will receive money (income). A budget balances when the projected expenses and income are equal.

There is a simple, two-step process for budget preparation that most small nonprofit organizations can use effectively. The process takes into account the largest number of variables without doing extensive research or developing elaborate spread-sheets. In some organizations a single staff member prepares the entire budget and presents it for board approval, but this is a large burden for one person. Therefore, the method presented here assumes that a small committee will undertake the budget-setting program.

Step One: Expenses Versus Income

The budget committee should first divide into two subgroups: one to estimate expenses and the other to project income. When these tasks are completed, the subgroups will reconvene to mesh their work (step two).

Estimating Expenses

The group working on the expense side of the budget prepares three columns of numbers representing "bare bones," "reasonable," and "ideal" expense figures (see sample, below). The "bare bones" column spells out the amount of money the organization needs to survive. Items here generally include office space, minimum staff requirements, postage, printing, and telephone. This column does not include the cost of new work, salary increases, additional staff, new equipment, or other improvements.

Next, the group prepares the "ideal" column: how much money the group would need to operate at maximum effectiveness. This is not a dream budget, but a true estimate of the amount of funding required for optimum functioning.

Finally, the committee prepares the "reasonable" column: how much money the group needs to do more than simply survive but still not meet all its goals. These figures should not be conceived of as an average of the other two columns. For example, an organization may feel that in order to accomplish any good work, the office needs to be larger, or in order to maintain staff morale, the organization must raise salaries. Because higher rent and increased salaries aren't necessary to a group's survival, they will not be included in the group's "bare bones" budget; however, they are important enough to the organization's work to be included in the "reasonable" budget.

The "bare bones," "reasonable," and "ideal" columns, then, give the range of finances required to run the organization at various levels of functioning.

The process of figuring expenses and income must be done with great attention to thoroughness and detail. For example, to estimate how much you will spend on printing, think through all the items you print and how many of each you will need. A simple mail appeal has at least four printed components — the letter, the reply card and return envelope, and the envelope the appeal is sent in. Planning for a newsletter, annual report, brochure, or flier must include costs of design, layout, and paste-up.

When you don't know how much something costs, do not guess. Take the time while creating the budget to find out. To assure completeness and accuracy in budget-setting, many organizations have found it helpful to send board and staff members to training sessions on financial planning.

SAMPLE EXPENSE PROJECTIONS

Item	Barebones	Reasonable	Ideal
Salaries			
Director			
Fundraising coordinator			
Support staff			
Program coordinator			
Benefits and taxes			
Total Personnel			
Office rent			
Office equipment			
Maintenance			
New (specify)			
Computer			
Office supplies			
Telephone (per month)			
Photocopy			
Typesetting			
Design and layout			
Printing			
Brochures			
Envelopes			
Mail appeals			
Annual report			
Newsletters			
Stationery			
Other			
Total Printing			
Postage			
First class			
Bulk mail			
Bulk mail permit			
Other (specify)			
Total Postage			
Bookkeeping contract			
Fundraising training for board			
Staff development			
Miscellaneous			
TOTAL			

Projecting Income

At the same time that the expense side of the budget is being prepared, the other half of the committee is preparing the income side. Crucial to this process is a knowledge of what fundraising strategies the organization can carry out and how much money these can be expected to generate. The income side is also estimated in three columns, representing "worst," "likely," and "best" (see sample below).

To calculate the income projection labeled "worst," take last year's income sources and assume that with the same amount of effort the group will at least be able to raise this amount again. In the case of foundation, corporation, or government grants it may be wise to write "zero" as the worst projection.

The "best" income projections are drawn up next. These figures reflect what would happen if all the organization's fundraising work was successful and every grant proposal submitted was funded. Again, this is

SAMPLE INCOME PROJECTIONS

Source	Explanation	Worst	Likely	Best
Major gifts				
New				
Renewing				
Membership				
New				
Renewing				
Special appeals				
Pledging				
Sale of products				
T-shirts				
Booklets				
Bumper stickers				
Special events				
Raffle				
Dance				
Conference				
Luncheon				
Board donations				
Fees for service				
Foundations				
Other (specify)				

not a dream budget. It does not assume events that will probably not occur, such as someone giving your group a gift of a million dollars. The ideal budget must be one that would be met if everything went absolutely right.

The "likely" column is a compromise. It estimates the income the organization can expect to generate with reasonable hard work, expanding old fundraising strategies and having success with some new strategies, yet with some things going wrong.

All income categories are figured on the basis of their gross: that is, the amounts you expect to earn from each strategy before expenses are subtracted. The expenses must be included in the expense side of the budget. Be sure that the committee developing the expense side of the budget includes expenses involved in carrying out fundraising strategies in the total expenses of the organization.

Step Two: Meet, Compare, Negotiate

Once income and expense projections have been completed, the two parts of the committee can share their results. When the income and expense sides of the budget have been figured separately in this way, there is less chance of giving in to the temptation to manipulate the figures to make them balance. For example, in one organization in which the budget committee of the board prepared income and expense estimates together, the income estimates were boosted several times during the process to ensure that income and expenses would come out the same on paper. Little thought was given to the reality of being able to raise so much more money, and the group was soon in financial trouble.

When the entire committee reconvenes, you hope to find that the "reasonable" expense column and the "likely" income column are close to the same. In that happy circumstance those figures can be adopted as the budget with no more fuss. Occasionally groups are pleasantly surprised to discover that their "likely" income projections come close to their "ideal" budget. However, compromises usually need to be made. In these cases, the expenses need to be adjusted to meet realistic income potential, not the other way around.

When no two sets of numbers are anywhere near alike, the committee will have to find solutions. There is no right or wrong way to negotiate at this point. If each committee has really done its job properly, there will be no need to review each item to see if it is accurate. However, with more research, committees may discover other ways to delete expenses or add income.

Expenses	Income
Barebones	Worst
Reasonable	Likely
Ideal	Best

Expenses	Income
Barebones	Worst
Reasonable	Likely
Ideal	Best

Expenses	Income
Barebones	Worst
Reasonable	Likely
Ideal	Best

Two case studies that illustrate different ways of reaching a workable budget using compromise and research are discussed below.

Neighborhood Advocacy

Neighborhood Advocacy was founded ten years ago. For the past five years, they have received a federal grant of $30,000 annually. Last year, however, with their budget at $73,700, they were informed that federal money was no longer available. This shortfall represented over 40 percent of their total budget. Their budget committee developed the following estimates:

Expenses		Income	
Barebones	$56,500	Worst	$43,700
Reasonable	$73,700	Likely	$45,000
Ideal	$103,000	Best	$50,000

All of their income projections were below the amount they needed in order to survive. Furthermore, their reasonable budget was their actual budget from the past five years, and their barebones budget represented significant cutbacks in service. After much discussion among the board and staff, the group decided that they wanted to continue operating at the current level to avoid undermining morale completely and curtailing the program. Therefore, the board asked the budget committee to develop a budget that would be between the existing "barebones" and "reasonable" options and to research some expanded fundraising programs, including seeking a loan.

The half of the committee working on expenses then created a budget called "Barebones Two," which called for renting part of their office to another group and reducing the hours of a clerical position. The half of the committee working on income investigated hiring a consulting firm to help implement a large membership recruitment drive using telephone and direct mail. The strategy would pay for itself the first year and begin making money the second year. The front money required for this consulting package was $10,000. The budget committee returned to the board with these figures:

Expenses		Income	
Barebones One	$56,500	Likely	$45,000
Barebones Two	$60,000	Best	$50,000
Loan Payments	$10,000	Loan	$10,000

When the full board met they first adopted the "Best" income projection and the "Barebones Two" expense budget. This involved risk, and board members all realized and agreed that their level of involvement in fundraising had to increase over that of previous years. They then committed themselves to the loan: a move of considerable risk, foresight, and courage. They reasoned that the worst that could happen was that they would have to cut their budget drastically and extend the loan payments. But with some luck and a lot of hard work, Neighborhood Advocacy would never be as dependent on one source of money again.

Their final decision was to adopt their Barebones Two expense and Best plus Loan income columns. They plan to pay the loan back starting in the second year and have it fully paid by the end of the third year, when the membership recruitment strategy begins to make more money.

Our School

Our School, an alternative private school, has been functioning for only two years. The first year the school was run entirely by volunteers, mostly parents of the students. In the second year, the board (also composed of students' parents) hired an administrator who also teaches classes. This sole staff member now needs an assistant. While the board has been successful in fundraising and a few parents have made significant financial contributions to the school, no one is certain that these gifts will be repeated. It is difficult for them to make fundraising projections based on past experience because they have so little to go on. A budget committee estimates these figures:

Expenses		Income	
Barebones	$28,000	Worst	$30,000
Reasonable	$40,000	Likely	$40,000
Ideal	$100,000	Best	$43,000

The only difference between the "Barebones" and "Reasonable" expenses is the cost of an assistant. Even though the "Likely" income can cover the "Reasonable" budget, the board elects to adopt the "Barebones" expenses for the first six months, and the "Likely" income. They reason that although their track record for fundraising is good, their fundraising program is not well enough established for them to draw conclusions about the future. Because the school has grown rapidly the board feels that taking on another staff person is ill-advised until they are sure of meeting their income goals. At a six-month income review, they will hire the assistant if they have raised at least half of their "Likely" goals. This gives the board some "breathing time" and assures the administrator that the issue of her work load is being addressed and can be solved in a short time.

These case studies illustrate that budgets are designed to be flexible, to serve as measurements of progress, and to provide structure for the way money is spent and raised. Using a budget this way makes it a helpful document rather than a club hanging over your head. Small organizations cannot know exactly how much money they will raise or spend beyond certain fixed costs such as rent or salaries, but they need parameters that a well-thought-out and realistic budget can provide.

32.

Creating a Fundraising Plan

Veteran fundraiser and organizer Gary Delgado says that there are four steps to successful fundraising:

    1. Plan
    2. Plan
    3. Plan
    4. Work

Because there is so much truth to this, it may surprise readers that this planning chapter is relatively short. That's because planning for fundraising is not difficult to explain, nor is it difficult to do. Not only is planning fully three-fourths of what makes for successful fundraising, it is also true that one hour of planning can save three hours of work. But the final and most important truth is that planning does not take the place of doing.

Given that an organization is going to have to work its plan in order to raise money, how can a workable plan be created? There are five steps:

1. Create a budget, based on the principles outlined in the previous chapter on budgetting.

2. From the amount of money you determine you must raise, subtract any amounts that will be raised from strategies not involving individual donors, such as income from foundation, corporate or government grants, product sales, fees for service, interest income, etc. The amount that remains is the amount that will form the basis of your fundraising plan. The other methods of income generation will be added to your plan during the last step.

3. Now divide the amount of money that must be raised from individuals into the proportions you can expect from different groups of givers as discussed in Chapter 14, Major Gifts Programs:

♦ 60% of your money will come from 10% of your donors — major donors

♦ 20% of your money will come from 20% of your donors — habitual donors giving through your retention strategies

♦ the remaining 20% of your money will come from 70% of your donors — first-time donors giving through acquisition strategies.

Next, analyze your current donor list to answer the following questions:

♦ How many donors do you have now in each of these three categories?

♦ What is your renewal rate? (It should be around 66%.)

♦ What is the organization's strength in working with donors? Do you do a good job in acquiring donors, but have a higher than normal attrition rate? Or, do you have a strong base of loyal habitual donors, but a lower than normal attrition rate (this would indicate a weakness in use of acquisition strategies)? Do you do a good job finding the top ten percent of donors and regularly seeking upgraded gifts and major gifts?

♦ Has the number of donors to your organization grown, decreased, or stayed the same in the last three years? If it has decreased, you are definitely not doing enough acquisition and you may also have a problem with retention of donors. If the number of donors has stayed the same, you are either doing a good job with retention or acquisition, but not both, because otherwise you would see an increase.

This analysis will give you a clearer sense of the strategies you need to employ to meet your financial goals.

4. Decide how many donors you need to meet your goals in each category, and match them with the strategies that work best for reaching those donors (see Chapter 3, Fundraising Needs and Strategies).

5. Put the plan onto a time line and fill out the tasks. Voila! A fundraising plan is born. (This is not to underplay the amount of time it will take you to do these five steps — a planning committee of the board will need to meet two or three times to get a plan of this specificity accomplished.)

The following example presents an illustration of the application of these steps.

Artworks is a community theater serving a town of 250,000 people. The theater performs works of local playwrights aimed at raising consciousness about, or demonstrating the talents of, disabled people, children and seniors. It has a budget of $150,000 a year and two paid staff people — an artistic director and an administrator. The administrator is also in charge of coordinating fundraising. The group has an active board of directors of thirteen people. Each year they raise $75,000 from ticket sales, small government grants, and fees from their acting classes, and the remaining $75,000 from community donations, which, until this year, included a $10,000 grant from a private foundation. With that grant not being renewed, Artworks needs to rethink its fundraising plan for community donations.

Using the formula in Step 3, they determine that they will need to raise $45,000 from major gifts, $15,000 from habitual donors, and the remaining $15,000 from three special events and their direct mail program. They are a highly visible organization in their community and currently have 1,000 donors. Of these, 600 give about $25 and 200 more give between $50 and $99. Many of these gifts are given at the end of performances when someone a board member comes on stage and asks people to make a gift beyond their ticket purchase. Among their donors, 50 people give $100 or more; the biggest gifts are $1,500 from a board member, two gifts of $1,000 from past board members, and two gifts of $750 from sisters who support all the arts programs in this community. Other funds come from their special events.

One major problem for this group is that their attrition rate for donors is more than 50 percent. For the past three years, they have steadily lost donors, decreasing from 1,500 to 1,250 and now to 1,000. Some board members have blamed this on the artistic director's choice of a disability rights play that some people complained was too strident, two avant garde plays that some people found too obscure, and a play about an aging priest and his struggle with and eventual expulsion from the Catholic Church because of his views on sexuality, that some found anti-Catholic, others found anti-gay, and others found too pro-gay. Because the director mixes these with works for the whole family and plays written and largely produced by children, other board members feel that the range of works is appropriate and suits the variety of people in the community. They also feel that since their mission is to raise consciousness, the plays that are chosen will necessarily raise hackles as well.

The board and staff have spent countless hours discussing these plays and audience reaction to them, and by and large have found these conversations helpful; however, fundraising has lagged. Now they have decided to focus on fundraising and then to determine whether the plays they are producing are the cause of the decline in their donor base, since there has been no decline in their audience numbers.

Applying the formula to their donor base of 1,000 donors, they come up with the following:

> 100 donors should give $100 or more for a total of $45,000
>
> 200 donors should give $25 to $100 for a total of $15,000
>
> 700 donors should give various amounts totalling $15,000.

If they project a normal attrition rate of 33 percent, they will need to acquire 300 new donors just to maintain their base at 1,000 donors.

Moving to Step Four, they draw up this outline:

> **Goal 1:** Double the number of major donors from 50 to 100 people.
>
> **Goal 2:** Maintain the number of donors giving $50 to $99 at 200 people.
>
> **Goal 3:** Attract 300 first-time givers, and strengthen retention strategies to ensure renewal of enough of the 700 donors (some of whom will become major donors) to make sure to maintain a base of 1,000 donors and not experience any more shrinkage.

To meet these goals, they choose the following strategies:

Conduct two major donor campaigns — one in the spring and one in the fall. They will create a gift range chart and seek 400 prospects who could give gifts in the range of $100 to $2,500 (projecting that half will decline to give and half of the positive responses will give less than the amount requested). Fifty of these prospects will be major donors asked to renew, 150 will be prospects identified from current donors who give less than $100, and the remaining 200 prospects will come from the community at large through board and staff contacts.

To retain donors, they will write to current donors three times during the year, describing different projects and different aspects of their work. They will introduce a pledge program and have a fundraising column in their newsletter.

Finally, they will continue to ask for donations at the end of shows, and will continue their three special events because they have had good luck acquiring donors this way.

Moving to Step Five, they are ready to put this plan on a time line.

On a calendar, they mark off when their plays are running. They note when their government grant applications are due, and when their special events are scheduled. Their quarterly newsletter goes out just before each play, and that is marked in. They schedule their three extra appeals for just after the first three plays, and make sure they will arrive at least three weeks before or after each special event. Finally, they schedule their major gift campaign in two small windows of "down" time: January 15 to February 15, and November 1 through Thanksgiving.

With this plan, the Artworks board divides itself into three committees: acquisition, retention and major donors (upgrades). With the help of the administrator, each committee prepares a task list and divides up the work.

By using these steps, the planning process can be both simple and accurate. Working together, people with little experience in fundraising can figure out what to do using easy-to-learn principles described in this book and in other fundraising literature.

The Children's Museum

How One Group Changed Their Fundraising Program Through Planning and Analysis

The Children's Museum is located in a small city of 550,000 people. Started two years ago, the museum is similar to those all over the country in which children are encouraged to touch and interact with the exhibits. The museum has a board of 40 committed people from all walks of life. Most have children. About half are involved as volunteers with other arts organizations in the community. All agree that board members should both give and help raise money.

Before understanding the larger issues in fundraising and learning the fundraising strategies discussed in this book, the fundraising committee (five board members and a staff person) presented monthly fundraising plans, mostly ideas for special events, at board meetings. They never planned more than two or three months in advance. In one year they had the following activities:

January-February: A Japanese restaurant offered a benefit sushi dinner for the museum. Tickets were $10 each. Board members were expected to sell five tickets each, which they did. Net: $1,950.

March: An expert schooner donated his time and yacht for a day of sailing on a nearby lake. The museum provided food and drink. Board members were expected to sell two tickets each at $25. Most board members bought one ticket and sold the other to their spouses. Net: $1,800.

April: A pancake breakfast was held in cooperation with five other arts organizations. The breakfast was widely advertised, but each organization had to guarantee to bring in 100 participants. No requirements were set, but most of the board members came with their families and a few friends. Cost: $4 for adults, $2 for children. Overall net: $2,000; Children's Museum: $400.

April-June: Membership campaign: board members held one extra meeting that month in order to help send out 4,000 invitations to join the museum. In addition, each board member was expected to enroll 15 new members at $25 each. All board members enrolled at least three new members and some got their full complement of 15. Total new members from all efforts: 200. Gross: $5,000. Cost of mailings: $1,500. Net income: $3,500.

July: The museum contracted with a circus company to set up their tents with Ferris wheels and other rides for the Fourth of July weekend. Admission was $2, with an additional charge for each ride. Booths for drinks, hot dogs, cotton candy and so on were staffed by museum board members and volunteers, with those proceeds going to the museum. In addition, ten percent of the proceeds from admissions and rides went to the museum. Anyone who worked at a booth could bring his or her family for free, plus each child of a volunteer worker got three free rides. Fifty volunteers were needed during the weekend; board members and spouses worked. Net: $7,500.

August: A well-deserved breather, except for the fundraising committee that planned the September event. No board meeting.

September: An art auction was held with paintings and sculpture by local artists. The museum paid for the rental of the auction gallery and for the publicity. The artists paid for the auctioneer and split the price of each item sold with the museum. Board members were each given 50 posters announcing the auction to display around town. For this task the fundraising committee assigned each person several square blocks near their home or work. Further, board members were to help stuff invitations. These had to be mailed first class because, as the committee explained, "This all came together very fast." Front costs were high. Because the museum did not have the money to front, each board member was asked for an interest-free, one-month loan of $100. Net: $2,000.

October-November: Two wonderful opportunities arose that the fundraising committee did not want to pass up. First, a fancy restaurant offered to donate its opening to benefit the museum if the museum could keep the restaurant full all night. Capacity of the restaurant was 200. The event was free for board members, $20 for others. No children were allowed. Each board member was encouraged to bring at least five friends. The museum succeeded in its bargain. Net: $3,200. The other opportunity was to sell bouquets of flowers at a shopping mall on three consecutive Saturdays. The museum would buy bunches of flowers at $1 and sell them for $2.50-5.00. Two volunteers for two-hour shifts were needed for three shifts per Saturday, or six volunteers per Saturday. The board dutifully signed up. Net: $400.

December: The board evaluated their fundraising efforts. Every event had been successful. A total of $20,250 had been raised, plus the museum had acquired over 600 new members, and massively increased its visibility.

Not surprisingly, however, in spite of their success, 36 of the 40 board members resigned at the end of the year, including three members of the fundraising committee. All cited overwork and too much fundraising as their primary reasons for leaving the board.

Almost miraculously, the museum recruited 36 more board members of the same high caliber (largely from their volunteer pool). With the help of a consultant the museum board evaluated and changed its fundraising plans considerably. First, they looked at the special events themselves. While all the events were appropriate, not all enhanced the image of the museum. Therefore, the new fundraising committee scrapped those events that did not include children, except the art auction, which promoted the museum in other ways. They scrapped the sushi benefit, the sailing adventure, and the restaurant opening (an unrepeatable event in any case).

The pancake breakfast, which had raised the least amount of money, was repeated with two changes: 1) as far as possible, the advertising was designed to attract new people, and 2) every family or adult attending would later be sent a fundraising appeal offering membership in all five arts organizations at a cost slightly higher than that of joining any two of them. Although this event would still not be a giant moneymaker, it would bring in many new members and increase visibility for all five organizations. Further, it promoted the sense that all the arts organizations were working in harmony. The flower selling was also repeated. Although labor intensive, the chance for volunteers to discuss the museum with so many people brought a notable rise in museum attendance in the weeks during and after the sale. Each bouquet was accompanied by a 3" by 5" card that briefly described the museum and listed its hours.

Board members divided themselves into committees, each of which helped the fundraising committee in different ways. The membership committee worked all year to increase membership through mail and phone solicitation. The major gifts committee solicited major gifts from current donors. The rest of the board worked on the special events, with no board member working on more than three events. An auxiliary of volunteers is now being formed to help with the planning and work of these events.

The fundraising calendar was prepared a year in advance and looked like this:

January-December: Ongoing membership recruitment. New members: 1,000. Net income: $12,000.

April: Pancake breakfast, with mail appeal follow-up. Net income: $1,000.

July: Circus with food booths. Net income: $9,500.

September: Art auction. Net income: $4,000.

September-November: Major gifts campaign. Net income: $25,000.

October-November: Three weekends of flower sales. Net income: $600.

Total income: $52,100

Total new members: 1500

At the end of the first year of the new fundraising plan only five board members resigned, all citing personal reasons.

SECTION 7
Special Circumstances

INTRODUCTION

Every nonprofit is unique. It brings together a combination of people for a particular purpose at a particular time in history — both the history of the world and the history of that organization. The configuration of people, place and time will not be repeated. Even if the same people team up again, it will be for a different project, and it will certainly be a different time. This uniqueness is positive. When used well, it gives the organization momentum and enables the board to "seize the moment" and address the social need or human interest that is the organization's purpose.

Every nonprofit also has much in common with every other organization. A small socialist feminist health collective in a big city has a great deal in common with a private Christian preparatory school in a rural area. Their needs for money and the strategies they use to raise that money will be similar.

Within the broad framework of similarities and differences, occasionally special circumstances make fundraising more difficult for certain kinds of organizations or at certain times in an organization's life. An accurate analysis of your fundraising situation is essential for planning long-term fundraising. For example, a group that feels it cannot raise money because of its board's inadequate fundraising efforts may in fact be hampered more severely by the local economy. In another instance, a group may feel that they can't raise money because no one agrees with their program, when in fact they have failed to articulate a clear case as to why they deserve support.

I have chosen six of the more common special circumstances that a group may find itself in, either temporarily (financial crisis) or permanently (rural). An entire book could be devoted to special circumstances, but these five should give you a sense of how to think through special circumstances of your own.

33.

Dealing with Anxiety

During the seventeen years I have been in fundraising, I have observed that the greatest factor causing people to leave fundraising, or to "burn out," is not the work itself, or even the challenge of having to ask for money. It is the constant, gnawing anxiety that the money won't come in, and the knowledge that once you have raised money for one month or one quarter you must simply turn around and begin raising it for the next period of time. There is never a rest, and lack of success shows up immediately.

Many paid fundraising staff have told me that they wake up in the middle of the night worrying, that they never feel really free to take a weekend off, let alone a vacation. Fundraising staff often watch their self-esteem eaten away by the constant pressure of a job that by its nature can never be finished.

There are four ways to deal with this anxiety short of psychotherapy or quitting one's job.

1. Remember that if you do your job, the money will come in. Of course some mail appeals will fail, some donors won't give and some grant proposals will be turned down. But your job is to generate enough requests for money that even when only a small portion are successful you will have the money you need. Fundraising is basically a numbers game — get the word out in as many ways and to as many people as you can, and you will get money back.

2. If your primary responsibility is to raise money, then every day that you come to work you need to set your priorities around that goal. Ask yourself, "Of all the tasks that I have to do today, which one will raise the most money?" Do that task first, then do the task that will raise the next most money, and so on. No one ever gets their whole job done. Make sure that the things you don't get done are things not related to fundraising.

In one organization, the director was the only staff person. Feeling responsible for everything, she did those things she knew how to do, and which she could finish. She kept accurate and excellent books, paid bills on time, got out minutes and agendas for meetings, and wrote, edited and produced the newsletter. The board did a lot of program work under her direction. Soon, the group had little money and was in danger of going out of business. This director quickly learned to change her priorities; now she works on fundraising at least five hours every day. If she has time, she does the books. Board meeting minutes and agendas are handled by the board secretary. At each board meeting, the director brings a fundraising to-do list for the board. While some board members object that they want to work on program and do not want to do fundraising, the director is teaching them that without money there is no program and no group. The first and primary responsibility of the board and staff of any organization is to keep the group going, and this usually means active ongoing participation in fundraising.

3. Try to detach from the results of your work. An unsuccessful proposal or mailing does not mean that you are a failure as a person or as a fundraiser. Not being able to do everything is not a condemnation of your worth as a person. Ask yourself whether it will be important in ten years whether you got the newsletter out today or next week. One person can only do so much. Do what you can do in the time allotted, and let the rest go. Too often, groups have fundraising goals that no one could reach. Re-evaluate your goal setting, instead of trying to live up to impossible expectations.

Some people have found it helpful to form support groups: either informal gatherings over happy hour, or more formal, structured meetings at a specific time and place. If you do use a support group, make sure it supports your work and helps with strategies. Do not use it as a gripe session to compare notes on how awful everyone's job is. That will only make you more depressed.

4. Take care of yourself. Don't always work overtime. Take vacations. Ask for help. Delegate tasks. The overall work of social justice is the creation of a humane and just society, where (among other things) work and leisure are balanced. If your work is none of those things for you, it is unlikely that your organization can have a positive role in creating social change.

34.

Challenges of Rural Areas

Just as cities and towns vary greatly one from another, so do rural areas, but there are some things many of them have in common. Six factors must be taken into account in doing nonprofit work in a rural community.

1. Everything takes longer. This applies not only to the obvious time involved in getting from one place to another when vast distances separate homes or towns, but also to rural hospitality, which is much more deliberate than that of city dwellers. For example, suppose you decide to visit a major donor on his or her ranch. You make an appointment, then drive one to three hours to the ranch. Once there, you do not chat briefly, ask for the gift and leave in 30 minutes, as you would in a city. The graciousness often customary in rural areas may lead your host or hostess to give you a tour of the ranch, invite you to stay for lunch or dinner and perhaps encourage you to spend the night. This graciousness is wonderful but time-consuming.

2. The necessities of ranch or farm life can create obstacles. Depending on the main economy of the area, there may be times — such as planting, harvesting, lambing or calving — when contact must be limited because people are working almost around the clock. Then, when none of those things are going on, the weather make may driving conditions so hazardous that volunteers cannot get to meetings, people cannot attend special events, and prospects cannot be visited.

3. Fundraising costs may be higher. The cityperson's idyllic notion that everything is inexpensive or free in a rural area is false. Almost all supplies have to be shipped in, adding freight to their cost. Lack of competition among businesses can also create high prices. While office space may be less expensive, there may not be any available. The distances between people and places make driving costs high, and the price of gasoline is higher per gallon.

4. Logistics are complicated. If you wish to print a newsletter, mail appeal, or flier, you may have to send it to the nearest city. If you need something sent or received quickly, there may be no overnight mail service from or to your community. The facsimile machine has helped to solve this problem to some extent, but only for groups that can afford one.

If your rural community or your constituency is made up of low-income families or individuals, logistical details can take on nightmarish proportions. For example, a small organization covering 20 counties in a southern state held an annual meeting. The meeting was timed perfectly between planting season and the onset of unbearably hot weather, and the organization offered to pay transportation costs for their low-income members. Five members decided to drive to the meeting together; none of them, however, had a car that could be trusted for the eight-hour trip. After the organization encouraged them to rent a car, they drove two hours to the nearest rental-car facility, only to be told that they must present a credit card, which none of them had. Finally, the organization called a credit card number to the rental car agency and the group made it to the meeting.

5. The culture plays an important role. When organizing and fundraising in a rural community, one must keep in mind that people often have known each other for many years; sometimes families have known each other for generations. People depend on each other for help in hard times or for assistance in emergencies. Thus, rural people are cautious about doing anything that might cause offense. If you live down the road from someone who is dumping effluent into your water source, you will think twice about publicly confronting this person when you know that if you have a medical emergency in the middle of winter and can't get your car started you may need to call on him or her.

This reluctance to challenge other people's actions often includes a hesitation to fundraise assertively or ask people for money directly. Fundraisers and organizers mistakenly interpret this reluctance on the part of volunteers as a sign that they are either conservative (wishing to maintain the status quo) or passive (willing to sit by while land is destroyed or peoples' rights are violated). In fact, this reluctance is a survival mechanism; it must be respected and taken into account. Because of these and other factors, change comes more slowly in rural communities.

6. Not everyone has equal loyalty to the area. One often thinks of residents of rural communities as people who have lived in the same place all their lives and make their living from farming or ranching. This is common, and these people usually have deep and abiding loyalty to their area. However, other circumstances of bring people to rural communities who do not develop such loyalty. For example, some rural areas are retirement communities; many of the people living in these communities are not from the region and have little loyalty to it. Some of them do have money and, being retired, they may also have time to volunteer. Other rural communities, such as those within a few hours of major cities such as San Francisco, Washington, D.C., or Boston, are bedroom communities for commuters who work in those cities. The increasingly common use of fax, computer and modem for business enables people to live in rural communities two or three hours' drive from their workplace and still carry on their business, commuting to the city one or two days each week. Their loyalty to their local community may depend on whether they are raising families there and how strongly they wish to be accepted and involved. While their time may be limited, they may have significant disposable income. The back-to-the-land "hippies" or small farmers are another population type in rural communities. Finances and values of these people are extremely varied.

There are also many rural communities where people make their living from mining (many of these people are now unemployed) or as workers on other people's farms or ranches, in some instances as sharecroppers. Increasingly, there are rural communities where the majority of the population are non-English-speaking immigrants or refugees from Mexico, Latin America, Cambodia and other countries.

Strategies for Raising Money

For groups in communities located near cities with populations of 100,000 or more, focus attention on raising money in those towns and cities where the financial base is strongest. Form support groups with people living in the town or city. Hold special events there and use direct mail to locate donors there.

In addition to raising money in the nearest population center, try to discover ways to raise money from people who pass through the community, particularly tourists and visitors. Some communities mount events just to attract tourists. For example, many communities have county fairs or various kinds of festivals, such as the Garlic Festival in California, the Ramp Festival in Georgia, the Storyteller's Convention in North Carolina. These attract tourists.If you live in a place where tourists come to see the natural beauty or to vacation (such as along the coasts, or near national parks or monuments), consider developing products that tourists will buy. Local crafts and homemade jellies and jams are always appealing.

If you live near a freeway or a frequently travelled road, set up a rest stop where truckers and tired drivers can buy coffee, doughnuts or other treats. This can be very lucrative in the cold winter months, particularly at night. It is also a community service that helps keep people from falling asleep at the wheel.

You can raise money from your local community as well. It is important to note that even in the poorest and most rural areas churches, volunteer fire departments, rescue squads, service clubs and the like are supported by local residents. Even the smallest, poorest towns in the Bible Belt, for example, support at least two churches. Even if they do not have paid clergy, the people manage to support a building.

Money can be raised locally through special events. This helps counter the reluctance rural people have for asking for money directly by providing a way to give something in return. Events such as raffles, car washes and bake sales can be good money makers. Many times people from rural community groups simply stand with buckets at busy crossroads and ask drivers to drop in spare change. Three hours at a crossroads on a shopping day can bring in $200 to $300. Flea markets are also popular. It is often easier for rural people to donate items rather than cash, and people always seem willing to buy each other's castoffs.

All of these are labor-intensive activities and make fundraising in rural communities even harder than it is elsewhere. We must face the fact that an organization located in a low-income, rural area doing work related to social justice issues (tax or land reform, appropriate economic development, peace and disarmament work, or opposing such things as hazardous waste dumping, clearcutting, or wildcat strip mining) will need to seek funding from foundations and from outside their immediate region. Unless the organization has a very low budget and no paid staff, it is unlikely that it will be able to become entirely self-sufficient. However, your community will support you and your work will be more successful if community members have bought into it with a donation.

35.

Fundraising for Coalitions

There are hundreds of organizations whose boards are made up of representatives of other nonprofits. For example, in most federated funds members of the federation form the majority of seats on their board. Almost every state has a Coalition Against Domestic Violence (CADV) for which directors of local battered women's shelters serve as board members. Most regional associations and national organizations operate the same way.

In terms of making policy and translating the mission and programs of the organization, or from the local level to the regional or national and back, or from the individual organization to the consortium and back, there are obvious advantages. A board or staff member of a local chapter of a regional or national group will be in the best position to represent the concerns of the local organization. This person will also well understand the need for a regional or national umbrella and will be committed to this part of the whole operation. Ideally this person will be the best qualified to make policy and help plan for the umbrella group and to translate the work of the umbrella group to the people at the local level.

From a fundraising point of view, however, this arrangement is difficult for the consortium because its executive director or development director is working with board members whose primary loyalty and main fundraising commitments lie with the organization they are representing. Getting such a board to raise money requires patience, perseverance and a degree of maneuvering. However, it can be done.

The first step is to examine the problem. Evaluate the excuses board members offer for not being able to raise money. Most will say they can't participate in fundraising because they have to raise money for their local group. They can't ask the same people to give money to the umbrella as to the local group.

Next they will point out that strategies other than face-to-face fundraising are difficult for a consortium to carry out. Special events, for example, require a local presence to generate interest in the event. Direct mail is not a good way to sell an umbrella group because the service is too complicated and local representatives are reluctant to provide names of possible donors.

On the surface, these excuses make sense. However, a closer examination of the people who complain most about how difficult it is to raise money for an umbrella organization reveals that these are people who are often not effective at raising much money at the local level either. Ironically, people who are very effective at their local level, with active fundraising committees and well-executed fundraising campaigns for their local organization, often make the best fundraisers at a regional or national level.

The reality of fundraising is that some people, foundations or corporations prefer to give locally, others have no preference and will give both locally and nationally, and still others would rather be part of a national picture.

Local organizations are in the best position to identify sources of funding in their communities whose primary commitments are regional or national. Those sources should be solicited for the umbrella group, provided that they are committed to the issues. Further, some donors will give to both the local group and the larger coalition and will understand the importance of both organizations.

Another common excuse from local people is that they don't have time to raise money in addition to all the other umbrella board responsibilities and their responsibilities at the local level. This is a legitimate problem, however these same people will spend hours debating personnel issues, discussing policy and program problems, and poring over the budget to see what can be cut. By shaving a few minutes off of each of those tasks, they would have some time for fundraising.

To be frank, you will fight an uphill and pointless battle if you spend all your time trying to get executive directors or very active board members of local groups to raise money for the umbrella group. It is better to spend time recruiting and developing other board members who will raise money for your umbrella group.

Some Solutions

First, every board of an umbrella group should have at least three slots reserved for "at-large" members — people who are not associated with a local group. These can be former staff, former board of local groups or simply people committed to the cause who don't happen to work for the cause. Their primary loyalty should be to your umbrella group, and their primary task should be fundraising. They should be recruited for this purpose.

Second, umbrella groups usually call for a "representative" of each local group to be on the umbrella board. Recruit someone who is not on the staff at the local level and is not an active board member. A person can represent their local organization who has been a staff person or a board member or who is a volunteer but not on the board.

One federated fund requests that member groups send as their representative someone who "does not have major responsibility for the health and well being of the local organization." Their board is very active in fundraising and they do not have the problem of divided loyalties. Board members are clear that they represent their local group, yet their primary task is to promote the umbrella organization. Further, they understand that they work best for their local group by being part of a strong umbrella organization.

Finally, it is critical to look closely at fundraising strategies and give all your board members tasks they can do. When people say, "I can't fundraise," ask what they mean. Do they mean they can't make coffee? Or take tickets at a special event? Or stuff envelopes? Or ask individuals for money? Usually it is the latter. If that is the case, find out which individuals they can't ask. Friends? Donors to their local groups? Strangers? Anyone? If they can't ask anyone, send them to a fundraising training so they can get over their fear and in the meantime give them a fundraising task that does not involve direct solicitation. Fundraising is a series of at least 1000 tasks and there is no one who cannot do something.

Working closely with individual board members, lobbying with member groups for who is to be nominated, and creating an "organizational culture" where people do fundraising will enable an umbrella organization to get maximum use of its board for fundraising.

36.

When Everyone Is A Volunteer

Thousands of very successful organizations are run entirely by volunteers. Service clubs, volunteer fire departments, PTAs, and neighborhood organizations have no paid staff. Many of these organizations have run successfully for years. They are designed by volunteers and designed to be run by volunteers. Other organizations may prefer to have paid staff but cannot afford them, so they, too, run on the energy of volunteers.

If you are such a group, here are five pointers.

1. Volunteers should think of themselves as unpaid staff. Staff people have jobs and tasks for which they are accountable. Volunteers have the same obligation as paid staff to do what they say they will do. Similarly, no one should tolerate incompetence and lack of follow through from a volunteer any more than they would from a paid person. In a group where everyone volunteers, it is really important to create an environment where people do the work they say they will do.

2. Volunteers have lives beyond the organization. They should not be encouraged to take on more work than they feel they can do. Suppose you know that Mary Jones would make a great treasurer but she says she hasn't got the time. You talk to her several times, beg her, tell her that no one else can do the job but her; finally she agrees to do it. Don't be surprised when Mary turns out not to be as good a treasurer as you had expected. As part of respect for each others' time, it is imperative to create and support an organizational culture that encourages people to finish the tasks they take on, even if that means taking on fewer tasks. Also, some people have more time than others and so some people may be able to take on more work than others. This needs to be all right in the group and people with less time must not be made to feel that they are not doing enough if they don't put in as much time as those with more time.

3. Volunteers should use their own and other people's time respectfully. Meetings should start and end on time. A facilitator or the chair of the meeting or the group as a whole should agree on how long each agenda item will take and try not to take longer than that. There is usually more to say, and one more way of looking at things, but unless you are an academic think tank, you can't explore every possibility.

4. People should take on particular responsibilities. Someone should be the treasurer, someone should prepare the agenda for meetings, someone should be the chair. Organizations working in a collective model can rotate these responsibilities (which need to be rotated occasionally anyway). The group should not have to wonder "Who is in charge of filing our 990?" or "Who has the check book?"

5. People should be particularly careful about writing things down. Turnover in all volunteer organizations is often high, and knowledge gets easily lost, particularly if there is no office or central place to keep files. If you do a special event or a direct mail appeal or write a proposal, keep track of everything someone else might want to know about it in order to do it faster and easier the next time. Preparing reports and narratives for the use of people who will come after you is the best way to ensure that your organization can continue to function well using volunteers and, in fact, helps to ensure that your organization can grow.

6. Volunteers should constantly seek to expand the number of volunteer workers. There is so much work to be done that a few initial dedicated volunteers will burn out quickly. You should be drawing new people into the organization all the time who can help share the work and broaden the organization's thinking and its access to funds.

All-volunteer organizations are not that different from many grassroots organizations that have one or two paid staff people. In fact, in many grassroots groups there are two kinds of staff — low-paid and unpaid. In all other grassroots groups there is one kind of staff — unpaid. The work is still valuable and people's time is very valuable. Keeping these pointers in mind will ensure that your organization is able to do the useful and important work it has set out for itself.

37.

Being Brand New

But where do I start?" is an excellent question that often follows reading fundraising books or attending fundraising lectures. There are so many possible starting places, but there is no money to meet start-up costs; little is known about what will attract money, but there is not much room for making mistakes. First, know that your group will make mistakes. Try to make new mistakes and not fall into predictable and avoidable traps.

Start by raising money from the founders of the organization — yourselves. Each person should pledge a certain amount per month or per quarter and should bring their pledge check to meetings or mail it to someone designated as the treasurer. Develop a culture of giving money among all who work with the group. Next, each founder or core volunteer should assess how much money he or she can raise from friends, family and acquaintances.

Each person should make a list of all the people she or he knows, without regard to whether these people believe in your cause or give money away. Just list the names of people who would recognize your name if you phoned them. Next to that list, mark all the people who you know believe in the cause your new group represents. If you don't know, put a question mark. Next to all the people who you know and you know agree with you, write an amount of money you think they might give. If you are not sure, keep it small. Is it $25? $50? $10? Remember that some friends and family will give you money just to be supportive of you. Finally, next to that column, note what method you will use to solicit this money. Will you invite them to a houseparty? Send a personal letter and follow-up with a phone call? Set up a meeting? Bring someone else with you? Here's what your list might look like:

Name	Believes in Cause?	Amount I will ask for	Method
Shakur	yes	$50	Meeting
Frank	?	15??	Mail appeal
Betty	no		
Gloria	yes	25	Phone
Charmaine	yes	10-35	Small party

People often object to raising money in this way for a brand new group by saying, "You can't just ask people for money without giving them something. We don't have a newsletter or a program or even an office. What are they giving to?" It is true that some people will not give until you are more established, however some people enjoy being in on the beginning of organizations. What you are giving to people is your conviction that your group will work; that the approach you have to address a certain issue or problem is feasible. You are asking them to step out in faith with you on this. Your friends will give money for the same reasons you will — just ask them.

The next step is to identify a few people or foundations who will give larger amounts of money ($1,000 or more) for start-up costs. Use the methods described under "Prospect Identification" for this step. For information on approaching foundations, go to your local Foundation Center collection, listed at the end of the bibliography. You will need to develop a case statement, including a preliminary budget. While your organization has no history, the people who are forming it have history. Each of the founders should be briefly described to give the impression that knowledgeable and experienced people are behind this idea.

From the beginning, appoint someone to keep records and make sure your records are accurate. Always write thank you notes, even before you get organizational stationary. Before you actually develop a newsletter, you can keep founding donors posted on your progress with a one- or two-page update.

Being a brand-new organization gives you a chance to do your fundraising the right way from the very beginning.

38.

What to Do in Case of Financial Trouble

F irst, don't panic. Every organization gets into difficult financial straits from time to time. Cash-flow problems are common among small nonprofit groups.

Next, carefully analyze the nature of the financial problem and how you got into it.

There are several kinds of financial troubles, ranging from simple cash-flow problems to serious mismanagement or even embezzlement of funds. I will discuss each of these major types of financial problems below. First, however, it is important to recognize that financial problems are usually symptomatic of deeper management difficulties. These difficulties usually show up first, and often most seriously, in the areas of fundraising and spending. The root cause may be the failure of the board of directors to plan the year thoroughly and thus anticipate the financial crisis; or it could be the reluctance of a staff person to discuss the finances of the organization honestly and fully with the board, leading them to approve an unrealistic budget. Sometimes the deeper problem is that fundraising projections are inaccurate because not enough research was done to make reasonable estimates of income. Whatever the problem turns out to be, it must be addressed and solved. If only the financial problem is solved and the underlying organizational issues remain unaddressed, the financial problems will recur, each time with increasing severity.

There are three main types of financial problems: cash-flow problems, deficit spending, and serious accounting errors or embezzlement of funds.

Cash-Flow Problems

Anticipated income is not coming in fast enough, creating a temporary lag in income in relation to spending. A cash-flow problem has an end in sight. You know that when a certain major donation or grant comes in, or reimbursement from the city, county, or state is received, you will be able to pay your bills and say goodbye to your problem. Until that time, however, the organization has to draw on its reserves; once the organization exhausts any savings it might have, then it is in a bind.

You have several choices at that point. You can try to put a freeze on spending and even up your income and expenses by ceasing to incur expenses. You can attempt to stall your creditors by paying bills in installments and by postponing as many bills as possible. (Call creditors and explain your situation, giving them a date by which you will pay the bill. Many times creditors will allow you to postpone payment if they believe you will have the money soon.) A third choice is to borrow money to cover your expenses and repay the loan when your cash flow improves. Depending on the size of the loan, you may be able to borrow the money from a loyal board member or major donor with little or no interest and no publicity. Foundations and corporations in some communities have "emergency loan funds" to help groups through cash-flow difficulties when those problems are not the organization's fault.

Deficit Spending

A deficit is a chronic cash-flow problem or a cash-flow problem with no end in sight. Every month your organization spends more than it brings in. Some organizations finance their deficit with money from their savings if they have any or with money earmarked for special programs (which is problematic for the special program and may cause distress to the person or grantmaking source for the program). At some point, however, the organization will run out of money and no longer be able to finance the deficit.

There is only one solution to deficit spending: spend only as much money as you raise. Permanently cutting down on spending may require radical alteration of the organization's spending habits. Examine where you are overspending and put a freeze on those areas. Designate one staffperson or Board member to authorize all expenditures over $10. In a low-budget organization, careful attention to money spent on photocopying, postage and office supplies can make a big difference.

Obviously, the fundraising plan and the income reports will have to be carefully examined and strengthened. Raising more money, however, is a long-term solution; deficits require immediate attention because the longer they continue the worse they get.

Serious Accounting Errors or Embezzlement of Funds

In these cases, the entire board must be notified immediately and the people responsible for the error or crime must be dealt with immediately. In the case of crime, the person must be fired. In the case of serious error, some mitigating circumstances may be taken into account (the person had never made an error before, the person admitted it immediately and took steps to remedy it, the error was clearly a mistake and not indicative of carelessness or deception), but probably the person should be suspended until the situation is resolved. In the case of fraud or theft, the board will have to decide whether to take legal action against the person or people responsible.

Board members should prepare a brief statement on what happened and what the organization is doing about it. This statement can be sent to funding sources and used should the story get into the newspapers or other media. Honesty and swift action are the best ways to ensure the fewest repercussions.

The more difficult problem to solve is how to make up the loss of money that this error or crime has caused. Loans, spending freezes, vacation without pay, or pay deferments for staff are some options; in the last resort, staff layoff may be necessary.

If the financial situation cannot be improved by any of the above means, the organization should consider closing. An organizational development consultant or a facilitator will be helpful in leading the board to a proper decision.

The most serious problem in this third case is the morale of all the people involved. Very little work goes on when the everyone in the organization is depressed and shocked. Morale will be boosted when the staff and board have decided on a course of action. If the organization is to stay alive, this must be decided quickly and the plan implemented immediately. A crisis of this magnitude can pull people together and strengthen the organization as long as those who stay with it agree that keeping the organization going is of the utmost importance.

Bibliography

The following list of materials is not exhaustive. It contains the books, magazines and other materials that I have found helpful or important for effective fundraising.

One of the most valuable ways to read more about fundraising is to visit the Foundation Center collection nearest you. The Foundation Center (main office in New York) is a nonprofit library service supported by foundations, fees for service, products for sale and other fundraising strategies, that collects and disseminates information about foundations, corporations, government and all other types of fundraising and grant-writing. A list of Foundation Centers and their cooperating collections (that is, public libraries or other locations that have materials from the Foundation Center) appears at the end of this bibliography.

Must Read

Achieving Excellence in Fundraising, Henry Rosso, 1991. 304 pgs. $37.95. Jossey-Bass, 350 Sansome St., San Francisco CA 94104.

America's Wealthy and the Future of Foundations, Teresa Odendahl, ed. 1987. 325 pgs. $24.95. The Foundation Center, 79 Fifth Ave., New York NY 10003.

Chronicle of Philanthropy. Bi-weekly publication. Annual subscription, $67.50. Chronicle of Philanthropy, 1255 Twenty-third St. NW, Washington DC 20037.

Designs for Fundraising: Principles, Patterns & Techniques, 2nd ed., Harold J. Seymour, 1988. 220 pgs. $41.50. McGraw-Hill, 1221 Avenue of the Americas, New York NY 10020. (Out of print, but you may be able to find a used copy.)

Giving USA Annual Report, American Association of Fundraising Counsel, Inc., published yearly. $40.00. AAFRC, 25 West 43rd St., New York NY 10036.

Grassroots Fundraising Journal, Kim Klein, publisher and editor. Bi-monthly periodical. 16 pgs. $25 annual subscription. *Special editions:* **The Board of Directors; Getting Major Gifts** ($10 each). GFJ, PO Box 11607, Berkeley CA 94712 (see order form at end of book).

Grassroots Grants, Andy Robinson, 1996, 208 pages. $25.00 Chardon Press, PO Box 11607, Berkeley CA 94712 (see order form at end of book).

How to Get Control of Your Time and Your Life, Alan Lakein, 1989. 160 pgs. $4.99. Penguin USA, PO Box 999, Dept. 17109, Berenfield NJ 07621.

How to Make Meetings Work, Michael Doyle and David Straus, 1986. 320 pgs. $4.99. Putnam Berkeley Publishing Group, 290 Murray Hill Parkway, East Rutherford NJ 07073.

How to Sell Anything to Anybody, Joe Girard and Stanley Brown, 1986. 240 pgs. $9.99. Warner Books, PO Box 690, New York NY 10019.

The Updated and Revised Grass Roots Fundraising Book, Joan Flanagan, 1992. 320 pgs. $14.95. Contemporary Books, 2 Prudential Plaza, Suite 1200, Chicago IL 60601.

Successful Fundraising: A Complete Handbook for Volunteers and Professionals, Joan Flanagan, 1991. 256 pgs. $12.95. Contemporary Books, 2 Prudential Plaza, Suite 1200, Chicago IL 60601.

Also Recommended

Activists' Guide to Religious Funders, Karen Livacoli, ed., 1990. 90 pgs. $27.00. Center for Third World Organizing, 1218 E. 21st St., Oakland, CA 94606.

The Board Members' Handbook, Brian O'Connell, 1993. 208 pgs. $24.95. Independent Sector, PO Box 451, Annapolis Junction MD 20701.

The Complete Guide to Planned Giving, Debra Ashton. 440 pages. $50.00 plus $4.00 shipping and handling. JLA Publications, 50 Follen Street, Suite 507, Cambridge MA 02138.

CBBB Standards for Charitable Solicitations. Free with SASE, Council of Better Business Bureaus, Inc., 4200 Wilson Blvd., Suite 800, Arlington VA 22203.

Filthy Rich: and Other Nonprofit Fantasies, Richard Steckel, et al, 1989. 223 pgs. $12.95. Ten Speed Press, PO Box 7123, Berkeley CA 94707.

Financial and Accounting Guide for Not-for-Profit Organizations, 4th ed., Malvern J. Gross, Jr., et al, 1991. 686 pgs. $105.00. John Wiley and Sons, 1 Wiley Drive, Somerset NJ 08875.

Give but Give Wisely. Annual subscription, $12.00, single issues $2.00. Council of Better Business Bureaus, Inc., 4200 Wilson Blvd., Suite 800, Arlington VA 22203.

How to Write Successful Fundraising Letters, Mal Warwick, 1994. 251 pgs. $12.95. Strathmoor Press, 2550 Ninth St., Suite 1040, Berkeley CA 94710.

The Legal Obligations of Nonprofit Boards: A Guidebook for Board Members, Jacqueline Covey Leifer and Michael B. Glomb, $26.00. National Center for Nonprofit Boards, 2000 L St., NW, Suite 411, Washington DC 20036.

Looking at Income-Generating Businesses for Small Non-Profit Organizations, 25 pgs. $2.00. Free to community-based organizations. Center for Community Change, 1000 Wisconsin Ave., NW, Washington DC 20007.

Money for Your Campus Ministry, Church or Other Nonprofit Organization — How to Get It, Tom Neuger Emswiler, 1981. $3.05 includes postage and handling. Wesley Foundation, 211 N. School St., Normal IL 61761.

Planned Giving for the One-Person Development Office, David Schmeling. $36.00. Deferred Giving Services, 614 South Hale St., Wheaton, IL 60187.

Responsibilities of a Charity's Volunteer Board. $2.00. Council of Better Business Bureaus, Inc., 4200 Wilson Blvd., Suite 800, Arlington VA 22203.

Securing Your Organization's Future: A Complete Guide to Fundraising Strategies, Michael Seltzer, 1993. 514 pgs. $24.95. The Foundation Center, 79 Fifth Ave., New York NY 10003.

Workplace Solicitation. For books and other information on this topic, write to National Committee for Responsive Philanthropy, 20001 S St., NW, Suite 620, Washington DC 20009.

Writing Effective News Releases, Catherine McIntyre, 1992. 176 pgs. $16.95. Picadilly Books, Box 25203, Colorado Springs CO 80936.

FOUNDATION CENTER COOPERATING COLLECTIONS   FREE FUNDING INFORMATION CENT█

The Foundation Center is an independent national service organization established by foundations to provide an authoritative source of informa█ on foundation and corporate giving. The New York, Washington, D.C., Atlanta, Cleveland, and San Francisco reference collections operated by █ Foundation Center offer a wide variety of services and comprehensive collections of information on foundations and grants. Cooperating Collec█ are libraries, community foundations, and other nonprofit agencies that provide a core collection of Foundation Center publications and a varie█ supplementary materials and services in areas useful to grantseekers. The core collection consists of:

THE FOUNDATION DIRECTORY 1 AND 2, AND SUPPLEMENT	THE FOUNDATION GRANTS INDEX QUARTERLY	THE LITERATURE OF THE NONPROFIT SECTOR
THE FOUNDATION 1000	FOUNDATION GRANTS TO INDIVIDUALS	NATIONAL DIRECTORY OF CORPORATE GIVING
FOUNDATION FUNDAMENTALS	GUIDE TO U.S. FOUNDATIONS, THEIR TRUSTEES, OFFICERS,	SELECTED GRANT GUIDES
FOUNDATION GIVING	AND DONORS	USER-FRIENDLY GUIDE
THE FOUNDATION GRANTS INDEX	THE FOUNDATION CENTER'S GUIDE TO PROPOSAL WRITING	

Many of the network members make available for public use sets of private foundation information returns (IRS Form 990-PF) for their state and/or neighbo█ states. A complete set of U.S. foundation returns can be found at the New York and Washington, D.C., offices of the Foundation Center. The Atlanta, Cleveland, and█ Francisco offices contain IRS Form 990-PF returns for the southeastern, midwestern, and western states, respectively. Those Cooperating Collections marked w█ bullet (■) have sets of private foundation information returns for their state and/or neighboring states.

Because the collections vary in their hours, materials, and services, *it is recommended that you call the collection in advance.* To check on new locations or cu█ information, call toll-free 1-800-424-9836.

REFERENCE COLLECTIONS OPERATED BY THE FOUNDATION CENTER

THE FOUNDATION CENTER	THE FOUNDATION CENTER	THE FOUNDATION CENTER	THE FOUNDATION CENTER	THE FOUNDATION CEN█
8th Floor	312 Sutter St., Rm. 312	1001 Connecticut Ave., NW	Kent H. Smith Library	Suite 150, Grand Lobby
79 Fifth Avenue	San Francisco, CA 94108	Washington, DC 20036	1422 Euclid, Suite 1356	Hurt Bldg., 50 Hurt Plaza
New York, NY 10003	(415) 397-0902	(202) 331-1400	Cleveland, OH 44115	Atlanta, GA 30303
(212) 620-4230			(216) 861-1933	(404) 880-0094

ALABAMA

■ BIRMINGHAM PUBLIC LIBRARY
Government Documents
2100 Park Place
Birmingham 35203
(205) 226-3600

HUNTSVILLE PUBLIC LIBRARY
915 Monroe St.
Huntsville 35801
(205) 532-5940

■ UNIVERSITY OF SOUTH ALABAMA
Library Building
Mobile 36688
(205) 460-7025

■ AUBURN UNIVERSITY AT
MONTGOMERY LIBRARY
7300 University Drive
Montgomery 36117-3596
(205) 244-3653

ALASKA

■ UNIVERSITY OF ALASKA AT
ANCHORAGE
Library
3211 Providence Drive
Anchorage 99508
(907) 786-1848

JUNEAU PUBLIC LIBRARY
292 Marine Way
Juneau 99801
(907) 586-5267

ARIZONA

■ PHOENIX PUBLIC LIBRARY
Business & Sciences Unit
12 E. McDowell Rd.
Phoenix 85004
(602) 262-4636

■ TUCSON PIMA LIBRARY
101 N. Stone Ave.
Tucson 87501
(602) 791-4010

ARKANSAS

■ WESTARK COMMUNITY
COLLEGE—BORHAM LIBRARY
Ft. Smith 72913
(501) 785-7133

■ CENTRAL ARKANSAS LIBRARY
SYSTEM
700 Louisiana
Little Rock 72201
(501) 370-5952

PINE BLUFF-JEFFERSON COUNTY
LIBRARY SYSTEM
200 E. Eighth
Pine Bluff 71601
(501) 534-2159

CALIFORNIA

■ VENTURA COUNTY COMMUNITY
FOUNDATION
Funding and Information Resource
Center
1355 Del Norte Rd.
Camarillo 93010
(805) 988-0196

■ CALIFORNIA COMMUNITY
FOUNDATION
Funding Information Center
606 S. Olive St., Suite 2400
Los Angeles 90014-1526
(213) 413-4042

GRANT & RESOURCE CENTER OF
NORTHERN CALIFORNIA
Building C, Suite A
2280 Benton Dr.
Redding 96003
(916) 244-1219

RIVERSIDE CITY & COUNTY PUBLIC
LIBRARY
3581 Seventh St.
Riverside 92502
(714) 782-5201

NONPROFIT RESOURCE CENTER
Sacramento Public Library
828 I Street, 2nd Floor
Sacramento 95812-2036
(916) 552-8817

■ SAN DIEGO COMMUNITY
FOUNDATION
Funding Information Center
101 West Broadway, Suite 1120
San Diego 92101
(619) 239-8815

■ NONPROFIT DEVELOPMENT CENTER
Library
1762 Technology Dr., #225
San Jose 95110
(408) 452-8181

■ PENINSULA COMMUNITY
FOUNDATION
Funding Information Library
1700 S. El Camino Real, R301
San Mateo 94402-3049
(415) 358-9392

LOS ANGELES PUBLIC LIBRARY
San Pedro Regional Branch
9131 S. Gaffey St.
San Pedro 90731
(310) 548-7779

■ VOLUNTEER CENTER OF GREATER
ORANGE COUNTY
Nonprofit Management Assistance
Center
1000 E. Santa Ana Blvd., Ste. 200
Santa Ana 92701
(714) 953-1655

■ SANTA BARBARA PUBLIC LIBRARY
40 E. Anapamu St.
Santa Barbara 93101
(805) 962-7653

SANTA MONICA PUBLIC LIBRARY
1343 Sixth St.
Santa Monica 90401-1603
(310) 458-8600

SEASIDE BRANCH LIBRARY
550 Harcourt St.
Seaside 93955
(408) 889-8131

SONOMA COUNTY LIBRARY
3rd & E Streets
Santa Rosa 95404
(707) 545-0831

COLORADO

PIKES PEAK LIBRARY DISTRICT
20 N. Cascade
Colorado Springs 80901
(719) 531-6333

■ DENVER PUBLIC LIBRARY
Social Sciences & Genealogy
1357 Broadway
Denver 80203
(303) 640-8870

CONNECTICUT

DANBURY PUBLIC LIBRARY
170 Main St.
Danbury 06810
(203) 797-4527

■ HARTFORD PUBLIC LIBRARY
500 Main St.
Hartford 06103
(203) 293-6000

D.A.T.A.
70 Audubon St.
New Haven 06510
(203) 772-1345

DELAWARE

■ UNIVERSITY OF DELAWARE
Hugh Morris Library
Newark 19717-5267
(302) 831-2432

FLORIDA

VOLUSIA COUNTY LIBRARY CEN█
City Island
Daytona Beach 32014-4484
(904) 255-3765

■ NOVA UNIVERSITY
Einstein Library
3301 College Ave.
Fort Lauderdale 33314
(305) 475-7050

INDIAN RIVER COMMUNITY
COLLEGE
Charles S. Miley Learning Resourc█
Center
3209 Virginia Ave.
Fort Pierce 34981-5599
(407) 462-4757

■ JACKSONVILLE PUBLIC LIBRARIES
Grants Resource Center
122 N. Ocean St.
Jacksonville 32202
(904) 630-2665

■ MIAMI-DADE PUBLIC LIBRARY
Humanities/Social Science
101 W. Flagler St.
Miami 33130
(305) 375-5015

■ ORLANDO PUBLIC LIBRARY
Social Sciences Department
101 E. Central Blvd.
Orlando 32801
(407) 425-4694

SELBY PUBLIC LIBRARY
1001 Blvd. of the Arts
Sarasota 34236
(813) 951-5501

■ TAMPA-HILLSBOROUGH COUNTY
PUBLIC LIBRARY
900 N. Ashley Drive
Tampa 33602
(813) 273-3628

COMMUNITY FOUNDATION OF
PALM BEACH & MARTIN COUNTIES
324 Datura St., Suite 340
West Palm Beach 33401
(407) 659-6800

■ ATLANTA-FULTON PUBLIC LIBRARY
Foundation Collection—Ivan Allen
Department
1 Margaret Mitchell Square
Atlanta 30303-1089
(404) 730-1900

DALTON REGIONAL LIBRARY
310 Cappes St.
Dalton 30720
(706) 278-4507

■ UNIVERSITY OF HAWAII
Hamilton Library
2550 The Mall
Honolulu 96822
(808) 956-7214

HAWAII COMMUNITY FOUNDATION
Hawaii Resource Center
222 Merchant St., Second Floor
Honolulu 96813
(808) 537-6333

■ BOISE PUBLIC LIBRARY
715 S. Capitol Blvd.
Boise 83702
(208) 384-4024

■ CALDWELL PUBLIC LIBRARY
1010 Dearborn St.
Caldwell 83605
(208) 459-3242

■ DONORS FORUM OF CHICAGO
53 W. Jackson Blvd., Suite 430
Chicago 60604-3608
(312) 431-0265

■ EVANSTON PUBLIC LIBRARY
1703 Orrington Ave.
Evanston 60201
(708) 866-0305

ROCK ISLAND PUBLIC LIBRARY
401 - 19th St.
Rock Island 61201
(309) 788-7627

■ SANGAMON STATE UNIVERSITY
Library
Shepherd Road
Springfield 62794-9243
(217) 786-6633

INDIANA

■ ALLEN COUNTY PUBLIC LIBRARY
900 Webster St.
Ft. Wayne 46802
(219) 424-0544

INDIANA UNIVERSITY NORTHWEST
LIBRARY
3400 Broadway
Gary 46408
(219) 980-6582

■ INDIANAPOLIS-MARION COUNTY
PUBLIC LIBRARY
Social Sciences
40 E. St. Clair
Indianapolis 46206
(317) 269-1733

IOWA

■ CEDAR RAPIDS PUBLIC LIBRARY
Foundation Center Collection
500 First St., SE
Cedar Rapids 52401
(319) 398-5123

■ SOUTHWESTERN COMMUNITY
COLLEGE
Learning Resource Center
1501 W. Townline Rd.
Creston 50801
(515) 782-7081

■ PUBLIC LIBRARY OF DES MOINES
100 Locust
Des Moines 50309-1791
(515) 283-4152

SIOUX CITY PUBLIC LIBRARY
529 Pierce St.
Sioux City 51101-1202
(712) 252-5669

KANSAS

■ DODGE CITY PUBLIC LIBRARY
1001 2nd Ave.
Dodge City 67801
(316) 225-0248

■ TOPEKA AND SHAWNEE COUNTY
PUBLIC LIBRARY
1515 SW 10th Ave.
Topeka 66604-1374
(913) 233-2040

■ WICHITA PUBLIC LIBRARY
223 S. Main St.
Wichita 67202
(316) 262-0611

KENTUCKY

WESTERN KENTUCKY UNIVERSITY
Helm-Cravens Library
Bowling Green 42101-3576
(502) 745-6125

■ LOUISVILLE FREE PUBLIC LIBRARY
301 York Street
Louisville 40203
(502) 574-1611

LOUISIANA

■ EAST BATON ROUGE PARISH LIBRARY
Centroplex Branch Grants Collection
120 St. Louis
Baton Rouge 70802
(504) 389-4960

BEAUREGARD PARISH LIBRARY
205 S. Washington Ave.
De Ridder 70634
(318) 463-6217

■ NEW ORLEANS PUBLIC LIBRARY
Business & Science Division
219 Loyola Ave.
New Orleans 70140
(504) 596-2580

■ SHREVE MEMORIAL LIBRARY
424 Texas St.
Shreveport 71120-1523
(318) 226-5894

MAINE

■ UNIVERSITY OF SOUTHERN MAINE
Office of Sponsored Research
246 Deering Ave., Rm. 628
Portland 04103
(207) 780-4871

MARYLAND

■ ENOCH PRATT FREE LIBRARY
Social Science & History
400 Cathedral St.
Baltimore 21201
(410) 396-5430

MASSACHUSETTS

■ ASSOCIATED GRANTMAKERS OF
MASSACHUSETTS
294 Washington St., Suite 840
Boston 02108
(617) 426-2606

■ BOSTON PUBLIC LIBRARY
Soc. Sci. Reference
666 Boylston St
Boston 02117
(617) 536-5400

WESTERN MASSACHUSETTS
FUNDING RESOURCE CENTER
65 Elliot St.
Springfield 01101-1730
(413) 732-3175

■ WORCESTER PUBLIC LIBRARY
Grants Resource Center
Salem Square
Worcester 01608
(508) 799-1655

MICHIGAN

■ ALPENA COUNTY LIBRARY
211 N. First St.
Alpena 49707
(517) 356-6188

■ UNIVERSITY OF MICHIGAN-ANN
ARBOR
Graduate Library
Reference & Research Services
Department
Ann Arbor 48109-1205
(313) 764-9373

■ BATTLE CREEK COMMUNITY
FOUNDATION
Southwest Michigan Funding Resource
Center
2 Riverwalk Centre
34 W. Jackson St.
Battle Creek 49017-3505
(616) 962-2181

■ HENRY FORD CENTENNIAL LIBRARY
Adult Services
16301 Michigan Ave.
Dearborn 48126
(313) 943-2330

■ WAYNE STATE UNIVERSITY
Purdy/Kresge Library
5265 Cass Avenue
Detroit 48202
(313) 577-6424

■ MICHIGAN STATE UNIVERSITY
LIBRARIES
Social Sciences/Humanities
Main Library
East Lansing 48824-1048
(517) 353-8818

■ FARMINGTON COMMUNITY LIBRARY
32737 West 12 Mile Rd.
Farmington Hills 48018
(313) 553-0300

■ UNIVERSITY OF MICHIGAN—FLINT
Library
Flint 48502-2186
(313) 762-3408

■ GRAND RAPIDS PUBLIC LIBRARY
Business Dept.—3rd Floor
60 Library Plaza NE
Grand Rapids 49503-3093
(616) 456-3600

MICHIGAN TECHNOLOGICAL
UNIVERSITY
Van Pelt Library
1400 Townsend Dr.
Houghton 49931
(906) 487-2507

SAULT STE. MARIE AREA PUBLIC
SCHOOLS
Office of Compensatory Education
460 W. Spruce St.
Sault Ste. Marie 49783-1874
(906) 635-6619

■ NORTHWESTERN MICHIGAN
COLLEGE
Mark & Helen Osterin Library
1701 E. Front St.
Traverse City 49684
(616) 922-1060

■ DULUTH PUBLIC LIBRARY
520 W. Superior St.
Duluth 55802
(218) 723-3802

■ SOUTHWEST STATE UNIVERSITY
University Library
Marshall 56258
(507) 537-6176

■ MINNEAPOLIS PUBLIC LIBRARY
Sociology Department
300 Nicollet Mall
Minneapolis 55401
(612) 372-6555

ROCHESTER PUBLIC LIBRARY
11 First St. SE
Rochester 55904-3777
(507) 285-8002

ST. PAUL PUBLIC LIBRARY
90 W. Fourth St.
St. Paul 55102
(612) 292-6307

■ JACKSON/HINDS LIBRARY SYSTEM
300 N. State St.
Jackson 39201
(601) 968-5803

■ CLEARINGHOUSE FOR
MIDCONTINENT FOUNDATIONS
University of Missouri
5315 Rockhill Rd.
Kansas City 64110
(816) 235-1176

■ KANSAS CITY PUBLIC LIBRARY
311 E. 12th St.
Kansas City 64106
(816) 221-9650

■ METROPOLITAN ASSOCIATION FOR
PHILANTHROPY, INC.
5615 Pershing Avenue, Suite 20
St. Louis 63112
(314) 361-3900

■ SPRINGFIELD-GREENE COUNTY
LIBRARY
397 E. Central
Springfield 65802
(417) 869-9400

MONTANA

■ EASTERN MONTANA COLLEGE
LIBRARY
Special Collections—Grants
1500 North 30th St.
Billings 59101-0298
(406) 657-1662

BOZEMAN PUBLIC LIBRARY
220 E. Lamme
Bozeman 59715
(406) 586-4787

■ MONTANA STATE LIBRARY
Library Services
1515 E. 6th Ave.
Helena 59620
(406) 444-3004

■ UNIVERSITY OF MONTANA
Maureen & Mike Mansfield Library
Missoula 59812-1195
(406) 243-6800

NEBRASKA

■ UNIVERSITY OF
NEBRASKA—LINCOLN
Love Library
14th & R Streets
Lincoln 68588-0410
(402) 472-2848

■ W. DALE CLARK LIBRARY
Social Sciences Department
215 S. 15th St.
Omaha 68102
(402) 444-4826

NEVADA

■ LAS VEGAS-CLARK COUNTY LIBRARY
DISTRICT
833 Las Vegas Blvd. North
Las Vegas 89101
(702) 382-5280

■ WASHOE COUNTY LIBRARY
301 S. Center St.
Reno 89501
(702) 785-4010

NEW HAMPSHIRE

■ NEW HAMPSHIRE CHARITABLE FDN.
One South St.
Concord 03302-1335
(603) 225-6641

■ PLYMOUTH STATE COLLEGE
Herbert H. Lamson Library
Plymouth 03264
(603) 535-2258

NEW JERSEY

CUMBERLAND COUNTY LIBRARY
New Jersey Room
800 E. Commerce St.
Bridgeton 08302
(609) 453-2210

■ FREE PUBLIC LIBRARY OF ELIZABETH
11 S. Broad St.
Elizabeth 07202
(908) 354-6060

COUNTY COLLEGE OF MORRIS
Learning Resource Center
214 Center Grove Rd.
Randolph 07869
(201) 328-5296

■ NEW JERSEY STATE LIBRARY
Governmental Reference Services
185 West State St.
Trenton 08625-0520
(609) 292-6220

NEW MEXICO

ALBUQUERQUE COMMUNITY
FOUNDATION
3301 Menual NE, Ste. 30
Albuquerque 87176-6960
(505) 883-6240

■ NEW MEXICO STATE LIBRARY
Information Services
325 Don Gaspar
Santa Fe 87503
(505) 827-3824

NEW YORK

■ NEW YORK STATE LIBRARY
Humanities Reference
Cultural Education Center
Empire State Plaza
Albany 12230
(518) 474-5355

SUFFOLK COOPERATIVE LIBRARY
SYSTEM
627 N. Sunrise Service Rd.
Bellport 11713
(516) 286-1600

NEW YORK PUBLIC LIBRARY
Fordham Branch
2556 Bainbridge Ave.
Bronx 10458
(718) 220-6575

BROOKLYN IN TOUCH
INFORMATION CENTER, INC.
One Hanson Place—Room 2504
Brooklyn 11243
(718) 230-3200

BROOKLYN PUBLIC LIBRARY
Social Sciences Division
Grand Army Plaza
Brooklyn 11238
(718) 780-7700

■ BUFFALO & ERIE COUNTY PUBLIC
LIBRARY
Business & Labor Dept.
Lafayette Square
Buffalo 14203
(716) 858-7097

HUNTINGTON PUBLIC LIBRARY
338 Main St.
Huntington 11743
(516) 427-5165

QUEENS BOROUGH PUBLIC LIBRARY
Social Sciences Division
89-11 Merrick Blvd.
Jamaica 11432
(718) 990-0761

■ LEVITTOWN PUBLIC LIBRARY
1 Bluegrass Lane
Levittown 11756
(516) 731-5728

NEW YORK PUBLIC LIBRARY
Countee Cullen Branch Library
104 W. 136th St.
New York 10030
(212) 491-2070

ADRIANCE MEMORIAL LIBRARY
Special Services Department
93 Market St.
Poughkeepsie 12601
(914) 485-3445

ROCHESTER PUBLIC LIBRARY
Business, Economics & Law
115 South Avenue
Rochester 14604
(716) 428-7328

ONONDAGA COUNTY PUBLIC
LIBRARY
447 S. Salina St.
Syracuse 13202-2494
(315) 448-4700

UTICA PUBLIC LIBRARY
303 Genesee St.
Utica 13501
(315) 735-2279

■ WHITE PLAINS PUBLIC LIBRARY
100 Martine Ave.
White Plains 10601
(914) 422-1480

NORTH CAROLINA

■ COMMUNITY FDN. OF WESTERN
NORTH CAROLINA
Learning Resources Center
14 College Street
Asheville 28801
(704) 254-4960

■ THE DUKE ENDOWMENT
200 S. Tryon St., Suite 1100
Charlotte 28202
(704) 376-0291

DURHAM COUNTY PUBLIC LIBRARY
301 North Roxboro
Durham 27702
(919) 560-0110

■ FORSYTH COUNTY PUBLIC LIBRARY
660 W. 6th St.
Winston-Salem 27101
(910) 727-2680

■ STATE LIBRARY OF NORTH CAROLINA
Government and Business Services
Archives Bldg., 109 E. Jones St.
Raleigh 27601
(919) 733-3270

NORTH DAKOTA

BISMARCK PUBLIC LIBRARY
515 North Fifth St.
Bismarck 58501
(701) 222-6410

■ NORTH DAKOTA STATE UNIVERSITY
LIBRARY
Fargo 58105
(701) 237-8886

OHIO

STARK COUNTY DISTRICT LIBRARY
Humanities
715 Market Ave. N.
Canton 44702
(216) 452-0665

■ PUBLIC LIBRARY OF CINCINNATI &
HAMILTON COUNTY
Grants Resource Center
800 Vine St.—Library Square
Cincinnati 45202-2071
(513) 369-6940

COLUMBUS METROPOLITAN LIBRARY
Business and Technology
96 S. Grant Ave.
Columbus 43215
(614) 645-2590

■ DAYTON & MONTGOMERY COUNTY
PUBLIC LIBRARY
Grants Resource Center
215 E. Third St.
Dayton 45402
(513) 227-9500 x211

■ TOLEDO-LUCAS COUNTY PUBLIC
LIBRARY
Social Sciences Department
325 Michigan St.
Toledo 43624-1614
(419) 259-5245

YOUNGSTOWN & MAHONING
COUNTY LIBRARY
305 Wick Ave.
Youngstown 44503
(216) 744-8636

MUSKINGUM COUNTY LIBRARY
220 N. 5th St.
Zanesville 43701
(614) 453-0391

OKLAHOMA

■ OKLAHOMA CITY UNIVERSITY
Dulaney Browne Library
2501 N. Blackwelder
Oklahoma City 73106
(405) 521-5072

■ TULSA CITY-COUNTY LIBRARY
400 Civic Center
Tulsa 74103
(918) 596-7944

OREGON

OREGON INSTITUTE OF
TECHNOLOGY
Library
3201 Campus Dr.
Klamath Falls 97601-8801
(503) 885-1773

■ PACIFIC NON-PROFIT NETWORK
Grantsmanship Resource Library
33 N. Central, Suite 211
Medford 97501
(503) 779-6044

■ MULTNOMAH COUNTY LIBRARY
Government Documents
801 SW Tenth Ave.
Portland 97205
(503) 248-5123

OREGON STATE LIBRARY
State Library Building
Salem 97310
(503) 378-4277

PENNSYLVANIA

NORTHAMPTON COMMUNITY
COLLEGE
Learning Resources Center
3835 Green Pond Rd.
Bethlehem 18017
(215) 861-5360

ERIE COUNTY LIBRARY SYSTEM
27 South Park Row
Erie 16501
(814) 451-6927

DAUPHIN COUNTY LIBRARY S
Central Library
101 Walnut St.
Harrisburg 17101
(717) 234-4976

LANCASTER COUNTY PUBLIC
LIBRARY
125 N. Duke St.
Lancaster 17602
(717) 394-2651

■ FREE LIBRARY OF PHILADELPHIA
Regional Foundation Center
Logan Square
Philadelphia 19103
(215) 686-5423

■ CARNEGIE LIBRARY OF PITTSBURGH
Foundation Collection
4400 Forbes Ave.
Pittsburgh 15213-4080
(412) 622-1917

POCONO NORTHEAST
DEVELOPMENT FUND
James Pettinger Memorial Library
1151 Oak Ave.
Pittston 18640-3755
(717) 655-5581

READING PUBLIC LIBRARY
100 South Fifth St.
Reading 19602
(215) 655-6355

MARTIN LIBRARY
159 Market St.
York 17401
(717) 846-5300

PROVIDENCE PUBLIC LIBRARY
150 Empire St.
Providence 02906
(401) 521-7722

ANDERSON COUNTY LIBRARY
202 East Greenville St.
Anderson 29621
(803) 260-4500

CHARLESTON COUNTY LIBRARY
404 King St.
Charleston 29403
(803) 723-1645

SOUTH CAROLINA STATE LIBRARY
1500 Senate St.
Columbia 29211
(803) 734-8666

NONPROFIT GRANTS ASSISTANCE
CENTER
Business & Education Institute
Washington Street, East Hall
Dakota State University
Madison 57042
(605) 256-5555

SOUTH DAKOTA STATE LIBRARY
800 Governors Drive
Pierre 57501-2294
(605) 773-5070
(800) 592-1841 (SD residents)

SIOUX FALLS AREA FOUNDATION
141 N. Main Ave., Suite 310
Sioux Falls 57102-1132
(605) 336-7055

KNOX COUNTY PUBLIC LIBRARY
500 W. Church Ave.
Knoxville 37902
(615) 544-5700

MEMPHIS & SHELBY COUNTY
PUBLIC LIBRARY
1850 Peabody Ave.
Memphis 38104
(901) 725-8877

NASHVILLE PUBLIC LIBRARY
Business Information Division
225 Polk Ave.
Nashville 37203
(615) 862-5843

TEXAS

COMMUNITY FOUNDATION OF
ABILENE
Funding Information Library
500 N. Chestnut, Suite 1509
Abilene 79604
(915) 676-3883

■ AMARILLO AREA FOUNDATION
700 First National Place
801 S. Fillmore
Amarillo 79101
(806) 376-4521

■ HOGG FOUNDATION FOR MENTAL
HEALTH
3001 Lake Austin Blvd.
Austin 78703
(512) 471-5041

TEXAS A & M UNIVERSITY AT
CORPUS CHRISTI
Library
Reference Dept.
6300 Ocean Dr.
Corpus Christi 78412
(512) 994-2608

■ DALLAS PUBLIC LIBRARY
Urban Information
1515 Young St.
Dallas 75201
(214) 670-1487

EL PASO COMMUNITY FOUNDATION
1616 Texas Commerce Building
El Paso 79901
(915) 533-4020

■ FUNDING INFORMATION CENTER
OF FORT WORTH
Texas Christian University Library
2800 S. University Dr.
Ft. Worth 76129
(817) 921-7664

■ HOUSTON PUBLIC LIBRARY
Bibliographic Information Center
500 McKinney
Houston 77002
(713) 236-1313

■ LONGVIEW PUBLIC LIBRARY
222 W. Cotton St.
Longview 75601
(903) 237-1352

LUBBOCK AREA FOUNDATION, INC.
502 Texas Commerce Bank Building
Lubbock 79401
(806) 762-8061

■ FUNDING INFORMATION CENTER
530 McCullough, Suite 600
San Antonio 78212-8270
(210) 227-4333

NORTH TEXAS CENTER FOR
NONPROFIT MANAGEMENT
624 Indiana, Suite 307
Wichita Falls 76301
(817) 322-4961

UTAH

■ SALT LAKE CITY PUBLIC LIBRARY
209 East 500 South
Salt Lake City 84111
(801) 524-8200

VERMONT

■ VERMONT DEPT. OF LIBRARIES
Reference & Law Info. Services
109 State St.
Montpelier 05609
(802) 828-3268

VIRGINIA

■ HAMPTON PUBLIC LIBRARY
4207 Victoria Blvd.
Hampton 23669
(804) 727-1312

■ RICHMOND PUBLIC LIBRARY
Business, Science & Technology
101 East Franklin St.
Richmond 23219
(804) 780-8223

■ ROANOKE CITY PUBLIC LIBRARY
SYSTEM
Central Library
706 S. Jefferson St.
Roanoke 24016
(703) 981-2477

WASHINGTON

■ MID-COLUMBIA LIBRARY
405 South Dayton
Kennewick 99336
(509)586-3156

■ SEATTLE PUBLIC LIBRARY
Science, Social Science
1000 Fourth Ave.
Seattle 98104
(206) 386-4620

■ SPOKANE PUBLIC LIBRARY
Funding Information Center
West 811 Main Ave.
Spokane 99201
(509) 838-3364

■ UNITED WAY OF PIERCE COUNTY
Center for Nonprofit Development
734 Broadway
P.O. Box 2215
Tacoma 98401
(206) 597-6686

GREATER WENATCHEE COMMUNITY
FOUNDATION AT THE WENATCHEE
PUBLIC LIBRARY
310 Douglas St.
Wenatchee 98807
(509) 662-5021

WEST VIRGINIA

■ KANAWHA COUNTY PUBLIC LIBRARY
123 Capitol St.
Charleston 25301
(304) 343-4646

WISCONSIN

■ UNIVERSITY OF
WISCONSIN-MADISON
Memorial Library
728 State St.
Madison 53706
(608) 262-3242

■ MARQUETTE UNIVERSITY MEMORIAL
LIBRARY
Funding Information Center
1415 W. Wisconsin Ave.
Milwaukee 53233
(414) 288-1515

UNIVERSITY OF
WISCONSIN—STEVENS POINT
Library—Foundation Collection
99 Reserve St.
Stevens Point 54481-3897
(715) 346-3826

WYOMING

■ NATRONA COUNTY PUBLIC LIBRARY
307 E. 2nd St.
Casper 82601-2598
(307) 237-4935

■ LARAMIE COUNTY COMMUNITY
COLLEGE
Instructional Resource Center
1400 E. College Dr.
Cheyenne 82007-3299
(307) 778-1206

■ CAMPBELL COUNTY PUBLIC LIBRARY
2101 4-J Road
Gillette 82716
(307) 682-3223

■ TETON COUNTY LIBRARY
320 S. King St.
Jackson 83001
(307) 733-2164

ROCK SPRINGS LIBRARY
400 C St.
Rock Springs 82901
(307) 362-6212

PUERTO RICO

UNIVERSITY OF PUERTO RICO
Ponce Technological College Library
Box 7186
Ponce 00732
(809) 844-8181

UNIVERSIDAD DEL SAGRADO
CORAZON
M.M.T. Guevara Library
Santurce 00914
(809) 728-1515 x 4357

Index

Dear Friends,

In 1982 I began publishing the *Grassroots Fundraising Journal* to share my experience of grassroots fundraising strategies and techniques with other small nonprofit groups. The *Journal* remains an excellent source of straightforward, down-to-earth information about methods grassroots nonprofits can use to become and remain financially stable. Every two months, the *Journal* contains articles by me and other experienced fundraisers on how to raise money from grassroots sources, along with book reviews, profiles of major donors and announcements of current opportunities in the fundraising world.

The *Journal* has also collected the best of its articles on two cornerstones of grassroots fundraising in two special editions: *The Board of Directors* and *Getting Major Gifts*. Use the order form on the following pages.

Thanks,

Kim Klein

About Chardon Press

Founded in 1988 by Kim Klein and Nancy Adess, Chardon Press publishes works relating to or funding the work of social justice and social change.

On Fundraising

Grassroots Fundraising Journal, (6 issues annually; Special editions: Board of Directors, Getting Major Gifts)

Grassroots Grants: An Activist's Guide to Proposal Writing, Andy Robinson (1996)

Fundraising for Social Change, Third Edition, Kim Klein (1995)

General Interest

In the Time of the Right: Strategies for Liberation, Suzanne Pharr (1996)

Volver a Vivir/ Return to Life, PROJIMO/Suzanne Levine, ed. (1996)

The Family Guide to the Point Reyes Peninsula, Karen Gray (1996)

Naming Our Truth: Stories of Loretto Women, Ann Patrick Ware, ed. (1995)

Homophobia, A Weapon of Sexism, Suzanne Pharr (1988)

Home on the Range: Recipes from the Point Reyes Community, Foreword by Ed Brown (1988)

Chardon Press

P.O. Box 11607
Berkeley, CA 94712
tel.: 510-704-8714
fax: 510-649-7913
e-mail: chardn@aol.com

Order Form

FUNDRAISING FOR SOCIAL CHANGE by Kim Klein

ISBN 0-9620222-3-3

_____ copies @ $25.00 _____

$2.00 postage/handling per book _____

(in CA add $2.00 tax per book) _____

Discounts: 5-9 books: 20%, $4 postage

_____ books @ $20 = _____ + $4 postage = _____

10+ books: 40%, $6 postage

_____ books @ $15 = _____ + $6 postage = _____

TOTAL $ _____

GRASSROOTS FUNDRAISING JOURNAL

_____ 1-year subscription: $25 _____

_____ 2-year subscription: $48 _____

Canada and overseas subscriptions, please pay in US dollars:

_____ One year ($32) _____ Two Years ($55) _____

TOTAL $ _____

SPECIAL EDITIONS:

_____ _The Board of Directors_ @ $10 _____

Shipping and handling, $2.00 _____

(in CA, add $ .82 tax each) _____

_____ _Getting Major Gifts_ @ $10 _____

Shipping and handling, $2.00 _____

(in CA, add $ .82 tax each) _____

Bulk orders available. Call for information

TOTAL $ _____

GRASSROOTS GRANTS by Andy Robinson

ISBN 0-9620222-5-X

_____ copies @ $25.00 _____

$2.00 postage/handling per book _____

(in CA add $2.00 tax per book) _____

Discounts: 5-9 books: 20%, $4 postage

_____ books @ $20 = _____ + $4 postage = _____

10+ books: 40%, $6 postage

_____ books @ $15 = _____ + $6 postage = _____

TOTAL $ _____

TOTAL ENCLOSED $ _____

Please fill out information on the next page and send with your order.

PLEASE FILL IN THE FOLLOWING INFORMATION.

_____

Name

_____

Organization

_____

Address

_____

City, State, Zip   Phone

Make checks payable to **CHARDON PRESS**

Credit Card Orders: ❑ MC   ❑ VISA

Acct. No. _____ Exp. date _____

Signature _____

_____

CHARDON PRESS   P.O. BOX 11607   BERKELEY   CA   94712
PHONE: 510/704-8714 • FAX: 510/649-7913